Theories of Terrorism

This new textbook provides students with a multidisciplinary theoretical and methodological introduction to terrorism studies.

The book identifies the main theories proposed in the field of terrorism studies as they relate to several issues:

- why and how individuals and organizations get involved in terrorism;
- the definition and concept of terrorism;
- state terrorism;
- leaving terrorism behind;
- counter-terrorism;
- manifestations of terrorism in time and space.

Terrorism studies is a highly heterogeneous field with a broad range of theories and disciplines, marked by ample debates. Beyond individual contributions and unique perspectives, however, it is difficult for students and interested readers to have a broader and structured grasp of the theoretical landscape within and behind the study of terrorism. This textbook offers a valuable new teaching tool which aims to provide students with the conceptual, theoretical, and methodological toolbox necessary to understand and research terrorism.

This book will be essential reading for students of terrorism studies, political violence, and counter-terrorism, and is highly recommended for students of security studies, criminology, politics, and international relations.

Daniela Pisoiu is a senior researcher at the Austrian Institute for International Affairs (oiip), Vienna, Austria. She obtained her PhD in international relations at the University of St Andrews and is the author of *Islamist Radicalisation in Europe: An Occupational Change Process* (Routledge, 2011) and editor of *Arguing Counterterrorism: New Perspectives* (Routledge, 2014).

Sandra Hain is affiliated with the Austrian Institute for International Affairs (oiip), Vienna, Austria.

'Pisoiu and Hain provide a comprehensive and valuable critical and comparative examination of the major theoretical approaches, their implications, convergences and insights for building a better understanding of terrorism, terrorists and organizations that employ terrorism. Students, scholars and policy analysts will all benefit from their careful analysis.'

Michael Stohl, University of California, Santa Barbara, USA

'One of the main criticisms of the terrorism studies field is that it lacks theoretical systematisation. *Theories of Terrorism* synthesises a vast amount of relevant social theory in an impressive attempt to overcome this weakness. Unique in the way it draws together orthodox and critical research on terrorism, and meticulous in its consideration of the wider literature, it provides multiple theoretical vantage points for understanding the highly variegated and complex phenomenon of terrorism. With the publication of this book, we can no longer say that terrorism studies lacks theory. A truly impressive accomplishment.'

Richard Jackson, University of Otago, New Zealand

Theories of Terrorism
An Introduction

Daniela Pisoiu and Sandra Hain

LONDON AND NEW YORK

First published 2018
by Routledge
2 Park Square, Milton Park, Abingdon, Oxon OX14 4RN

and by Routledge
711 Third Avenue, New York, NY 10017

Routledge is an imprint of the Taylor & Francis Group, an informa business

© 2018 Daniela Pisoiu and Sandra Hain; individual chapters, the contributors

The right of Daniela Pisoiu and Sandra Hain to be identified as authors of this work
has been asserted by them in accordance with sections 77 and 78 of the Copyright,
Designs and Patents Act 1988.

All rights reserved. No part of this book may be reprinted or reproduced or utilised
in any form or by any electronic, mechanical, or other means, now known or hereafter
invented, including photocopying and recording, or in any information storage or retrieval
system, without permission in writing from the publishers.

Trademark notice: Product or corporate names may be trademarks or registered trademarks,
and are used only for identification and explanation without intent to infringe.

British Library Cataloguing-in-Publication Data
A catalogue record for this book is available from the British Library

Library of Congress Cataloging-in-Publication Data
Names: Pisoiu, Daniela, author. | Hain, Sandra, author.
Title: Theories of terrorism : an introduction / Daniela Pisoiu and Sandra
Hain.
Description: Abingdon, Oxon ; New York, NY : Routledge, 2018. | Includes
bibliographical references and index.
Identifiers: LCCN 2017024654| ISBN 9780415826075 (hardback) | ISBN
9780415826082 (pbk.) | ISBN 9780203536599 (ebook)
Subjects: LCSH: Terrorism.
Classification: LCC HV6431 .P5726 2018 | DDC 363.32501--dc23
LC record available at https://lccn.loc.gov/2017024654

ISBN: 978-0-415-82607-5 (hbk)
ISBN: 978-0-415-82608-2 (pbk)
ISBN: 978-0-203-53659-9 (ebk)

Typeset in Times New Roman
by Fish Books Ltd.

Printed and bound by CPI Group (UK) Ltd, Croydon, CR0 4YY

Contents

List of tables		vii
List of boxes		viii
List of contributors		x
List of acronyms		xi
Glossary		xii
Acknowledgements		xviii
	Introduction	1
1	The making of terrorism	11
2	Defining terrorism ASTA MASKALIŪNAITĖ	25
3	Studying terrorism	37
4	Determining *individual* terrorism	50
5	Choosing *individual* terrorism	65
6	Relational *individual* terrorism	77
7	Determining *organizational* terrorism	94
8	Choosing *organizational* terrorism	108
9	Relational *organizational* terrorism	123
10	Individual disengagement, de-radicalization, and counter-radicalization	137
11	State terrorism	152

vi *Contents*

12 Terrorism in time and space 165

13 Counter-terrorism 179
ASTA MASKALIŪNAITĖ

Index 197

List of tables

8.1	The strategies of terrorism as reviewed by Kydd and Walter	115
13.1	Comparison of three studies into the end of terrorism	180

List of boxes

1.1	School shooters and terrorism	12
1.2	The critical discourse analysis method	16
1.3	Paradigmatic dimensions of comparison	18
2.1	Defining terrorism in Spanish legal discourse	27
2.2	French revolutionary terror	28
3.1	The IRA and Martin McGuinness	38
3.2	Jihadi cell member skills, aptitudes, and roles in Petter Nesser	41
3.3	A weak rationality concept	45
4.1	The case of Anders Breivik	53
4.2	The Nuclei Armati Rivoluzionari in Italy	55
4.3	History repeats itself	59
5.1	Heroic role models and community approval: The case of Middle Eastern terrorists in Israel	67
5.2	On the seamless transition to terrorism in Horgan	68
5.3	The four stages of a terrorist event in Horgan	69
5.4	Grounded theory	70
5.5	SAT in action	74
6.1	Frames and framing	81
6.2	*Delinquent Boys: The Culture of the Gang* (1955)	85
6.3	Cognitive dissonance theory	87
7.1	Poverty, education, and terrorism	95
7.2	Democratic peace theory	98
7.3	The case of Benno Ohnesorg	102
8.1	The Beirut barracks bombings	112
8.2	Al-Qaeda's strategy	114
8.3	Inter-organizational rivalry in Northern Ireland	119
9.1	Revolutionary violence in Italy and the loss of support from the radical milieu	126
9.2	Indirect frame diffusion in Turkey—from the Arab–Israeli War to the Anti-Sixth Fleet demonstrations	127
10.1	Social learning	141
10.2	Governmental counter-terrorism programs in the UK and Denmark	147
10.3	State of exception	149

11.1	Interpretations of the French revolutionary terror	152
11.2	The Algerian War 1954–1962	153
11.3	Perpetuating terror	160
11.4	The terror foundations of the modern state	161
12.1	Czar Alexander II and the failed transformation of the system in Russia	166
12.2	The group Irgun Tz'va'i Le'umi and the struggle against the British	167
12.3	Weathermen aka Weather Underground and their 'Declaration of War' against the US	169
13.1	Suffragette bombers	181
13.2	Club de Madrid: tackling the socio-economic and political causes of terrorism	184
13.3	Italian legal inducements to quit terrorist organizations	187
13.4	Playing to the audience	190
13.5	Three foreign policy discourses after 9/11	193

List of contributors

Authors

Daniela Pisoiu is a senior researcher at the Austrian Institute for International Affairs (oiip) in Vienna, Austria. She obtained her PhD in International Relations at the University of St Andrews, Centre for the Study of Terrorism and Political Violence. She is the author of *Islamist Radicalisation in Europe: An Occupational Change Process* (Routledge, 2011), and editor of *Arguing Counterterrorism: New Perspectives* (Routledge, 2014). Her research interests include terrorism, radicalisation, extremism, comparative regional security, and American and European foreign and security policy.

Sandra Hain is affiliated with the Austrian Institute for International Affairs (oiip) in Vienna, Austria. She is a recent graduate of the MSc Security Studies program at the School of Public Policy of University College London (UCL). Her research interests include international security, terrorism, intelligence and foreign policy analysis.

Contributor

Asta Maskaliūnaitė is a senior lecturer in War and Conflict Studies at the Baltic Defence College, Tartu, Estonia. She obtained her PhD from the Central European University in 2007 with the thesis focusing on the role of ETA in Spanish politics. She is editor-in-chief of the *Journal on Baltic Security*. Her research interests include terrorism, especially its historical dimension, revolutions, and security studies.

List of acronyms

CCCT	Cabinet Committee to Combat Terrorism
CTS	critical terrorism studies
EOKA	Ethniki Organosis Kyprion Agoniston
ETA	Euskadi Ta Askatasuna
FARC	Fuerzas Armadas Revolucionarias de Colombia
FBI	Federal Bureau of Investigation
FLN	Front de Libération Nationale
GAL	Grupos Antiterroristas de Liberación
GDP	gross domestic product
GT	grounded theory
Hamas	Ḥarakat al-Muqāwama al-Islāmiyya
IDF	Israel Defense Forces
INLA	Irish National Liberation Army
IPLO	Irish People's Liberation Organisation
IR	international relations
IRA	Irish Republican Army
IS	Islamic State
ISIS	Islamic State of Iraq and Syria
LTTE	Liberation Tigers of Tamil Eelam
MENA	Middle East and North Africa
NAR	Nuclei Armati Rivoluzionari
NGO	non-governmental organization
QCA	qualitative comparative analysis
PADS+	Peterborough Adolescent and Young Adult Development Study
PLO	Palestine Liberation Organization
PIRA	Provisional Irish Republican Army
RAF	Red Army Faction
RB	Red Brigades
SAT	situational action theory
TOP	Terrorist Organization Profile
UAE	United Arab Emirates
UDA	Ulster Defense Association
UN	United Nations
UVF	Ulster Volunteer Force
WSPU	Women's Social and Political Union

Glossary

Agency A concept used in philosophy and sociology meaning the capacity of an agent to act (i.e. a person or entity). A moral dimension to the ability to make a choice is not implied in the capacity to act. In sociology, an agent is an individual that engages with the social structure. Agency may be classified as unconscious, involuntary behavior, or intentional (purposeful, goal-directed activity).

Anarchism A political philosophy that advocates non-hierarchical stateless societies. Anarchism holds the state to be unnecessary or harmful and does not offer a fixed body of doctrine. There are many types and traditions of anarchism that vary greatly and support anything from individualism to collectivism. Anarchism is often considered a radical left-wing ideology and its philosophy reflects anti-authoritarian interpretations of for example communism and collectivism.

Anti-colonialism A movement that opposes any form of colonialism. It aims to free the colonized from the colonizers.

Attrition Constant demoralization through wearing down with the aim to weaken or destroy (often used as the phrase 'war of attrition').

Clandestine organization An organization that keeps its affiliations and its activities secret, often by going underground, in order to avoid punishment by law enforcement.

Cognitive restructuring A psychotherapeutic process that includes learning to identify and dispute irrational or maladaptive thoughts. This can, for example, be all-or-nothing thinking or magical thinking, commonly associated with many mental health disorders.

Conservatism A political philosophy that opposes radical change and aims to preserve the best in an established society. Modern European conservatism evolved between 1750 and 1850 as a response to a rapid series of changes in European societies, i.e. the ideas of the Enlightenment, industrialization, and/or extended, usually male, suffrage.

Constructivism A political theory which asserts that human knowledge and understanding are constructed through social institutions and practices. It is assumed that knowledge of the material world becomes reality not through the discovery of truths and facts that are observable, but through intersubjective socialization and constructed understanding. As a result, constructivists question any claims of objective reality or knowledge. They

Glossary xiii

maintain that humans interpret, construct, and invent their knowledge of the material world, which in turn influences political actions and social thinking at a normative and political level.

Contentious politics Disruptive techniques used to make a political point, or to change the policies of governments. This can be demonstrations, general strikes, riots, terrorism, but also revolution or insurrection. It is often used by social movements.

Counter-culture A culture that deviates from a mainstream culture, with values and norms of behavior that differ from those of the mainstream society. When oppositional forces reach a critical mass, counter-cultures can also bring about dramatic cultural changes.

Critical discourse analysis An interdisciplinary approach to the study of discourse that focuses on language as a form of social practice and on the ways social and political domination are reproduced in text and talk. Since 1989 critical discourse analysis has been deployed as a method of multidisciplinary analysis throughout the humanities and social sciences. The overriding assumption shared by practitioners is that language and power are linked.

Critical theory A social theory that emphasizes critiquing and changing society, rather than merely understanding or explaining it, as in traditional theory. It encourages a multi-disciplinary approach to better understand society, and it stresses the need to analyse the totality of society in its historical context, including how it came into being.

Democratic peace theory A theory of liberal internationalist thought that asserts that liberal democratic states do not go to war with each other because of numerous factors, such as shared political and economic interests, or because democratic leaders want to avoid a potential public backlash after significant war losses. The validity of the democratic peace thesis has been fiercely debated in the international relations literature.

Fatwa A ruling or legal statement issued by an Islamic scholar.

Frames A pattern of interpretation that enables people to locate, perceive, identify, and label occurrences. They give meaning to events or occurrences and thereby organize experience and guide action.

Freedom fighter Refers to individuals that are engaged in a struggle to achieve political freedom for themselves or for others. The usage of the term is commonly restricted to those who are actively involved in an armed rebellion, and does not include those who campaign for freedom by peaceful means. Freedom fighters are commonly seen as people who use physical force in order to change the political or social order. They are also often called rebels, insurgents, or terrorists.

Free rider dilemma This occurs when someone benefits from resources, goods, or services without paying for the cost of the benefit. The term 'free rider' was first used in the economic theory of public goods, but it now also applies to other contexts like psychology or political science. The free rider dilemma is considered a problem when it leads to the under-provision of goods or services, or when it leads to overuse or degradation of a common resource.

xiv *Glossary*

French Revolution This refers to the period of radical social and political upheaval that lasted from 1789 until 1799. It led to the collapse of the monarchy that had been in power for centuries, and thus to a considerable change in the structure of society. The revolution was an important factor in the spread of major modern political political ideologies, such as liberalism and nationalism, and also precipitated the rise of republics and democracies around the world.

Genocide Acts that intentionally destroy a national, ethnic, racial, or religious group. The United Nations Convention on the Prevention and Punishment of the Crime of Genocide, which took place in 1948, led to the first legal definition of this crime.

Group polarization A concept of social psychology that refers to the tendency for groups to make decisions that are more extreme than the original inclination of its members. If the individuals' initial tendencies were to be risky, the extreme decisions are of greater risk. If they were initially rather cautious, the extreme decisions are of greater caution. It also holds that a group's attitude toward a situation may change in the sense that the individuals' initial attitudes have strengthened and intensified after group discussion.

Groupthink A psychological phenomenon that occurs when a group of people trying to minimize conflict and reach a consensus. The desire for harmony or conformity in the group results in an incorrect or deviant decision-making outcome because of an uncritical evaluation of alternative ideas or viewpoints and because people isolate themselves from external influences.

International conventions A general treaty between states, often the result of an international conference. It may set out goals or proceedings with the aim to develop future actions or may prohibit certain actions.

Islamic Salafi ideology and Salafi jihad Salafism is described as a purer, stricter, and more fundamentalist version of the Quran and hadith. Islamic Salafi ideology, jihad as a call for violence and revolution, as well as transnationalism, are characteristics of global Salafi jihad groups. Adherents include purists who emphasize non-violent means and education, politicos who stress the Salafi creed to politics, irredentist jihadis who fight foreign invaders to Islamic territory, and internal jihadis who strive to introduce Sharia law to their country. Global Salafi jihad groups strategically aim to defeat the 'far enemy' (Western countries) first before fighting the 'near enemy,' meaning their own, often authoritarian, governments.

Jihad Means 'struggle' in Arabic and can refer to an internal struggle of an individual to be a better Muslim, a struggle to make society more closely align with the teachings of the Koran, or a call to arms to wage a war in self-defense of an Islamic community under attack.

Just war theory A doctrine that aims to ensure a war is morally justifiable according to certain criteria. The theory asserts that war, despite being abominable, is not always the worst option, as there are cases where it can prevent further atrocities, for example.

Liberalism A political philosophy that emphasizes the equality of rights and personal liberty. It has focused on the space available to individuals to pursue their own lives, or their own conception of the good. The arbitrary will of a monarch was seen as a threat to this 'space' and led liberals to consider the limits of political power. Religious or social intolerance were seen as further threats. In general, liberalism has tried to draw the line between the public and the private. They also focused on the relationship between legitimate power and consent, and the rule of law. Liberalism also asserts that the most effective economic system is one that is market-driven and (neither domestically or internationally) subordinated to bureaucratic regulation and control.

Narcissism An excessive admiration of oneself. A personality disorder that is characterized by an abnormal sense of self-importance, a need for admiration, and lack of empathy. The technical term is *narcissistic personality disorder*. In psychoanalytic theory it derives from a fixation on or a regression to an infantile stage of development.

New Left A movement that challenges the doctrines, methods of organization, and styles of leadership of the 'old' left. It emerged from the disintegration of Soviet hegemony after 1956, the East European revolts and the Soviet response and the repercussions that caused in the individual communist parties. It influenced feminism, green parties, Euro-communism, and a renaissance in intellectual thought on the left in general.

Positivism A form of strong empiricism that rejects metaphysics and theology as methods of seeking knowledge. It holds that experimental investigation as well as observation are the only legitimate sources of substantial knowledge. Furthermore, positivism maintains that society is analagous to the physical world, in that also functions according to general laws.

Post-structuralism An intellectual movement that developed in Europe in the 20th century. Its predecessor is structuralism. Post-structuralists argue that human culture may be understood by means of a structure—modeled on language—that differs from reality and abstract ideas. Post-structuralists maintain that meanings and intellectual categories shift and are unstable. They critique structuralism insofar as they reject the self-sufficiency of the structures and an interrogation of the binary oppositions that constitute those structures.

Power The ability to change the (intended) actions of people (or things). Arguably the first person who wrote about power was Niccolò Machiavelli in the late 15th century. The modern concept of power was recognized in 1748, with the publication of Hume's essay *Of the Original Contract*. Hume argued that all existing governments have been founded on usurpation or conquest, without fair consent or the voluntary subjection of the people. Political power refers to the authority of a certain individual or group that enables the implementation of policies and the administration of public resources.

Psychological warfare Psychological warfare uses various techniques to influence the value system, belief system, emotions, motives, reasoning, or behavior of the audience of a target. It is applied to induce confessions or reinforce attitudes and behaviors that favor the objectives of the conductor. Target audiences can be governments, organizations, groups, as well as individuals.

xvi *Glossary*

Rational choice An approach to the study of politics which focuses on the individual actor as the basic unit of analysis. It models economic and political behavior and assumes that individuals behave rationally. Rationality is usually defined in terms of transitivity and consistency of choice.

Reign of Terror Also known as 'The Terror,' this was a period of violence from 5 September 1793 to 28 July 1794. It occurred after the onset of the French Revolution and was incited by conflict between the Girondins and the Jacobins as rival political factions. The Reign of Terror was marked by mass executions of 'enemies of the revolution.' The death toll ranged in the tens of thousands across France.

Relative deprivation The deprivation of something that an individual believes himself or herself to be entitled to. The experience can lead to the feeling of discontent when people compare their achievements to others and realize that they have less of what they believe themselves to be entitled to.

Rogue state A term used by some theorists for states that are considered to threaten world peace. States that are labeled as rogue states usually meet certain criteria, like being ruled by authoritarian regimes that restrict human rights, that sponsor terrorism, or proliferate weapons of mass destruction. The term is mostly used by the United States, but the US State Department officially quit using the term in 2000. The term is also applied by other countries as well.

Sampling bias A systematic error that occurs when one studies a nonrandom sample of a population.

Selective incentives They can be used to correct the free rider problem. Selective incentives are a way of encouraging people to contribute to a common good, by either rewarding participants, or punishing individuals that do not participate.

Social contract A contract between individuals in a situation that is characterized by a pre-political or pre-social condition. It specifies the terms upon which they are willing to enter society or submit to a political authority. The term is often used to illuminate the transition from a state of nature to a social and/or political existence.

Social movement A political formation that aims to bring about political change or new ways of thinking to the political agenda through direct action, with loose and informal organizational structures. Social movements are organized around ideas which give adherents a new social and political identity.

Structure This exists independently of the actor (i.e. a social class). It is an important determinant in the nature of the action (e.g. a revolution).

Subculture A group of people within a culture that differentiates itself from the mainstream culture. It is also defined as a group within a culture that has its own culture, with different beliefs or interests.

Subjectivity A fundamental philosophical concept that refers to the perception of truth based on the perspective of a subject. It is commonly used to explain the influences and biases that affect the way individuals experience truth and reality. In contrast, objectivity describes views of truth or reality that are devoid of any individual's influence.

War on Terror A term that was invented by the Bush administration after the attacks on the World Trade Center in New York on September 11, 2001. It refers to military, political, and legal actions taken by the US and its allies to fight terrorism in general and Islamic-inspired terrorism in particular.

Acknowledgements

This book is dedicated to three important women and a dad who, at various stages in our lives, have encouraged us to pursue our dreams and believe in ourselves: Aurora, Manuela, Anita, and Dorin.

The authors would like to thank their colleagues at the Austrian Institute for International Affairs for their support and inspiring working atmosphere, especially our director Dr Ilse König for her leadership and commitment to the empowerment of women. The authors are also thankful to Reem Ahmed, Hakan Akbulut, Benedict Etz and Stefan Meingast for their careful and patient reading of the manuscript and their precious advice.

The book has been produced as part of the cooperation between the Austrian Institute for International Affairs (oiip) and the Danube University Krems.

Introduction

Terrorism studies is a highly heterogeneous and amply debated field. Often driven by events or policy interests, terrorism scholarship is developing at various paces with various emphases in different parts of the world. Another typical feature is the incredibly high number of theories and disciplines which have something to say about terrorism, to an extent more or less covering the entire range of social sciences and humanities. At the same time, terrorism often surprises through its *lack of explicit reference to theory*. The following four scenarios can occur: concepts and theories pertaining to the broader social science scholarship are used without naming the original theories and sources; these concepts and theories are named, yet in a small number and with a narrow view on the broader scholarship; terrorism-specific theories are proposed without mentioning how they replicate or draw on broader social science theories; the works are purely empirical and/or historical with no mentioning whatsoever of any particular theory. There are of course also plenty of works which explicitly name their theoretical sources, or even place themselves in a theoretical tradition. Beyond these individual contributions and unique perspectives, however, it is difficult to have a broader and structured grasp of the theoretical landscape within and behind the study of terrorism.

The idea for this book has emerged from rather practical considerations and is also meant to address the practical needs of students or any other readers interested in grasping the field and its workings. It is a general introduction to the kinds of questions, approaches, and to a lesser extent methods used in the field, but it particularly focuses on theories and aims to achieve the following:

- it identifies the main theories proposed in the field of terrorism studies;
- relates these theories (or traces them back) to political science, sociological, psychological, criminological and broader social science theories;
- sets these theories in the broader paradigmatic perspectives of the more traditional vs. the critical terrorism studies scholarships;
- proposes an orientation tool in the form of a typology for the classification of theories addressing the questions 'why' and 'how' of terrorism and counter-terrorism.

Clearly, a lot has been written on terrorism, and the scholarship is on a steady rise. No book can include all of this production and a selection needs to take place in some way. Some of the orientation points taken in selecting works for this book have been, apart from the books and authors which have been influential for our own development, books and authors which are generally acknowledged as representative for certain perspectives on theories, as well as

2 *Introduction*

contents of individual syllabi. The book does not stand in competition but rather complements available handbooks, which are in the main collections of existing 'primary documents' as it were—influential articles and book chapters, or empirical and/or historical accounts. What it does is help the student of terrorism better understand and use these and other material.

The book aims to address some of the main topics and aspects of terrorism studies: non-state but also state terrorism; majorly terrorism but also counter-terrorism; positivist and critical approaches. Above all, the book introduces a paradigmatic triad which can itself also be traced back to broader social science paradigms and their assumptions about agency, structure, and causality. In this book, we have called this: the deterministic, intentional, and relational approach. The terms, as such, have been already used by social movements scholars in the attempt to more clearly delineate their work from that of others, namely deterministic and rational choice. We have opted for intentional instead of 'rational choice' in order to avoid the immediate association with mathematical models and the economic understanding of rational choice more broadly, which would have been a rather narrow understanding of what we actually mean by 'intentional.' This classification is a heuristic tool which should help readers better locate and understand the assumptions behind any particular text they are reading. Scholars usually do not mention these terms in their studies, with the exception of social movement scholars as mentioned, and others working through a 'strategic' lens, for example. This separation itself is also heuristic, since one and the same work can contain elements of two or even three approaches. Such is, for example, the case of Wiktorowicz's (2005) radicalization model, which starts off with a deterministic phase—various personal crises which determine religious seeking; continues with a relational phase—the indoctrination carried out by movement entrepreneurs; and progresses towards an intentional approach—paradise as rational choice. The theory proposed by Pisoiu (2012) also follows a mixed approach, by combining elements of rational choice in criminology (intentional approach) with relational elements pertaining to framing theory.

The structure of the individual chapters involves the presentation and discussion of the main theories of terrorism pertaining to that particular topic, a genealogy of 'where they are coming from,' the kinds of methods usually used in the field, empirical examples, further reading and questions. We have attempted to include both positivist and critical approaches, concepts and theories in all of the chapters. The first chapter discusses these paradigms in more detail. The second chapter deals with the definition of terrorism, which it assesses along several levels of analysis. The third chapter deals with broader questions regarding the study of terrorism and introduces the triad of approaches. We have structured the causes and processes of terrorism along two dimensions: individuals (Chapters 4, 5, and 6) and organizations (Chapters 7, 8, and 9), and by these approaches: deterministic individual (Chapter 4), deterministic organizations (Chapter 7), intentional individual (Chapter 5), intentional organizations (Chapter 8), relational individual (Chapter 6), and relational organizations (Chapter 9). Disengagement from terrorism and counter-terrorism are also analyzed along these three dimensions and by looking at individuals (Chapter 10) and organizations (Chapter 13). We finally look at state terrorism (Chapter 11) and terrorism in time and space (Chapter 12).

Before engaging with the core of the book, it is important to discuss some issues connected to the traditional vs. critical terrorism studies debate, and introduce the triad of deterministic, intentional, and relational approaches.

Traditional vs. critical terrorism studies

One of the main things that 'traditional' terrorism studies scholars did in reply to the critique advanced by the critical terrorism studies (CTS) school was to contest the novelty the latter claimed for themselves and their work. Indeed, there had been studies on state terrorism before, and quite a few scholars outside CTS have and continue to work with interpretative methods; most even pay attention to context. In short, not all traditionals are quantitative and not all think the Western state is beyond reproach. Some of the exchanges became unnecessarily personal and it is understandable that some scholars might have felt uncomfortable in one way or another. At the same time, it might be pointed out that paradigmatic separations and contradictory discussions exist in all fields. Indeed, critical theory has been present in a number of other disciplines and fields, so it was really just a matter of time until this kind of approach would also focus on terrorism studies. Obviously, there are some critical specificities and these are clearly reflected in the CTS scholarship too, such as, for example, the emphasis on the normative dimension, but also ontological specificities, according to which, for example, calling something 'terrorism' is a social convention. This clearly has effects on the kinds of questions CTS scholars ask and the kinds of theories and methods they choose to employ. One manifestation of this is, for example, the relatively lesser interest in investigating the 'causes' of terrorism, whereas a lot more effort is invested in understanding how something gets called 'terrorism' in the first place, and what consequences this labeling has on politics and society. There are, however, also commonalities, such as, for example, when critical scholars also wish to understand the pathways of individuals towards violence. The critical scholarship is in general not that far from the 'relational approach' (see below), from the perspective of the relationship to context, as well as the embedding of terrorism in broader kinds of political violence, and also the consideration of subjectivity to some extent. In general, however, it remains focused on broader kinds of questions related to structure and power, rather than the destiny of individuals or individual movements.

Deterministic, intentional, and relational approaches

Although not the central question shaping the interests of CTS, even these scholars have acknowledged that "The question of what causes terrorism is one of the most important and hotly debated topics in terrorism studies" (Jackson et al. 2011: 198). We also dedicate in this book several chapters to the various approaches to not only the causes and motivations but also the processes of involvement in terrorism; we also extend the typology to the analysis of counter-terrorism and how terrorism ends. We furthermore differentiate between individuals and organizations and propose a typology of *deterministic, intentional*, and *relational* approaches. We have included the *critical* scholarship dedicated to these questions under *relational* approaches due to the commonalities they share in terms of assumptions.

The three approaches are neither theories nor paradigms, but heuristic devices that can help classify and understand the underlying assumptions of theories at hand with regard to, for example, the role of agency and structure. 'Agency' refers to the capacity of individuals to act independently and make their own independent choices, whereas 'structure' is a more general depiction of systemic factors which affect individual behavior. The structure vs. agency debate, which one offers a more credible and fitting explanation, is age-old in social science and is naturally reflected also in the terrorism literature, which is in effect only a kaleidoscope of various fields of social science. Matching this broader divide in social science, some theories of terrorism prioritize structure over agency (deterministic approaches), and others emphasize agency over structure (intentional approaches). A central concept to mark the difference between deterministic and intentional approaches, between the effect of structure vs. agency, is the concept of choice. In determinism, there is no choice: given one or more conditions, terrorism will occur. With intentional approaches, there is choice, terrorism can or cannot be the option to take, the individual or the organization decides. Here, the individual (as actual individual or group) and their conscious deliberation are at the forefront, rather than some external factors or unconscious psychological forces. Furthermore, the assumption here is that individuals and groups aim towards something in the future, rather than reacting mechanically to something that occurred in the past or exists in the present. That is, deterministic approaches are in this sense 'reactive,' while intentional ones are 'purposive.' A third category (relational approaches) is a union in that it acknowledges intentionality, i.e. that individual actions have a purpose rather than being the result of some external forces, yet they see individual choice as shaped and thus limited by various types of contexts, whether they pertain to the terrorist organization itself, the broader political system, ideology, or something else. Additionally, agency is always seen as formed by the relations in which it engages. Critical approaches also fit here, as they consider both grievance and opportunities, and, more broadly, structure and agency. Jackson et al. (2011: 201), for example, outline that "The critical approach we take in this book looks at both structural and agency-based explanations, situating agents within their structural contexts while recognizing that these contexts are, in part, shaped by the actions of those agents."

Scholarship has studied both individuals and organizations from these three perspectives. It is, however, interesting to note that the 'popular wisdom' in the scholarship tends to see individuals as driven towards terrorism, while organizations are rather seen as strategic actors. On the reverse, most approaches to disengaging individuals assume them to be rational and offer them incentives, whereas more often than not the underlying logic of counter-terrorism addressing organizations is more of a deterministic nature. Running through all three approaches is a specificity dilemma: on the one hand, explanations specific to terrorism are being sought to realize that in fact most of the empirical manifestations of it are not specific at all. On the other hand, approaches that start off with the assumption that there is little specificity to terrorism eventually have a hard time explaining why the kinds of manifestations under study eventually end up in terrorism rather than something else.

Apart from the question 'why'—what are the causes and motivations to engage in terrorism, there is also the question 'how'—what is the process of it? Process can obviously be conceptualized in a number of ways; here we mean by 'process' the broad conceptualization of an evolution in time of this involvement in terrorism. This has concretized in different ways in the literature, depending on the approach and research tradition. Relational approaches focus on process *par excellence*, as it has at its core interactions between the various actors and mechanisms, such as socialization into certain views and behaviors, which necessarily occur over time. Process and its component concepts such as that of 'mechanism' are often positioned as an alternative to cause–effect relationships. Intentional approaches have also acknowledged process more explicitly, by outlining how individual involvement, for example, often occurs as a 'drift' or 'small steps,' and by differentiating between the point in time when one joins and later points in time when one commits acts of violence, for example. Another instance here are the decision-making processes of organizations as they relate to engagement in terrorism. Deterministic approaches also consider process, but they are more interested in the initial phase and the determining factors that lead to involvement in terrorism in the first place.

The classification we have proposed here is not entirely new. Indeed, social movement scholars have already proposed the term 'relational' to describe their approach and have more generally differentiated themselves from what they label 'deterministic' and 'rational choice' approaches. The term 'intentional' has been also used before as a further qualification of what Martha Crenshaw termed "the instrumental approach": "In this perspective violence is seen as intentional. Terrorism is a means to a political end" (Crenshaw 2001: 13). Her approach is focused on a specific formula involving a calculation of benefit, cost, and probabilities and functions in relation to political goals of organizations. We understand 'intentional' in a broader way to include goals beyond those ideologically declared, of various types, including personal, and also applying to individuals. We acknowledge the explanatory power of mathematical models, yet do not explicitly focus on them in this book.

To put our classification into perspective, we mention here another similar categorization which has been proposed in sociology by differentiating between 'substantialism' and 'relationalism,' itself drawing on more fundamental philosophical delineations (Emirbayer 1997). Substantialism assumes that 'substances' of various kinds (things, beings, etc.) are the fundamental units of analysis. Here we have first of all the rational choice theory, which assumes that actors are rational and calculating, with given goals and interests. Second, there is critical theory which conceives of individuals as driven by norms or social ideals. A further category of substantialism looks at action among entities, "much like billiard balls or the particles in the Newtonian mechanics" (ibid: 286). This is the 'variable-centered approach' whereby not the substances but the causation occurring among them is of interest—essentially our deterministic approach. Finally, in the 'transactional' or 'relational' approach "the very terms or units involved in a transaction derive their meaning, significance, and identity from the (changing) functional roles they play within that transaction. The latter, seen as a dynamic, unfolding process, becomes the primary unit of analysis rather than the constituent elements themselves" (ibid: 287). In the relational approach, agency itself is defined by the relations in which it enters:

> the relational point of view sees agency as inseparable from the unfolding dynamics of situations, especially from the problematic features of these situations ... Agency is always a dialogic process by which actors immersed in the *dureé* of lived experience engage with others in collectively organized action contexts, temporal as well as spatial.
>
> (Emirbayer 1997: 294)

In fact, individual entities are not seen as given at all, but always defined by transactional contexts, such that their very being is given by "the relations in which they are engaged" (ibid: 287). To be entirely fair, the operationalization of relations in the relational studies that we will discuss in this book does not go so far as to 'constitute' individuals and organizations; the latter are rather influenced by these relations in various ways.

The genealogy of the three approaches is multifold and multidisciplinary. *Deterministic* accounts are traceable to political science analyses of collective violence more broadly and which are in search of macro-variables such as relative deprivation, lack of democracy, etc., but also psychology and especially psychoanalysis. In an early overview of the research on terrorism, Ted R. Gurr, the inventor of relative deprivation theory, indicates at the same time some of the basic principles and methods of the deterministic approach—without naming it as such of course. Interestingly, and not unlike later scholars, he criticizes the lack

6 *Introduction*

of first-hand data in terrorism research, which effectively takes this line of argumentation from the exclusive possession of CTS. Indeed he notes:

> Careful gleaning of the literature turns up sound quantitative, comparative and historical studies of terrorist phenomena. But the fact remains that the research questions raised in the literature are considerably more interesting than most of the evidence brought to bear on them. With a few clusters of exceptions there is in fact a disturbing lack of good empirically-grounded research on terrorism.
>
> (Gurr 1988: 115)

His methodological account reveals the positivist assumptions behind this approach, namely: looking for explanations, the focus on quantitative methods, and the research design revolving around hypothesis testing. He contends that methodology "does not mean simply the analysis of quantitative data," but that, however, "the most technically sophisticated methods are those designed to generate and analyse quantified information" (ibid: 117). With respect to research design, methodologies "assume the existence of an analytical question and a body of relevant information which bears on the question" (ibid: 117). Most importantly as an indicator for the features of this approach and the criteria for inclusion therein, is the aim to discover what determines terrorism. This is pursued at different levels, with different units of analysis, and much of the (quantitative) work would also be simply descriptive in nature—in the sense of descriptive statistics. Importantly, however, we are not looking here at decision-making processes or interactions and we do not aim to 'understand' but to explain. We find here also terms which are more specific to other approaches, such as 'context.' Here context, however, plays the role of determining variable. To illustrate this, at the national level of analysis, Gurr mentions the 'political context,' which can appear in research questions such as:

> In what kinds of political systems are oppositional and state terrorism most likely? What are the relationships between the state's use of coercion and violence and the resort to oppositional terrorism? More generally, what kinds of conflicts are most likely to give rise to terrorist campaigns?
>
> (Gurr 1998: 123)

As another example of overlap with other approaches, at the individual level of analysis, Gurr enumerates perceived deprivation, but also rational choice or group solidarity as possible motivational factors (ibid: 137).

The main tenets of the *intentional* approach to organizational involvement in terrorism can be traced directly to the resource mobilization theory in social movements. At the time (the 1970s), new perspectives on collective action emphasized assumptions concerning actors' rationality and the strategic nature of their actions. J. Craig Jenkins (1983) lists the main elements of the theory in the following manner:

> (a) movement actions are rational, adaptive responses to the costs and rewards of different lines of action; (b) the basic goals of movements are defined by conflicts of interest built into institutionalized power relations; (c) the grievances generated by such conflicts are sufficiently ubiquitous that the formation and mobilization of movements depend on changes in resources, group organization, and opportunities for collective action; (d) centralized, formally structured movement organizations are more typical of

modern social movements and more effective at mobilizing resources and mounting sustained challenges than decentralized, informal movement structures; and (e) the success of movements is largely determined by strategic factors and the political processes in which they become enmeshed.

(Jenkins 1983: 528)

It is this literature, but also criminology and economics, which have debated and found a solution for individual involvement in a type of activity that invites free riding, namely the construct of selective incentives. This conceptualization of the free rider dilemma and its solution goes back to the work of economist Mancur Olson, which was then used in social movement resource mobilization theory. Mancur Olson presented his (revised) study *The Logic of Collective Action: Public Goods and the Theory of Groups* in 1971. In this influential but also criticized work he examines *inter alia* labor unions, trade associations, and professional associations. He finds that in large groups there can be no collective action in the pursuit of a collective good (a non-excludable, public good) because rational, self-interested individuals seek to maximize their gains while minimizing their costs. As the contribution of each single member in large groups is small, their participation is not decisive for the overall outcome which provokes some group members to free ride, meaning that they enjoy the public good provided through the action of others. Olson states that this free rider dilemma can only be overcome in large groups by forcing the members to contribute to the achievement of the collective good or by offering them selective incentives, e.g. prestige or money. To the contrary, Olson assumes that this is somewhat different in small groups as there can be a group interest which makes coercion or selective incentives unnecessary to achieve the collective good. This is so because first, some group members might have such a high interest in achieving the goal; second, the return to each group member is much higher in small groups; third, the organizational costs are lower in small groups; and finally, because it is easier to influence group members in smaller units.

According to the narrative of contemporary scholars using *relational approaches* to explain terrorism, this approach has emerged as an alternative to pre-existing deterministic and rational choice models. More recently, these scholars have also made a point out of criticizing 'orthodox' terrorism scholars and in so doing aligned themselves with the critical terrorism scholars. Both of these camps share an interest in context and advocate the application of existing social science research to what they view as essentially yet another type of political violence. Inevitably, however, the relational scholarship on terrorism—in essence the social movement relational scholarship on terrorism—is not uncharted territory. Indeed, on a closer look, many of the ideas, concepts, and mechanisms advanced in relational approaches find parallels in the deterministic and intentional approaches. For example, the ideas of resources and opportunities influencing organizational decision-making, and indeed the consideration of organizational decision-making in the first place, share commonalities with intentional approaches. More than anything, however, relational approaches to terrorism draw on relational approaches in social movements, which stress first and foremost the idea of process. Terrorism is not the expression of a cold and calculated strategy—at least not exclusively—and is not caused by external factors. Just like any other type of political violence, terrorism emerges out of processes of contention and as a matter of escalation of other repertoires of protest.

This focus on continuities with other types of violence, as well as the openness to broader theoretical approaches, and the interest in context, are elements that CTS also favors. Unlike

8 *Introduction*

social movement relational scholars, however, CTS scholars' stance on causality is more nuanced:

> Some are skeptical on the entire notion, regarding it as too embedded in positivist, problem-solving perspectives ... Instead of seeking to *explain* patterns of violence by identifying regularities, their focus is on understanding the meaning of the violence, usually through an emphasis on discourse analysis or ethnographic fieldwork ... These scholars are wary of generalizations and the quest for a unified explanatory framework and prefer to look at each instance of violence as self-contained and embedded in a particular web of local meanings. ... Scholars from a Critical Theory background tend to be more accepting of the notion of causation and acknowledge there exist human regularities on which tentative causal generalizations may be made. But they reject the positivists' desire to turn these tentative generalizations into "objective" laws and insist on taking both local meaning and their own (scholarly) subjectivity into account.
>
> (Jackson et al. 2011: 202)

The consequence of the critical theoretical and methodological stances they follow, limits to a certain extent the kinds of questions they ask and the methods they use to answer them. At the same time, the increased reflexivity with regard to the effect of context and the effect of discourse on policy explanations broaden the scope of the analysis on terrorism these scholars undertake.

As will become clear in the course of the book, it is these authors' belief that both the traditional or better-said 'classical' terrorism studies literature and the critical literature have brought important contributions to the study of this phenomenon. Importantly, their contributions should not necessarily be seen in competition with each other, but rather as complementary. The different theoretical and methodological traditions have influenced the kinds of questions and approaches scholars have taken up, even in relation to the same object of study. Not only have critical scholars preferred to look at counter-terrorism, rather than terrorism, at groups rather than individuals, at the discourse rather than at the behavior, but they also have a different interest in individual involvement in terrorism, for example, when that becomes the object of study, such as, for example, political structures, power, and resistance. A topic of hot dispute remains of course the definition of terrorism, but in general it would be fair to say that, not unlike other fields of study, terrorism has finally become researchable and researched in the entire range of social science perspectives, with the various constellations of research questions, theories, and methods. This is a sign of a field having reached maturity.

References

Crenshaw, M. (2001). Theories of Terrorism: Instrumental and Organizational Approaches, in Rapoport, D.C. (ed.) *Inside Terrorist Organizations*, 2nd Edn, London/Portland: Frank Cass, pp. 13–31.

Emirbayer, M. (1997). Manifesto for a Relational Sociology. *American Journal of Sociology*, 103(2), pp. 281–317.

Gurr, T.R. (1988). Empirical Research on Political Terrorism: The State of the Art and How it Might be Improved, in Slater, R.O. and Stohl, M. (eds) *Current Perspectives on International Terrorism*, Basingstoke, Hampshire: Macmillan, pp. 115–154.

Jackson, R., Jarvis, L., Gunning, J. and Breen Smyth, M. (2011). *Terrorism. A Critical Introduction*, New York: Palgrave Macmillan.

Jenkins, J.C. (1983). Resource Mobilization Theory and the Study of Social Movements. *Annual Review of Sociology*, 9, pp. 527–553.

Olson, M. Jr. (1971). *The Logic of Collective Action: Public Goods and the Theory of Groups*, Revised Edition, New York: Schocken Books.

Pisoiu, D. (2012). *Islamist Radicalisation in Europe. An Occupational Change Process,* Abingdon/NewYork: Routledge.

Wiktorowicz, Q. (2005). *Radical Islam Rising: Muslim Extremism in the West*, Oxford: Rowman & Littlefield.

1 The making of terrorism

Terrorism has become a very popular term, in spite of, or perhaps precisely because of its negative connotation. In some opinions, we live in the era of Islamist terrorism and most countries around the globe are currently having some type of contact with it. 'What is terrorism?' is an important and legitimate question and most books on the topic start off with a section on definitions. We consider it more useful to begin our journey through terrorism studies by discerning terrorism from other phenomena in the popular understanding and that of terrorists themselves. Following this, we identify 'labeling' as a central concept and mechanism underlying the 'making' of terrorism in popular and political discourse. We then trace it back to some foundational social science theories in the positivist and critical theory traditions, and then discuss the latter paradigms along their ontological, epistemological, and normative dimensions.

Most people associate terrorism with something bad. Particularly in our times, marked by the rise to prominence of the so-called Islamic State (IS) terrorist group and their long trail of death and atrocity, it would be quite difficult to think otherwise. In most countries and also at the level of international organizations such as the United Nations (UN), terrorism is a crime. In fact, under the influence of recent threat assessments, most Western countries have extended the definition of terrorism in their criminal codes to include actions which are associated with terrorism, without being terror attacks proper, such as training in terror camps. Typical actions which have been categorized as terrorism are otherwise, for example, bombings, kidnappings, hostage takings, assaults, etc. In the general under-standing, the condition for these acts to be categorized as 'terrorism' is their political motive. In other words, a kidnapping for ransom would be a 'regular' crime, since it has been committed for the purpose of self-enrichment, whereas if the same kidnappers have political demands instead, this would be terrorism. Oftentimes this distinction can be blurred, however, by the fact that the activities of terror groups usually also include purely criminal acts. Robbing a bank or the aforementioned kidnapping can be carried out for material reasons and in order to ensure the survival or expansion of the group, whose ultimate purpose is nevertheless of a political nature. Furthermore, the activities of some groups such as the FARC (Fuerzas Armadas Revolucionarias de Colombia) become so much entangled with organized crime that it is difficult to draw the line. In general, however, the rule of thumb is to say—as long as there is an ideology behind the crime, we are dealing with terrorism.

That said, it is apparent that media, politics, and also academia are often biased in their labeling of criminal acts with an ideological background as terrorism vs. something else, such as extremism or amok. In particular in relation to crimes motivated by right-wing extremist ideology, a certain 'blindness in the right eye' has been accused. Concretely, attacks motivated by Islamist ideology tend to be labeled as 'terrorism,' regardless how ideological the person was, or how close their connections to a terrorist group were. In contrast, attacks motivated by right-wing extremist ideology are rarely labeled as 'terrorist,' except when the number of victims is exceptionally high, or the attack is in another way 'noteworthy.' Such events also tend to capture less media and public attention. School shootings are another kind of violent criminal act which rarely receives the label of terrorism, although some of the perpetrators have an explicit political agenda. Leena Malkki (2014) has dealt at length with this issue and has outlined, among others, that there are parallels between terrorist and school shooting events, in terms of both empirical manifestation (see Box 1.1) and of the theoretical explanations offered, such as marginality and personal problems (see Further reading and Chapter 4 in this book).

Box 1.1 School shooters and terrorism

Malkki investigated in her study *Political Elements in Post-Columbine School Shootings in Europe and North America* (2014) common and prevalent political elements in school rampage shootings after the Columbine shootings in 1999, one of the most deadly school rampage shootings in US history that often served as a model for other perpetrators. She conducted a comparative case study with 28 school rampage shootings in Europe, Canada, and the US between 1999 and 2001. School rampage shootings are defined as acts that are "(at least partly) indiscriminate shootings perpetrated by former or current students of that school. They are 'attacks on whole institutions – schools, teenage pecking orders, or communities'" (ibid: 186–187) and are intended to reach a wider audience and not only the immediate victims; it is a form of symbolic violence. This is a commonality they have with terrorism. Malkki found that none of the perpetrators were involved in political action before, or tried to join an organization with political objectives. Yet, in two cases the offenders had some correspondence with political organizations or people. In four cases, the perpetrators left behind communication including political elements as an explanation for the shootings. The main reasons for the offenders to conduct the shootings were that the school shooters mixed personal grievances (i.e. because of bullying, failure to integrate, and rejection) and political grievances (i.e. because of collective de-individualization, the system, corrupt and totalitarian regimes, tyrants and gangsters that create slaves, and the rule of idiocracy). Many of them called for a revolution and stated that they would hope that others might follow their example. One of them, Pekka-Eric Auvinen, who conducted the Jokela High School shootings in Finland in 2007, even explicitly stated that his act would be a mass murder and political terrorism.

Calling names

Ordinarily, terrorists are eager to differentiate themselves and their actions from regular criminals. Ulrike Meinhof, one of the leading members of the terrorist group Red Army Faction (RAF), founded in the 1970s in West Germany, coined the phrase: "If you throw a stone, it's a crime. If a thousand stones are thrown, that's political. If you set fire to a car it's a crime; if a hundred cars are set on fire that's political" (cited in Aust 2008: 36). The phrase marked a turning moment in her biography and that of the group. She wrote this after the attempted assassination of the student leader Rudi Dutschke by a right-wing extremist and, in her and others' interpretation at the time, at the instigation of an anti-student movement campaign in the *Bild* newspaper. The phrase marked the acceptance of the use of violence against the perceived authoritarian and 'Nazi' government. The group obviously did not see itself as terrorist; on the contrary, it was the 'pig' state which was guilty of aggression against its people and those of other nations—the RAF saw the German government at the time in an 'imperialist' alliance with the US.

The RAF is just an example of the ways in which terrorist groups label their enemies with terms usually derived from the animal kingdom. The term 'pig society' is, for example, typical for historical left-wing groups, such as the RAF. Ulrike Meinhof is quoted to have said:

> As for the cops in this context, it is argued that they are naturally brutal because of their job, beating and shooting people is their job, repression is their job, but then again that's only the uniform, only the job, and the man who wears the uniform and does the job may be a perfectly pleasant character at home ... This is the problem, and of course we say the cops are swine, we say a man in uniform's a pig, not a human being, so we must tackle him. I mean we mustn't talk to him; it's wrong to talk to these people at all, and of course there may be shooting.
>
> (cited in Aust 2008: 11)

Contemporary jihadi groups also use the term 'pig' or 'monkey' to designate the '*kafir*' (unbelievers). Terrorism scholars have interpreted this kind of euphemism as an attempt on the part of the terrorists to deny guilt by denying humanity to their victims. Bonnie Cordes (1987) undertook to examine instances 'when terrorists do the talking' and found that this denial strategy became necessary in a political context where terrorism was not the only avenue to express grievances. Concretely, this refers to the fact that terror groups that act within democratic states could theoretically express their disagreement and protest through legal means, such as demonstrations, in parliament, or through civil society campaigns. Instead, they opt for armed struggle as if these democratic options do not exist. In the process, they furthermore commit acts of violence against state institutions and citizens, something that becomes not only legally, but also morally problematic. In order to overcome this dilemma of consciousness, terrorists need to frame the state and in some cases also its people as 'evil.' Unlike criminals, who may accept the label 'criminal,' terrorists deny their appellative and generally come to see their violence in other terms to the rest of the population. Terrorist communiqués oftentimes label the opposing state as terrorist and criminal and themselves as freedom fighters or revolutionaries, and their actions as part of a revolutionary struggle. The audience of these messages of persuasion is not just external, but also internal—terrorists need to also convince themselves that they are doing the right thing. This kind of analysis needs to be of course contextualized in its own historical moment: the 1980s were (still) marked by the allure of left-wing terrorism in its 'pure' form in Germany, Italy or the US, or alongside the more underlying cause of national liberation in Ireland or the Middle East (see Chapter 12 for more historical detail). While these kinds of terrorism have not died out, at least in the popular perception and according to some analysts, it is religious terrorism that occupies the frontlines. In its contemporary form, religious terrorism is global and also targeting 'foreign' states and civilian populations more than state institutions. The mechanism of labeling remains the same, though, as jihadi terrorists presumably also need to dehumanize their victims as they leave mass graves and burned cities behind.

14   *The making of terrorism*

Almost 20 years after Cordes wrote her piece, a series of critical scholars have undertaken to perform a reverse analysis and show how the state can use dehumanizing rhetoric to justify actions which are not entirely within the spectrum of legality or morality for that matter. The *pièce de resistance* in these analyses has been Guantanamo Bay and the labels the American government came up with in order to justify the treatment of prisoners there. Richard Jackson (2005) engaged in an assiduous effort to uncover how the state, in this case the US, similarly produced negative enemy labeling within an overall narrative of a 'just war.' *Writing the War on Terrorism: Language, Politics and Counter-Terrorism* details the ways in which 9/11 was constructed as an act of war, in response to which the US counter-terrorist campaign emerged as a war of self-defense, not unlike historical instances such as World War II. Jackson shows how, to this end, the US government made use of several rhetorical instruments such as: framing the military attack in Afghanistan as abiding to international law norms; the use of metaphors and mythologies around the ideas of justice, freedom, and liberty; invoking global support; formulations of winnability; and means of last resort or divine calling. Central to this construction of the just war narrative was the framing of a particular type of enemy, which involved attaching binary labels for the terrorists and the victims respectively, such as barbarism vs. civilization, or evil vs. good. Terrorists were furthermore dehumanized (e.g. parasites, scourge), portrayed as alien and filled with hatred, devious and mad. On the reverse, the American nation was depicted as freedom loving, courageous, innocent, and decent.

The theory behind

So far it would seem that terrorists and governments are essentially doing the same thing: attaching negative labels to the other party and seeing themselves as waging a just war. Cordes (1987) calls this 'the war of labels,' as state authorities and terrorists compete for the sympathy of the public. How might we think about this, and who is right? One criterion to consider might be the legitimacy of the cause—a task which is, however, in most cases not easy to handle. The legitimacy question becomes even more complicated in cases where the state is the perpetrator of violence, since, in principle, the state has legitimacy and further-more detains the monopoly of violence. Another option, which has been mostly taken up by scholars dealing with the definition of terrorism, including state terrorism, is to consider the nature of the means, or more precisely the victims. In this reading, violence against civilians with the purpose of intimidating a broader audience is terrorism, whether perpetrated by the state or by non-state actors. This also solves the dilemma of state terrorism in that state legitimacy does not necessarily imply the legitimacy of the means it employs. Finally, critical scholars would argue it is a question of power and would often look at state actions as a manifestation of unchecked, hegemonic, self-serving power. This is typical of a broader phenomenon whereby the study of 'terrorism' and 'counter-terrorism' largely occurs in separation from one another.

In terrorism studies, the labeling made by terrorists has been studied with the application of concepts from social cognitive psychology by Albert Bandura (1998). Social cognitive psychology refers to the study of human behavior at the intersection of cognition (how people understand the world) and social interaction. Bandura's theory of moral disengage-ment, as outlined in his chapter 'Mechanisms of moral disengagement' (1998), posits that, ordinarily, human conduct is regulated by moral standards (self-sanctions) which are adopted during socialization. A different type of socialization, namely what he calls "intensive psychological training in moral disengagement" (ibid: 163), can, however, lead to the adoption of particular neutralizing mechanisms. Two of the mechanisms Bandura describes are 'moral justification' and 'dehumanization.' The first refers to a 'cognitive restructuring' of violence into moral violence, whereby "people see themselves as fighting ruthless oppressors who have an unquenchable appetite for conquest, protecting their cherished values and way of life, preserving world peace, saving humanity from subjugation to an evil ideology, and honoring their country's international commitments" (ibid: 165). That is, perpetrators of terrorism would cast themselves in the positive light of the rescuer, of the fighter for good and dignity, thus attaching to themselves and their actions a positive moral value. This obviously involves the picturing of the enemy in the exact opposite terms, as the evil oppressor. This alone, however, usually does not suffice to cross the boundary of violence. Not dissimilar to psychological mechanisms used by soldiers at war, terrorists also need to 'dehumanize' in order to be able to kill. This disengagement mechanism functions in the following way: as non-humans, victims are not perceived as "persons with feelings, hopes, and concerns" but as "mindless 'savages', 'gooks', 'satanic fiends', and the like" and therefore "insensitive to maltreatment and capable of being influenced only by harsh methods" (ibid: 181). The underlying psychological reaction that this mechanism is meant to neutralize is empathy. It is assumed that witnessing another person's pain affects the perpetrators' self-esteem, and that this would conversely not occur if the victim were non-human or distant (ibid: 180).

The bulk of Bandura's psychological analysis of moral disengagement is illustrated with instances of non-state terrorism. However, since his theoretical standpoint is not fixed on particular units of analysis but draws on general social cognitive psychology, the same mechanisms could in principle be easily applied to state actors, too. In fact, his chapter contains an explicit section on the 'moral justification of counter-terrorist measures' and the citation above illustrating moral justification contains instances that are clearly only applicable to states. He differentiates between democracies and other states though, and argues that the mechanism occurring in the former case is "utilitarian justifications." Faced with the possibility of killing innocents during counter-terrorist operations, these states would argue "in terms of the benefits to humanity and the social order that curbing terrorist attacks will bring" (ibid: 167). Seemingly, a qualitative difference is made here between democracies and other states, whereby the former are assumed to possess increased sensitivity to legal and moral standards. This *a priori* assumption of 'goodness' associated with Western democracies—in a sense understandable from the perspective of the overall bi-polar political constellation at the time of the original formulation—permeates the pre-critical scholarship and also explains why there was comparatively less preoccupation at the time with problematic acts perpetrated by these states.

This changed with the advent of the War on Terror, which offered plenty of opportunity to engage with the actions and discourse of Western democratic states. Settled in the overall critical theoretical approach, this analysis naturally unfolded at the level of discourse (rather than behavior) and resorted to post-structuralist thought, in particular the writings of Michel Foucault and his concepts of 'exclusion' and 'power.' Drawing on Foucault, Jackson (2005) argues that language has an effect on the ways we think and the kinds of choices we make:

> By using a restricted set of words and word formations, some choices can appear perfectly reasonable and commonsensical while others appear absurd. Expressed another way, the language we use at any given moment privileges one viewpoint over others, naturalizing some understandings as rational and others as nonsensical.
>
> (Jackson 2005: 22)

16   *The making of terrorism*

These acts of labeling have then effects in 'real' life, by allowing or making possible certain actions at the expense of others. Critical scholars have pointed out how labeling something or someone in a certain way fixes their meaning and automatically excludes other possible meanings. Concretely, the language of terrorism excludes other depictions such as freedom fighters, militants, or revolutionaries. Clearly, and this is another point they make, the fact that it is government representatives, individuals with political authority and credibility that exercise this labeling, increases its chances of success. Jackson (2005) offers a good example of 'exclusion' and its consequences, whereby he shows how the depiction of the enemy in certain ways practically excluded alternative depictions and therefore also alternative policy measures:

> the practice of counter-terrorism is predicated on and determined by the language of counter-terrorism. The language of counter-terrorism incorporates a series of assumptions, beliefs and knowledge about the nature of terrorism and terrorists. These beliefs then determine what kinds of counter-terrorism practices are reasonable or unreasonable, appropriate or inappropriate: if terrorists are assumed to be inherently evil, for example, then eradicating them appears apposite while negotiating with them appears absurd.
>
> (Jackson 2005: 8–9)

He shows how in the US the construction of a moral struggle between the forces of good and those of evil allowed the silencing of dissent both at home and abroad along the lines of 'you are either with us or with the terrorists.' Labeling terrorism as 'evil' involved the necessity to 'get rid of it' in a radical and uncompromising way. This then had legal effects in that enemy combatants were not afforded protection by the international law regime, in particular due process and the laws of war. This in turn allowed for the possibility of atrocities such as torture in the Guantanamo Bay detention camp or in the Abu Ghraib prison in Iraq, but also of a number of limitations to human rights and civil liberties at home.

In proving his points, Jackson makes use of the critical discourse analysis method. Discourse analysis refers to several sociolinguistic approaches which analyze the use of discourse beyond the basic meaning of the sentence. As Jackson (2005) explains, critical discourse analysis is both a technique for analyzing texts and a broader ontological and epistemological view in which discourse is a form of social practice which constitutes and is constituted by the social world. Importantly, discourse reflects and helps constitute power relations, thus the aim of critical discourse analysis is to reveal these relationships of power and try to affect social change for the better. Technically, critical discourse analysis operates at several levels: the text proper, with its grammar, vocabulary, and syntax; the discursive practices; and the broader perspective of culture, politics, and society (see Box 1.2 for an account of this method).

Box 1.2 The critical discourse analysis method

In his article *Constructing Enemies: 'Islamic Terrorism' in Political and Academic Discourse*, Richard Jackson (2007) explains in detail the origins and features of the critical discourse analysis method and illustrates it with practical examples. Sourced in the broader critical theory, this method aims to depict textual and social processes, as well as how representations occur and with what consequences. Given its non-positivistic nature, the method does not look for causality, but functions according to an interpretive logic. Its theoretical commitments include an

> understanding of language as constitutive or productive of meaning; an understanding of discourse as structures of signification that construct social realities, particularly in terms of defining subjects and establishing their relational positions within a system of signification; an understanding of discourse as being productive of subjects authorized to speak and act, legitimate forms of knowledge and political practices and importantly, common sense within particular social groups and historical settings; an understanding of discourse as necessarily exclusionary and silencing of other modes of representation; and an understanding of discourse as historically and culturally contingent, intertextual, open-ended, requiring continuous articulation and re-articulation and therefore, open to destabilization and counter-hegemonic struggle.
>
> (Jackson 2007: 396)
>
> The concrete examination of the discourse on Islamic terrorism in this study was carried out along three steps. First, the texts were screened for "labels, assumptions, narratives, predicates, metaphors, inferences and arguments they deployed and the kinds of existing cultural-political narratives and pre-existing texts they drew upon" (ibid: 396). Jackson calls this 'grounded theory' because of the mechanism of saturation—the data collection was deemed complete when new texts did not add any more contributions to the exiting categories. In a second step, a first order critique aims to identify the internal contradictions, mistakes, and misconceptions in the text, in order to show its political nature. Finally, the second order critique goes beyond the text and shows the effects in real life, namely how discourse is used to "structure the primary subject positions, accepted knowledge, commonsense and legitimate policy responses to the actors and events being described; exclude and delegitimize alternative knowledge and practice; naturalize a particular political and social order; and construct and maintain a hegemonic regime of truth" (ibid: 397).

The two approaches to labeling, positivist and critical, also work with different assumptions with regard to the nature of the actors involved. According to Cordes (1987), the terrorists' justificatory practices are not only aimed at persuading audiences, but also at convincing themselves. In other words, they are essentially moral actors who need to find a solution for their guilt. This falls in line with basic assumptions in social learning theory (on which social cognitive psychology rests) according to which cognitions and behaviors are not inborn, but learned during socialization processes. Drawing on Bandura's work, Cordes suggests that terrorists are not necessarily evil or immoral, but learn how to, in this case, neutralize moral inhibitors. Underlying the critical approach is an ideological layer depicting the Western state not as morally neutral or 'learning,' but as pursuing hegemonic ends through the accumulation and exercise of material and immaterial power. Here, the state does not engage in justificatory practices in order to 'feel better' and it is of little interest whether or not the agents of the state actually believe what they are saying. The focus of the investigation lays in showing how discourse is instrumentalized in order to create acceptance of the state agenda.

18 *The making of terrorism*

The paradigm behind

Having touched upon the kinds of questions critical vs. the more 'traditional' terrorism scholars deal with, it is apparent that the former are significantly more interested in analyzing state actions, whereas the latter largely focus on non-state actors. A reason for this might be the historical context in which the CTS school emerged, namely some highly problematic counter-terrorism state actions. But there is also a more underlying, paradigmatic reason behind these differences in treatment. CTS distinguishes itself through a rather strong normative component. Unlike positivists or even those who use interpretive methodologies, critical scholars understand their work not only as a matter of explaining or understanding things, but also from the perspective of an emancipatory mission. This means that the bulk of this critical scholarship has not only focused on the way governments, media, and society construct the understanding of the term 'terrorism,' but also understand their work as part of a broader perspective of resisting and exposing unchecked power. This is the most obvious difference between critical and more 'traditional' terrorism scholars; but there is also a series of ontological and epistemological particularities which differentiate the two.

Ontologically, positivists assume that reality exists independently of our knowledge of it and is thus not socially constructed. Critical theorists, similar to other post-positivist strands such as constructivists or feminists, would outline the socially constructed nature of reality. In other words, positivist terrorism scholars would say: there is terrorism, we can see it, we can see its consequences, and the only problem is to figure out the most appropriate way to conceptualize it. Critical scholars would argue that terrorism, like any other social phenomena is embedded in cultural, historical, and power contexts and does not exist out there, outside human interpretation. For the most part, this does not mean to say that there is no act of violence being carried out, but that whether or not we call this 'terrorism' or something else, is a social convention. Positivists will attempt to establish causal relationships between phenomena, such as for instance terrorism and grievance. The task of the critical academic is to inquire into the conditions for knowledge and challenge power relations. For positivists, it is possible to separate empirical from normative questions, which in turn means that social science can and should be objective. For critical theorists, epistemological and normative assumptions are interrelated. In critical theory, the normative objective of 'emancipation' is key and it has a central role also in critical approaches to terrorism (see Box 1.3 for some concrete examples of how traditional and critical scholars' statements can be related to these basic assumptions).

Box 1.3 Paradigmatic dimensions of comparison

Traditional and critical ontological, epistemological, and critical normative stances as voiced by Paul Wilkinson (2011) in *Terrorism vs. Democracy: The Liberal State Response* and Richard Jackson, Lee Jarvis, Jeroen Gunning and Marie Breen Smyth (2011) in *Terrorism: A Critical Introduction*.

Ontology

Traditional terrorism studies

Some so-called "post-modernists" reject the concept of terrorism on the grounds that it is purely "subjective", implying that there are no independent objective verifiable criteria to enable us to distinguish terrorism from other forms of activity ... common sense indicates that the general public in most countries in the world can recognize terrorism when they see campaigns of bombings, suicide bombings, shooting attacks, hostage-takings, hijackings and threats of such actions, especially when so many of these actions are deliberately aimed at civilians.

(Wilkinson 2011: 4)

Critical terrorism studies

Terrorism is fundamentally a social fact rather than a brute fact, because deciding whether a particular act of violence constitutes an "act of terrorism" relies on judgments about the context, circumstances and intent of the violence, rather than any objective characteristic inherent to it ... while acts of violence are a brute physical fact for the victims and onlookers, the meaning or labeling of the acts – as "crime", an act of "war" or an act of "terrorism", for example – is a social process that depends upon different actors making judgments about its nature.

(Jackson et al. 2011: 35)

Epistemology

Traditional terrorism studies

It is true that in the burgeoning of modern international terrorism in the late 1960s and early 1970s many efforts to obtain international agreements and conventions on the prevention and suppression of terrorist crimes were stymied by governments which, for their own political and ideological reasons, wished to block such measures by claiming that there was no internationally accepted definition of terrorism. Since then almost all the major democracies have developed national anti-terrorist legislation and many individuals have been convicted of terrorist offences.

(Wilkinson 2011: 4–5)

Critical terrorism studies

Theory and knowledge always comes *from* somewhere; that is, it is located in, and reflects, the values and assumptions of the particular historical and social context in which it emerges. [And] also question who benefits by claiming that it is.

(Jackson et al. 2011: 20)

Linkages between power and knowledge, particularly in terms of the different ways in which knowledge can be employed by actors as a political tool of influence and domination. CTS scholars are critical of the way in which certain kinds of knowledge claims about terrorism – the widely accepted knowledge that terrorism poses a serious ongoing or even existential threat to Western societies, for example – have been used by governments to increase their own power, suppress opposition and restrict civil liberties.

(Jackson et al. 2011: 37)

Normative stances

Critical terrorism studies

CTS scholars for the most part see emancipation as a process of trying to construct "concrete utopias" by realizing the unfulfilled potential of existing structures, freeing individuals from unnecessary structural constraints and the democratization of the public sphere.

(Jackson et al. 2011: 41)

[E]mancipation expresses itself in a variety of ways, including, among others: efforts to end the use of terrorist violence whether by state or non-state actors; the promotion of human rights and well-being in situations of terrorist and counter-terrorist violence; the refusal to sanction illegal and immoral practices such as targeted killings and torture; explorations in non-violent and conflict-resolution-based responses to terrorism; and addressing the conditions that might impel actors to resort to terrorist tactics.

(Jackson et al. 2011: 42)

While these paradigmatic principles are helpful in understanding the different takes on terrorism, research interests, and methodological preferences, they should not be always taken literally. Subsequent to the release of the CTS manifesto, several of the traditional scholars took a stand and deplored the perceived attempt to split the field and furthermore proceeded to challenge some of the claims made by the CTS school, in particular their claim to novelty. Some of the arguments advanced pointed out, among other things, that the traditional school has also been at times critical of governmental decisions, has inquired into the historical and cultural contexts of terrorism, included state terrorism in their analyses and also resorted to ethnographic methods (for more details on the issues raised during this debate, see Further reading). These are all valid points and have to do with the fact that terrorism studies prior to the 'critical turn' are not simply positivist (although it shares many of this paradigm's features). This is because, although evolved into a sub-field of international relations (IR), terrorism studies has not grown out of a particular IR theoretical tradition. It combines various branches of political science, whilst also including approaches pertaining to other disciplines, such as psychology, sociology, criminology, or history. Therefore, assumptions and methods are multiple and difficult to subsume into one paradigm. Significantly, many of the traditional scholars work from interpretivist perspectives, and therefore aim to understand, rather than explain, and use qualitative methodologies and soft data, such as interviews or participant observation, rather than large-N data and statistics. The critical scholarship, in turn, is also heterogeneous and differs in particular concerning the ontological role of language.

Harmonie Toros (2012) took up this issue and showed how critical terrorism scholars are divided between post-structuralists and 'minimal foundationalists.' Post-structuralists would only operate at the discursive level and argue that terrorism and terrorists are constituted through language, i.e. through the application of these labels in discourse to acts of violence which are thus pathologized. The minimal foundationalist approach would start off with the consensus definition in 'traditional' terrorism studies: "*the threat or use of politically motivated violence aimed at affecting a larger audience than its immediate target that is broadly deemed legitimate*" (ibid: 40, original emphasis). Added to that would be then the critical touch, namely the consideration of the social, political, economic, and human contexts, as well as of the respective power relationships. That is, minimal foundationalists do not deny the existence of something out there, most of the times brute violence, but challenge the specific meaning contained in the concept of terrorism. Toros argues in favor of this latter approach, as, in her view, the post-structuralist understanding of terrorism, by reducing it to discourse, would suffer from two drawbacks: it ignores the category of violence that exists out there and is different to others; and reduces responses to discursive ones only, i.e. deconstructing the terrorism discourse. In line with several other critical scholars, Toros pleads for 'de-exceptionalizing' terrorism and thus integrating its study within broader political and social theories.

We can derive from the above that, especially in terms of ontological assumptions, the two scholarships show some degree of overlap. There are, however, also clear differences, especially in epistemological and normative terms. 'Traditional' terrorism works are generally also interested in context, power, and oppression, but not in an epistemologically *a priori* manner. Also, whilst at times critical of human rights abuses and foreign occupation, they largely subscribe to the overall normative mission of combating terrorism, rather than that of constant critique of the dominant political order. Critical scholars take context and power as *a priori* conditions for 'knowing.' Furthermore, the normative invective of emancipation means that the researcher should not take the prevailing order, including the state privilege in the use of violence, as a given, but continuously investigate the contexts in which it has emerged, question, and challenge it. Two prominent ways in which these scholars understand to follow this principle are the sustained focus on state terrorism and the refusal to work for and therefore further empower a potentially oppressive establishment. Importantly, this principle also applies for the case of Western democracies. Before 9/11, only a handful of scholars investigated acts of state terror in the West or side-effects of Western counter-terrorism campaigns with similar consequences in terms of human rights. Prompted by the atrocities committed within the War on Terror, and arguably their increased visibility as compared to previous decades, an increasing number of scholars have taken particular interest in the terror activities of Western states in an overall very critical stance of Western foreign policy in general. This, however, should not be understood as a reification of terrorism as state terrorism, but rather as the attempt to fill in a gap in research, as well as, of course, as part of the broader emancipatory mission.

So how should a student of terrorism position him/herself, and is such a positioning necessary? Arguably, especially considering the commonalities between these two approaches, taking sides would be highly unproductive. While some authors would clearly state their attachment to particular paradigms, most would integrate along what could be labeled as a continuum between radical positivist and radical critical stances. As regards the ontological and epistemological dimensions of terrorism, a middle way is perhaps a more useful avenue to pursue. For example, while not negating the 'reality' of terrorism, we might accept the fact that labeling it terrorism or something else, and the concrete signification attached to it, is essentially a matter of human attribution of meaning, in a process that involves several facets, not least human agency, cultural background, historical context, institutional embedding, or relationships of power. That is, whenever reading a definition of terrorism, we should ask who has formulated the definition, with what purpose, and on which background. Finally, while emancipation is not the only possible normative stance, sensitivity to the possible uses of research as well as reflection on one's own socialization and biases is necessary in any research endeavor.

22 *The making of terrorism*

Summary

This chapter has been about perspectives. We have dealt with:

- the state and terrorist perspectives of each other;
- the issue of reciprocal 'labeling' and traced it to labeling theories in social cognitive psychology and discourse analysis;
- the positivist and critical theory research traditions, the ontological, epistemological and normative assumptions they rely on, and how they influence what and how we research;
- the argument against a strict and artificial separation between 'traditional' and 'critical' terrorism studies, given the multitude of approaches each of them entails.

Exercises

1.1 A common example of 'where you stand is where you sit' is also institutional embedding. Compare and discuss the different labeling of targets and perpetrators in relation to the institutional missions of the Department of State, Department of Defense, the Federal Bureau of Investigation (FBI), and the Department of Homeland Security.

Mission	Definition
Department of State	
The Department's mission is to shape and sustain a peaceful, prosperous, just, and democratic world and foster conditions for stability and progress for the benefit of the American people and people everywhere. (DOS 2016)	(1) the term "international terrorism" means terrorism involving citizens or the territory of more than one country; (2) the term "terrorism" means premeditated, politically motivated violence perpetrated against non-combatant targets by subnational groups or clandestine agents; and (3) the term "terrorist group" means any group practicing, or which has significant subgroups which practice, international terrorism. United States Code, Title 22, Section 2656f(d). (DOS 2013)
Department of Defense	
The mission of the Department of Defense is to provide the military forces needed to deter war and to protect the security of our country. (DOD 2017)	The unlawful use of violence or threat of violence to instill fear and coerce governments or societies. *DOD Dictionary of Military and Associated Terms,* 8 November 2010, as amended through 15 June 2013. (DOD 2013) *Note the lack of specification of whether the target should be non-combatant*

Mission	Definition
FBI	
The Director of the Federal Bureau of Investigation shall: ... Exercise Lead Agency responsibility in investigating all crimes for which it has primary or concurrent jurisdiction and which involve terrorist activities or acts in preparation of terrorist activities within the statutory jurisdiction of the United States.	Terrorism includes the unlawful use of force and violence against persons or property to intimidate or coerce a government, the civilian population, or any segment thereof, in furtherance of political or social objectives. (C.F.R. 1969)
Department of Homeland Security	
Homeland security is a widely distributed and diverse—but unmistakable—national enterprise. The term "enterprise" refers to the collective efforts and shared responsibilities of Federal, State, local, tribal, territorial, nongovernmental, and private-sector partners as well as individuals, families, and communities to maintain critical homeland security capabilities. (DHS 2010: ii)	Domestic terrorism: Any activity that involves an act that is dangerous to human life or potentially destructive to critical infrastructure or key resources, and is a violation of the criminal laws of the United States or of any state or other subdivision of the United States and appears to be intended to intimidate or coerce a civilian population to influence the policy of a government by intimidation or coercion, or to affect the conduct of a government by mass destruction, assassination, or kidnapping. (DHS 2011)

1.2 Compare and contrast the arguments put forward by the traditional and the critical terrorism scholars. Do you think the study of terrorism should be normative?

1.3 Yasser Arafat is a good example of the many perspectives that can be applied to the same person, from terrorist, to freedom fighter, to state official. Follow his path in time and observe how appellatives changed depending on who was speaking and when.

References

Aust, S. (2008). *Baader-Meinhof. The Inside Story of the RAF*, London: The Bodley Head.

Bandura, A. (1998). Mechanisms of Moral Disengagement. In W. Reich (ed.) *Origins of Terrorism. Psychologies, Ideologies, Theologies, States of Mind*, Washington, DC: Woodrow Wilson Center Press, pp. 161–191.

C.F.R. (1969). 28 C.F.R., Code of Federal Regulations, Section 0.85, General functions, www.law.cornell.edu/cfr/text/28/0.85.

Cordes, B. (1987). *When Terrorists do the Talking: Reflections on Terrorist Literature*, Santa Monica: RAND.

DHS (2010). Quadrennial Homeland Security Report, www.dhs.gov/sites/default/files/publications/2010-qhsr-executive-summary.pdf.

DHS (2011). Domestic Terrorism and Homegrown Violent Extremism Lexicon, 10 November, https://info.publicintelligence.net/DHS-ExtremismLexicon.pdf.

DOD (2013). DOD Dictionary of Military and Associated Terms. www.dtic.mil/doctrine/dod_dictionary/data/t/7591.html.

DOD (2017) U.S. Department of Defense, About the Department of Defense, www.defense.gov/about/#mission.

DOS (2013). Office of the Coordinator for Counterterrorism, Country Reports on Terrorism 2012, May 30, www.state.gov/j/ct/rls/crt/2012/209990.htm.

DOS (2016) U.S. Department of State, Department Mission Statement, www.state.gov/s/d/rm/index.htm#mission.

Jackson, R. (2005). *Writing the War of Terrorism: Language, Politics and Counter-Terrorism*, Manchester, New York: Manchester University Press.

Jackson, R. (2007). Constructing Enemies: 'Islamic Terrorism' in Political and Academic Discourse. *Government and Opposition*, 42(3), pp. 395–426.

Jackson, R., Jarvis, L., Gunning, J. and Breen Smyth, M. (2011). *Terrorism: A Critical Introduction*, New York: Palgrave Macmillan.

Malkki, L. (2014). Political Elements in Post-Columbine School Shootings in Europe and North America. *Terrorism and Political Violence*, 26(1), pp. 185–210.

Toros, H. (2012). *Terrorism, Talking and Transformation. A Critical Approach*, London, New York: Routledge.

Wilkinson, P. (2011). *Terrorism vs. Democracy: The Liberal State Response*, Abingdon, New York: Routledge.

Further reading

Baele, S.J. (2014). Are Terrorists "Insane? A critical analysis of mental health categories in lone terrorists' trials. *Critical Studies on Terrorism*, 7(2), pp. 257–276.

Blakeley, R. (2008). The Elephant in the Room: A response to John Horgan and Michael J. Boyle. *Critical Studies on Terrorism*, 1(2), pp. 151–165.

Booth, K. (2008). The Human Faces of Terror: Reflections in a cracked looking glass. *Critical Studies on Terrorism*, 1(1), pp. 65–79.

Horgan, J. and Boyle, M.J. (2008). A Case Against 'Critical Terrorism Studies'. *Critical Studies on Terrorism*, 1(1), pp. 51–64.

Malkki, L. (2016). School Shootings and Lone Actor Terrorism. In M. Fredholm (ed.) *Understanding Lone Actor Terrorism: Past Experience, Future Outlook, and Response Strategies*, Abingdon, New York: Routledge, pp. 182–205.

Wieviorka, M. (1988). *The Making of Terrorism*, Chicago, London: The University of Chicago Press.

2 Defining terrorism

Asta Maskaliūnaitė

The previous chapter has already provided a glimpse into the difficulties of defining terrorism. This chapter delves deeper into this issue and looks at five approaches to the definition of terrorism. First it looks into list-type of approaches, which simply enumerate the acts and actors to be named terrorist; second, it provides a historical overview of how terror and terrorism have been conceived over time; third, it looks into attempts to create an analytical definition of terrorism; fourth, it looks at the normative type of definitions and assesses the arguments for adding the normative dimension; and finally, it elaborates on the CTS approach to this issue.

Terrorism scholarship has put a lot of emphasis on the search for common understanding of what is meant by the term. The problems in defining terrorism are numerous. First, differently from many other political concepts, it is used freely in everyday parlance and, given its psychological underpinnings, means different things to different people. Second, it carries a strong charge. Indeed, one can hardly imagine the term 'terrorism' or 'terrorist' being used in a positive manner in either public or private contexts. This negativity is inherent also in expressions such as, 'one man's terrorist is another man's freedom fighter.' As was discussed in the previous chapter, this desire to control labeling of terrorism is an inherent part in the making of terrorism presented as the ultimate 'Other' of the state.

The contamination with negative emotional charge and the prevalence of its everyday use makes it difficult to consider terrorism as an academic term. Some authors even advocate the abandonment of the notion altogether and see it as a pejorative term with no academic validity (Bryan 2012). Other scholars deal with the negative charge of the concept by simply avoiding its usage in their work. For example, instead of talking about terrorists, some authors prefer to discuss the situation of European jihadis, Irish republicans, or leftist militants. In other instances, a more general notion of clandestine political violence or just political violence is used instead.

Those who advocate for the continued use of the term, including from the side of the CTS, argue that the abandonment of the term would preclude dialogue between academic researchers, policy-makers, and the general public. In addition, the abandonment of the term may lead to the dismissal of an already established tradition of terrorism studies, which, though flawed in many ways, also provides numerous important insights into the phenomenon. The debate about the continued utility of the term, or lack thereof, is therefore still raging and both sides of it have powerful ammunition to spend.

If we choose to pursue the definition of terrorism, there are some avenues to explore. In their *Introduction to Political Terrorism*, Weinberg and Davis (1989) distinguish between four approaches to the definition of terrorism: list-type—providing a listing of situations in which the event may be called terrorist; historical—seeking to provide an understanding of terrorism through the historical usage of the term; and analytical (or what could be called 'positivist') definitions of terrorism—trying to envelop the concept into neutral terms and to provide an as comprehensive as possible account of the phenomenon; and normative— distinguished by an employment of just/unjust, moral/immoral, etc. dichotomies. This typology will be used to explore definitional issues in the rest of this chapter, adding in the end the contributions of CTS to this debate.

List-type definitions

One way to escape the politicization of the concept is to apply the so-called list-type definitions of terrorism. Such definitions are an attempt at listing all or most of the acts that can be called terrorist, not considering their aims. As the means of the struggle are emphasized and aims are left aside, it is argued, it is easier to look neutrally on the subject. Thus, for example, every plane hijacking, hostage taking, or attack on diplomats becomes a terrorist act no matter what the motives. Such ideas are best expressed in international conventions, for example, the Convention for the Suppression of Unlawful Acts against the Safety of Civil Aviation, signed at Montreal on 23 September 1971 or the Convention for the Suppression of Unlawful Seizure of Aircraft, signed at The Hague on 16 December 1970, as well as in legal acts of the various states of the world. In such cases, notwith-standing the objectives of the performers of the acts and the support or rejection of the public of their aims, they will be considered terrorist. This way, it becomes possible to leave aside political sympathies and antipathies and to assess the doers of the acts with blindfolded justice.

In another version of list definitions, states and international organizations look at the actor, not the act, and create lists of designated terrorist organizations. In this case, the actions themselves may be as innocent as distributing flyers in the street, but their perpe-trators could be taken in under terrorism laws, as everything that is done on behalf of a terrorist organization is considered terrorism, and even belonging to such an organization is already considered a crime.

The two types of lists thus bring with them numerous, though different, types of problems. For the former, it is not always easy not to take into consideration the ends of the act. For example, if robbers attack a diplomat not even knowing that she is a diplomat, it is not considered terrorism but robbery, an act to be punished by other criminal laws than the ones concerning terrorism. For the latter, when everything an (often self-proclaimed) militant does is considered terrorism, the concept of terrorism becomes overly stretched and can become unconvincing. Indeed, the list of activities that were or are at one time or another considered terrorist could be nearly infinite and the activities of terrorist organizations can be very varied.

An additional problem associated with list-type definitions based on actors relates to the fact that it is either states or international organizations that create such listings. It is often argued that this reflects more on the idea that the state has of itself than on the groups or actions it wants to define. The twists and turns around terrorism definitions in Spain are a good example here (see Box 2.1).

Box 2.1 Defining terrorism in Spanish legal discourse

The Spanish case offers an example of both the narrowing down and the widening up of the definition of terrorism to suit a state's needs. In the first case, the 1990s trials of GAL (Grupos Antiterroristas de Liberación—Antiterrorist Liberation Groups) are illustrative. This organization was a paramilitary entity which was created with the idea of ending the seeming immunity of the Basque separatists, who used violence in Spain and often crossed the border into France, making it impossible for the Spanish authorities to pursue them. GAL, which was revealed to have had roots in the Spanish national political establishment, was supposed to address this issue by attacking Euskadi Ta Askatasuna (ETA/Basque Homeland and Freedom) members in their sanctuary in France. It used kidnappings, shootings, and even bombings of cafes and other public places to achieve this objective, in the process killing 27 people. The courts decided that the organization could not be called 'terrorist' because, it was argued, its aim was not to destroy the Spanish state but to serve it. The conceptualization of terrorism here was narrowed to apply not so much to violence but to certain political objectives.

Almost a decade later, the Spanish authorities declared that until then legal organizations promoting the cause of Basque independence, such as the political party Batasuna, youth organizations, and prisoner support groups, should all be declared illegal as a part of the terrorist strategy. The two moves—declaring GAL not-terrorist and declaring the political parties and other organizations terrorist, criminalized or de-criminalized not violence but the objectives for which violence was perpetrated. For the Spanish state, it appeared, it was not the violence itself but the striving for independence that was dangerous.

Historical approach

The second approach to defining terrorism is a historical one, looking deeper into the usage of the word over time and, in so doing, de-essentializing the term. As a political term, this concept became entrenched in the vocabulary during the French Revolution of the 18th century and initially was associated with the actions of the state. Before the Revolution, the notion had four different meanings, some of which became politicized during the Enlightenment: the terror of helplessness, the terror of eternity, the terror of arbitrary government, and the terror of aesthetic witness (Thorup 2010). These were woven into the political understanding of the concept during the Revolution and after.

The terror of helplessness, terror as fright, appeared in the European languages in the 14th century and was used synonymously with fear for most of its existence. It indicated a 'heightened state of fear' and remained largely as such throughout the coming centuries. In political philosophy, the term appeared with a somewhat more political meaning in the work of Hobbes. Terror here is "fear in its most basic sense ... fear of death or even violent death," but "its presence ... is what guarantees social peace" (Thorup 2010: 81). Terror was thus essential for maintaining the social contract. Similarly, the terror of eternity or, in other words, the fear of God has such a function. The fear of divine retribution serves to keep people in tow with the Commandments and away from sin, thus maintaining the social order. One can find echoes of these notions in the contemporary focus on security.

Keeping the individual in a constant fear of loosely defined danger, the state can exercise control and keep social order.

While the first two notions have a political component indirectly, the third—terror of arbitrary government—has politics written all over it. Though it was not the primary use of the word, this type of conceptualization appears first in Montesquieu's *The Spirit of the Laws*, where he established terror as a principle of a despotic government, as opposed to honor in a monarchy, or virtue in a republic. Montesquieu's use of terror can thus be seen as quasi-political, as Thorup suggests, seeing it "as an expression of state power, as an instrument or technique for political and social dominance" (Thorup 2010: 86). It was used, however, to exaggerate and create a straw man of such a power, in which both despotism and its principle 'terror' go outside the political realm, making political institutions meaningless. Montesquieu subverts the Hobbesian notion of fear as a mobilizing factor in human societies, helping people to 'be good' and obedient to the state for their own sake, into a paralyzing impulse which destroys any social and cultural creativity. Inasmuch as they portray the omnipotence of the state to silence dissent and create hegemonic discourses around the practices of counter-terrorism, one can see echoes of Montesquieu's notion of terror in the CTS descriptions of state terror today.

Terror of the sublime is often overlooked, but can be linked to the contemporary depiction of terrorism as a theatre. One of the most influential elaborations on terror in its relation to aesthetics is found in the work of Edmund Burke. Burke connects the notion of the sublime to that of terror, arguing that the human being is the only creature in the world who, looking at a particularly dangerous spectacle, such as a tempest, can grasp the beauty in it and elevate his soul. The general fascination of the media with terrorism and the continuous replaying of images from the attacks can also be seen in this light.

The meaning of terror underwent a change with the French Revolution, even though the traces of previous understandings remained. The period September 1793 to July 1794 was characterized already at the time as a 'Reign of Terror' (see Box 2.2).

Box 2.2 French revolutionary terror

The French Revolution started in 1789 with the storming of the Bastille, but also with the Declaration of the Rights of Man. By 1793 France was, however, in chaos, faced with war on all fronts outside and civil war inside, and periodic outbreaks of violence in the countryside, but especially in Paris. To reassert control over the country and the Revolution, the leaders of the French Revolution aimed to create strong institutions capable of administering the country, coordinating the war effort, curbing popular violence, and dealing with subversion. The latter two efforts where concentrated in the institution of the Revolutionary Tribunal, at the inauguration of which Danton famously pronounced "let us be terrible so that the people do not have to be."

Throughout 1793, such institutions were consolidated and the ideological foundations for the regime were created, with terror as one of the important elements of the regime. In 1794, the consolidation of power continued and the Revolutionary Tribunal was used to eliminate political dissent from both those who thought that the government was not doing enough and those who thought that it should stop (including the author of the Tribunal, Danton). On 10 June 1794 (22 Prairial in the Revolutionary calendar) the Law of Suspects was expanded to make prosecution and execution of 'suspects' easier, inaugurating the period of the great Reign of Terror.

> This period lasted until 27 July 1794, when Robespierre and his closest associates were themselves arrested and guillotined the next day. The question of how the revolutionaries who were opposed to the death penalty in 1789 ended up asking for more heads in 1794 continues to fascinate researchers to this day.

The concept of terror is inextricably linked to the figure of Maximilien Robespierre. On 5 February 1794, Robespierre made one of his most famous speeches, 'On the principles of political morality,' which he pronounced in the name of the Committee of Public Safety. In it, comes the most quoted passage on terror:

> If the mainspring of popular government in peacetime is virtue, amid revolution it is at once virtue and terror: virtue, without which terror is fatal; terror, without which virtue is impotent. Terror is nothing but prompt, severe, inflexible justice; it is therefore an emanation of virtue. It is less a special principle than a consequence of the general principle of democracy applied to the country's most pressing needs.
>
> It has been said that terror was the mainspring of despotic government. Does your government, then, resemble a despotism? Yes, as the sword which glitters in the hands of liberty's heroes resembles the one with which tyranny's lackeys are armed. Let the despot govern his brutalized subjects by terror; he is right to do this, as a despot. Subdue liberty's enemies by terror, and you will be right, as founders of the Republic. The government of the revolution is the despotism of liberty against tyranny.
>
> (Robespierre 2007)

Several elements are important in this passage. First, some authors include the pursuit of justice into their definitions of terrorism. Because terrorism involves engagement in a kind of 'selfless' violence, i.e. violence not for their own sake, but for the sake of some larger community, there has to be some powerful motive behind it. This motive often has something to do with justice or lack thereof. Second, for those justifying the use of terror, this type of violence cannot be judged within the confines of existing legal systems. Because its aims to transcend time (establishment of a state for one's community, creation of more equal and just society, etc.), it cannot be confined by the legal requirements of the day. Hence, for example, members of many terrorist groups declare that they do not recognize the authority of the state to judge them when they are taken to court.

Finally, though the use of terror as a principle of the government is not new and Robespierre refers here to Montesquieu, he twists the latter's argument so that terror becomes a neutral tool that can be used by the despots to prolong their torture of the people and by the founders of the Republic alike, who can wield it in order to protect virtue. It is used here to describe the harsh measures that the establishment of a Republic requires. As Thorup writes, Robespierre and his allies "turn the concept from a description of what various actors and events caused of fear in the individual, into a political concept about how this fear might help create the future. Terror is an instrument of bringing about a new society" (Thorup 2010: 93).

This element of hastening the future, which is already on the way, is also present in most terrorist organizations' idea of themselves and their purpose in the world. Add to this the fact that those who 'ran' systems of terror were a small minority of the French elite, that their notion of the guilty who deserved a visit to the guillotine was often based on a broad suspicion (class status or relation to the emigrés); and that terror was envisaged as an emotion-based management of the Revolution (the blade of the guillotine was not meant only to punish the guilty, but also to intimidate the potential enemy) and the similarities between the French revolutionaries and current terrorist movements become apparent. From investigations into the notion of terror during the French Revolution, thus, a lot can be learned not only about what the revolutionaries themselves tried to do, but also about what the current terrorists are trying to achieve. With the fall of Robespierre, the term received the negative connotation it retains to this day.

Towards the end of the century, terrorism came to be associated with the anarchist 'propaganda by the deed' bringing a new element into the concept of terrorism—that of communication, of violence being used when other forms of communicating grievance fail to impress. The advent of World War I saw a sharp decline in anarchist violence. The groups coming to the scene after this conflict made a conscious effort to avoid being seen as 'terrorist' and managed to imprint a much more positive notion of 'freedom fighters' as a designation of their struggle.

When political violence came back to haunt the Western states in the late 1960s, the question of how to characterize these actions and their perpetrators started to arise. Because most political violence before that time occurred in the de-colonizing 'Third World,' the dominant paradigm was to look at them as insurgencies, which may not always be palatable, but often understandable and not difficult to explain. This changed with the Munich events of 1972, when members of the Palestinian Black September Organization massacred members of the Israeli Olympic team. With this event, both the media and the political discourse started referring to terrorism as shocking, irrational violence.

Analytical definitions

The third type of approach to defining terrorism is analytical, which implies trying to locate those elements of the phenomenon that make terrorism what it is and which would allow one to distinguish terrorism from, for example, insurgency or political assassination. Alex Schmid has made probably the most extensive survey of terrorism definitions and examined 250 different definitions of terrorism proposed by researchers in the field. A table of major elements appearing in these definitions with more or less frequency contained 22 entries. The attempt to create a consensus definition led to the definition of terrorism as:

> on the one hand to a doctrine about the presumed effectiveness of a special form or tactic of fear-generating, coercive political violence and, on the other hand, to a conspiratorial practice of calculated, demonstrative, direct violent action without legal or moral restraints, targeting mainly civilians and noncombatants, performed for its propagandistic and psychological effects on various audiences and conflict parties.
>
> (Schmid 2011: 86)

This definition, however, requires 11 further points to describe other important aspects:

1 the context in which terrorism can be used, for example, that it can be employed by the state, by non-state actors outside war and as a tactic in war;

2 the violence used can take different forms;

Defining terrorism 31

3   it involves communication processes, i.e. demand-making on the government and society, and support-seeking from the constituent group on whose behalf the group acts;

4   at heart, terrorism is about terror;

5   the main victims here are usually civilians;

6   the direct victims are not the main targets of the attack, they are used as message-generators;

7   the perpetrators can be individuals, groups, networks, or state-supported clandestine actors;

8   while there can be similarities with organized crime, the motivation is political;

9   the immediate intent of the action is to terrorize with the hope of provoking a reaction that helps achieve certain aims;

10   motivations are a broad range of alleged grievances;

11   acts of terrorism usually form part of a campaign of violence, are not stand alone events and, through this, can create a climate of fear, allowing the terrorists to manipulate the political process.

Arguably, a less comprehensive definition of terrorism can also be used. The majority of the definitions of this phenomenon include only three or four elements of this definition; most commonly violence, political reasons and an attempt to create an atmosphere of fear. These are the elements that appear in more than half of the definitions of terrorism and, in fact, the only elements which go over the 50 per cent threshold (the next ones being threat at 47 per cent and psychological effects and anticipated reactions at 41.5 per cent) (see Schmid 2011: 74).

While having a clear advantage of parsimony, these shorter definitions leave a lot of questions unanswered, the main one being, probably, why these elements do not appear in all the definitions. Terrorism is seen as a form of violence, while the other characteristics of it are used essentially to distinguish it from other forms of violence. However, even this element is not encountered in all the definitions. For example, in a definition by R.P. Hoffman, one finds neither violence nor force; he defines terrorism as "a purposeful human political activity which is directed towards the creation of a general climate of fear, and is designed to influence, in ways desired by the protagonist, other human beings and, through them, some course of event" (cited in Schmid 2011:125).

In this understanding, fear (from which the word 'terrorism' itself derives its meaning) can be created also through other types of actions, not only violent ones. The question of what is violence itself is also hardly straightforward and is especially important for the debate on whether the attacks against property should be covered by the terrorist definition.

Political motives, another element at the core of most terrorism definitions, are also sometimes problematic as motives are not always easy to fathom. Cases such as Anders Breivik's attacks in Norway could be considered here. Were his actions political or just the rampage of a madman? The same question could be asked about the Nice truck attack. Especially in cases of so-called 'lone-wolf' terrorists, the reasons for the attack and their political nature cannot always be easily pinpointed. Yet, while establishing the motives is not always easy, there is a wide agreement among scholars that taking away politics would rob terrorism of its essence. This is also a move that is strongly resisted by the designated terrorists themselves. The dirty protests and hunger protests of the Irish republicans, when the authorities decided to remove their status as political prisoners, can be an example here.

32 *Asta Maskaliūnaitė*

The third in the list of important elements—creation of an atmosphere of fear—is even more subjective than the previous two and even more dependent on the context. It could be argued that there are simply too many aspects of contemporary life that create such fears. Sometimes, for example, the media is accused of creating an 'atmosphere of fear' by reporting and over-reporting certain negative developments.

The discussion on caveats could go on and scholars do not seem to tire from deliberations of what should and what should not be in the definition of terrorism. Schmid's approach of setting a more generic definition and then providing a context for its use is a rather fruitful approach to the issue, allowing one to avoid accusations of not being conscious of the context and at the same time keeping to some standards of parsimony. No matter how complicated in practice, analytical definitions of terrorism should contain elements of violence, political goals, and the creation of an atmosphere of fear at their core.

Normative definitions

While the definitions discussed above try to offer a neutral presentation of the phenomenon, normative or even condemnatory elements often find their way into definitions. The most common of such elements are the adjectives 'illegal' and 'illegitimate' attached to the word 'violence,' and 'innocent' or 'innocent civilians' attached to the definition as a description of the targets of terrorism.

The first term—illegal, illegitimate—is used to distinguish the perpetrators of the attacks as mainly non-state actors, and is therefore often criticized for excluding state actions by definition. In addition, the term 'illegality' adds a criminal element to the definition, thus putting an emphasis not on the 'political' side of the struggle, but on the criminal aspects of it. Adding 'illegal' to the definition puts a negative tinge not only on the violence, but also on the political objectives for which such violence is perpetrated. Finally, historical readings of the notion of terror do not provide an accurate description of the phenomenon, as violence here is seen not so much as 'illegal' but 'rather as extra-legal,' going beyond the everyday understanding of legality.

The question of the 'innocent' or 'innocent civilian' victims of terrorism is somewhat more complicated. We can distinguish two types of definitions employing such wording. First, simply the condemnatory definitions which are already designed to shock and awe the reader. For example, Benjamin Netanyahu in 1986 defined terrorism as "the deliberate and systematic murder, maiming, and menacing of the innocent to inspire fear for political ends" (cited in Schmid 2011: 127). Given the emphasis on the graphic description of "murder, maiming and menacing of the innocent," by the time the reader reaches political ends, the idea of cruel, irrational, and senseless violence is already instilled. Powerful imagery is used to bring up the pictures of bloodied children and the author does not need to employ any more arguments as to why terrorism as such is unacceptable.

The second way of looking at the 'innocents' in the definitions of terrorism is encountered in some works of philosophy that examine the concept. It is linked with the just war theory tradition and uses the notion of 'innocence' not so much to evoke images of childhood, but rather as a shortcut to the distinction between legitimate and illegitimate targets. Classical just war theory distinguishes first the moral justifications for the wars themselves (*ius ad bellum*) and then the moral justifications for the killing in a war (*ius in bello*). The former is based strongly on the idea of self-defense—only wars that are waged for self-defense or in order to stop some atrocities are justifiable. The latter puts an emphasis on the just conduct of the war, regardless of how just the cause of the war is itself. The *ius in bello*, in consequence, is strongly built upon the idea that combatants in the war are legitimate targets of attack and that non-combatants casualties should be avoided. Thus, building upon the tradition of just war theory, the notion of innocence is not so much linked to some kind of moral innocence as such, but to the status of non-combatants and the immunity which that status confers.

Prima facie this does not solve the issue of making moral condemnation part of the definition, as by emphasizing the attack on non-combatants, the definition of terrorism already makes it into an unjust, morally repugnant action. Igor Primoratz's (1997) article 'The Morality of Terrorism' is a good example here. While the author starts from what he suggests is a morally neutral definition of terrorism, he nevertheless includes the category of innocent in this definition. Later in the article, discussing Trotsky's ideas about revolution, war, and terrorism, he claims that:

> In war and revolution ... intimidation is (or can and should be) effected by the attacks on legitimate targets: on members of the enemy's armed forces, on other military targets (e.g. arms factories), and on his political leadership ... Terrorism, on the other hand is always an attack on illegitimate targets, on innocent people, with the aim of intimidation and coercion.
>
> (Primoratz 1997: 226)

Moreover, such a distinction helps him dismiss Trotsky's argument that if terrorism is always impermissible, the same should be the case for wars and revolutions. Trotsky suggests that it is difficult to distinguish between combatants and non-combatants in contemporary conflicts, especially as modern armies often consist of many soldiers that were drafted by force, who do not agree with the position of their government and the devastating effects of war necessarily fall on all the population. In his view, such circumstances dictate that either war and revolution are also seen as (always) morally wrong, or that terrorism is viewed as (sometimes) morally right.

Primoratz dismisses this idea, arguing that victims in wartime or revolution should be viewed differently than victims of terrorism. In wartime, he argues, civilians may be 'collateral damage,' but their deaths are not used (or at least should not be used) to advance some objective, while terrorism, already by definition, targets these innocent civilians as a means of advancing some agenda. The definition thus predetermines the view on the subject. Yet, it does not solve the issue of 'naming' the acts 'terrorist.' Many terrorist groups choose to attack military or security forces, either as primary targets, or at least as some of the targets. To include these in a definition of terrorism alongside 'innocent civilians' requires a larger scope, which usually also includes the idea that no official state of war was declared (argument used for declaring attack against the USS Cole a terrorist act in 2000) or that military personnel were off-duty (argument used in the case of the Berlin disco bombing in 1986).

The critical studies approach to defining terrorism

The definition of terrorism has been one of the major criticisms of 'orthodox' terrorism studies addressed by CTS. The first major criticism that was launched was directed to the lack of 'state' in most definitions of the phenomenon. CTS argued for the inclusion of the state in the definition of terrorism and for shifting the focus to state terror in general. The discussion about the inclusion of the state in the definition often took place within the 'positivist' field of studies as well, with some researchers arguing for the inclusion of the state and others suggesting that because the state was so much more powerful than its asymmetric challengers that its use of violence against its own civilians should be called something else. This notion can be linked to the discussion of the previous section; while the notion of 'innocents' or 'civilians' as the targets of terrorism is dubious in the general definitions of terrorism, in the case of state terror such targets become an essential part of the definition.

CTS does not represent a unified field in terms of definition, notwithstanding the attempts to create such. For example, Richard Jackson called for the creation of a unified concept of terrorism, around which CTS could converge. Yet, as in the 'positivist' paradigm, a unified definition has been elusive and the debates reflect to a large degree those taking place in 'positivist' terrorism studies. The focus on the state can serve as a unifying factor in these approaches, but beyond this focus, a large divergence exists.

First, the critical studies field is divided into those who think that the notion of terrorism as such is obsolete and those who think that it should be used, just differently defined or described rather than defined. Some scholars, such as Dominic Bryan, argue that terrorism as a term should be completely abandoned. According to him, this term carries such a negative load and is used as such a condemnatory tool, that its use by scholars is inherently compromised. He suggests that this term should be abandoned when talking about political violence as the use of said term immediately labels the act or the actor, and conditions very particular responses from the public, the authorities, and the victims themselves (Bryan 2012: 18).

Second, though sometimes linked to the first, there is a divide between those who see terrorism as a 'social fact,' but a fact nonetheless, and those who advocate a 'completely constructivist approach' to the study of terrorism (Stump 2013). The first group aims to explore the dynamics between violence 'out there' and the meaning conferred on this violence by observers, and explore its changing nature. The second group considers that such an approach is not critical enough and comes up with definitions that are in fact very similar to those advanced in mainstream terrorism studies. The alternative proposed is to look exclusively at discourse and ask not 'what is terrorism?' but how certain acts become labeled 'terrorism' and why such labeling is successful in some circumstances but not in others. Terrorism in such a view is nothing else but a category of discourse. Harmonie Toros, as discussed in the previous chapter, provides a persuasive critique of this approach as it ignores the social fact of violence and argues for the responses to it only on the discursive level. Yet, while the meaning of terrorism is indeed socially constructed, the fact of violence is real for those who perpetrate it and even more so for those who are caught up in it.

Summary

In this chapter, the different ways of defining terrorism were discussed following five different approaches:

- list-type definitions that are often used in the legal domain and involve categorizing some actions as 'terrorist' and some organizations or groups as 'terrorist organizations';
- historical developments of the notion of terrorism and how the different elements in the historic definitions filtered through to today's practices;
- analytical definitions that usually center on three major characteristics of terrorism: violence, political purposes, and the intent to create an atmosphere of fear;

- normative definitions that use notions that are coupled with terrorism in analytical definitions, but also add additional weight to the illegitimacy of terrorist violence and on the targets of terrorism that are identified as 'innocent civilians';
- CTS approaches that put more emphasis on the state and discuss whether terrorism can be viewed as a 'social fact' or should be seen exclusively as a category of discourse.

Exercises

2.1 If one focuses on the objectives of violence, 'one man's terrorist' becomes 'another man's freedom fighter.' Why, for some, does violence in politics seems acceptable? How widespread do you think this opinion is?

2.2 Historically, the use of terror has been associated with the pursuit of justice and the attempt to 'hasten' history's course. Does this still hold for contemporary groups? Are such pursuits part of the appeal of terrorist groups?

2.3 So-called 'lone wolves' are especially difficult to qualify as 'terrorists.' Discuss the case of Anders Breivik and the arguments given for and against calling him 'a terrorist.' Also, discuss what implications such naming has.

References

Bryan, D. (2012). A Landscape of Meaning: Constructing understandings of political violence from the broken paradigm of 'terrorism'. In Jackson, R. (ed.) *Contemporary Debates on Terrorism*, London: Routledge, pp. 17–23.

Jackson, R., Jarvis, L., Gunning, J. and Breen-Smyth, M. (2011). *Terrorism: A Critical Introduction*, Basingstoke: Palgrave Macmillan.

Primoratz, I. (1997). The Morality of Terrorism. *Journal of Applied Philosophy*, 14(3), pp. 221–233.

Robespierre, M. (2007). On the Principles of Political Morality that should Guide the National Convention in the Domestic Administration of the Republic. In Robespierre, M., *Slavoj Žižek presents Robespierre: Virtue and Terror*, London: Verso, pp. 108–125.

Schmid, A. (2011). *The Routledge Handbook of Terrorism Research*, London: Routledge.

Stump, J.L. (2013). On the Future of Critical Terrorism Studies: A response to Richard Jackson's minimal foundationalist redefinition of terrorism. *Behavioral Sciences of Terrorism and Political Aggression*, 5(3), pp. 217–224.

Thorup, M. (2010). *An Intellectual History of Terror: War, Violence and the State*, London: Routledge.

Weinberg, L. and Davis, P. (1989). *Introduction to Political Terrorism*, New York: McGraw-Hill.

Further reading

Bryan, D., Kelly, M. and Templer, S. (2011). The Failed Paradigm of 'Terrorism.' *Behavioural Sciences of Terrorism and Political Aggression*, 3(2), pp. 80–96.

Findley, M.G. and Young, J.K. (2012). Terrorism and Civil War: A spatial and temporal approach to a conceptual problem. *Perspectives on Politics*, 10(2), pp. 285–305.

Guelke, A. (1995). *The Age of Terrorism and the International Political System* (Vol. 2), London: I.B. Tauris.

Jackson, R. (2011). In Defence of 'Terrorism'': Finding a way through a forest of misconceptions. *Behavioural Sciences of Terrorism and Political Aggression*, 3(2), pp. 116–130.

Merari, A. (1993). Terrorism as a Strategy of Insurgency. *Terrorism and Political Violence*, 5(4), pp. 213–251.

Richards, A. (2015). *Conceptualizing Terrorism*, Oxford: Oxford University Press.

Robin, C. (2004). *Fear: The History of a Political Idea*, Oxford: Oxford University Press.

Tarrow, S. (2007). Inside Insurgencies: Politics and violence in an age of civil war. *Perspectives on Politics*, 5(03), pp. 587–600.

Woodworth, P. (2001). *Dirty War, Clean Hands: ETA, the GAL and Spanish Democracy*, Cork: Cork University Press.

3 Studying terrorism

In the previous two chapters, we have talked about how terrorism is 'made,' how terrorism is defined, and the different paradigmatic approaches to it. This chapter deals with the practical questions related to the study of terrorism, such as what should be analyzed and how. As previously indicated, the literature of terrorism is very broad in terms of disciplines, theories, and methods. In order to facilitate access to it, navigate it more efficiently, but also as a guide for one's own research, we propose here a typology of approaches: deterministic, intentional, and relational. These categories are not essentially new; in one way or another, they can be related to similar ones proposed by other authors (see more on this in the Introduction). These categories are not specific to the 'positivist' literature, but, with the exception of determinism, are also suitable to classify studies in the critical tradition, or which use theories and methods claimed by CTS.

Having been sensitized to the different perspectives, definitions, and broader paradigms that can influence the ways in which we relate to our object of study, we turn now to the more practical dimension of terrorism research. Suppose you have in front of you a terrorism-related topic: how do you go about studying it? A good starting point are the five basic questions in social science: who, what, when, where, and how. Starting with the *who*, it is obviously terrorist individuals and groups that form the main focus of attention in terrorism studies, but clearly also states are known to have engaged in acts of terror and even terrorist campaigns. As we have seen in the previous chapters, it is not always easy to clearly delineate who is a terrorist and who is not; terrorists themselves rarely accept this label, while the political constellations influencing who the 'good guys' and the 'bad guys' are, can change. A classic example here are the Taliban in Afghanistan, who were initially supported by the US during the Cold War against the Soviet Union, to be then later on battled in the War on Terror. At the international level, there is also little agreement on who should be on the list of designated terrorist organizations. How should we then decide whom to study when dealing with terrorism? The most straightforward way of selecting one's 'unit of analysis'—that is, whom or what to analyze, is to look at official designations of individuals and groups, as well as previously produced scholarship. In some cases, there will be a generally accepted depiction of 'terrorist'—for example in the case of al-Qaeda or IS. In most cases though, caveats will have to be introduced for various reasons, such as the nature of the organization or the subjective positioning of the researcher. Most 'terrorist' organizations also engage in other activities but terrorism, be it social welfare or education, or also at one time or another hold political offices in legal politics. Hezbollah has for instance only recently been introduced on the European Union list of designated terrorist organizations and only with respect to its military wing. The reason for this is that, while we use the criterion

38 *Studying terrorism*

'terrorism' to select our units of analysis, terrorism is not something that individuals and organizations *are*, but something that they *do*. Terrorism is consequently also something that they can stop doing (see Box 3.1).

Box 3.1 The IRA and Martin McGuinness

Martin McGuinness was a former member of the PIRA (the Provisional Irish Republican Army, a left-wing paramilitary organization in Ireland) and later a member of the Legislative Assembly in Northern Ireland for Sinn Féin (Ourselves). He was one of the main actors in the peace talks that eventually led to the Good Friday Agreement (Northern Ireland Peace Agreement). The violent conflict in Northern Ireland, also known as 'The Troubles,' lasted from 1968 to 1998. At the core of the conflict was the constitutional status of Northern Ireland. The Unionists and the Protestants, who formed the majority in the region, demanded to remain part of the United Kingdom whereas the Nationalists, the republican and Catholic part of the population, demanded to become part of the Republic of Ireland. The conflict was not a religious one, but a territorial one about national identity and national belonging in the course of which about 3,600 people died and 50,000 were injured. The conflict was resolved by the already mentioned Good Friday Agreement, also known as the Belfast Agreement. This peace agreement was established because of a stalemate in the conflict. As a result, multi-party talks had been established in 1996 and subsequently the IRA had restored its ceasefire in July 1997. In September of the same year, the representatives of the IRA and the loyalist paramilitaries finally engaged in peace talks at Stormont in Belfast. Signed by the two Irish states on 10 April 1998, the agreement marks the will to lay down arms and to continue the struggle in the political arena. McGuinness stated on repeated occasions that it was his and others' assessment at the time that peace talks were strategically necessary. He came to the conclusion that a military stalemate had been reached, a situation where military victory was not possible for either the British Army or the IRA, which then led to thoughts of how the conflict could be resolved in a peaceful way through peace negotiations.

What we can derive from all this then is that terrorism is not a compulsive behavior, but one that occurs for particular purposes and under particular circumstances; there is, in other words, an instrumental rationality for the use of terrorism. Not all approaches to the explanation of terrorism share this assumption though, or at least not completely. Some psychological approaches for instance would argue that one is or becomes a terrorist as a consequence of particular psychological features. Also somewhat questioning the mere instrumentality of terrorism, some individuals come to identify themselves as 'terrorists,' thus making it part of their identity. Consider the following citation which is an extract from an autobiography written by Kamel Daoudi, a person tried and convicted for participation in an al-Qaeda plot to blow up the American Embassy in Paris. Here, it is interesting to see how, rather than contesting the label 'terrorist,' he identifies with it, yet in an overall positive self-appraisal:

> My ideological commitment is total and the reward of glory for this relentless battle is to be called a terrorist. I accept the name of terrorist if it is used to mean that I terrorize a one-sided system of iniquitous power and a perversity that comes in many forms. I

have never terrorized innocent individuals and I will never do so. But I will fight any form of injustice and those who support it. My fight will only end in my death or in my madness.

(cited in Sciolino 2002)

There are two ways to think about how this re-definition of identity might occur, both uncovered by della Porta (2012) in her work on the left-wing terrorism of the 1970s. One mechanism is inherent to the specific conditions of underground organizations. Given their isolation, selective information processing, and intensive material and emotional commitment, individuals in underground groups gradually identify with a 'community of the armed struggle.' Their statements could then be interpreted in this case not just as moral excuses, but as actual illustrations of self-perception as warriors in an eschatological war. A second mechanism has to do with outside labeling and is called 'secondary deviance.' Remember the discussion on labeling in the first chapter, how this is used as a marker for the enemy and how exclusive knowledge can lead to problematic political decisions? Here we approach labeling from the perspective of how it can affect individual progression towards terrorism. Della Porta took the concept of secondary deviance to show how the deviant identities of the left-wing terrorists of the 1970s were created as a result of state overreaction. For the German and Italian left-wing terrorist groups, it was the difficult prison conditions and the long sentences in particular which solidified the identities of 'freedom fighters' and 'soldiers of the revolution.' In her view, these are instances of secondary deviance insofar as the individuals ended up by identifying with their primary deviance and the underground organization they served.

Secondary deviance is a concept originating in criminology and in particular from the work of David Matza. In *Becoming Deviant*, Matza (1969: 157) differentiates between the logic of nature and that of human activity, between "natural selection" and "signification," the first "blind, fortuitous and without purpose" and the second marked by human agency. His point is to show the importance of meaning for the understanding of human behavior, as opposed to natural phenomena which can be explained through laws of determination. In the context of understanding how and why individuals become criminals, Matza develops the concept of secondary deviance: individuals who engage in their first criminal activity (primary deviance) are subsequently labeled as criminals and thus solidified in their identity as criminals: "To be cast a thief, a prostitute, or more generally, a deviant, is to further compound and hasten the process of becoming that very thing" (ibid: 157). In rather flowery language, Matza describes how the authority of the ones who exercise the labeling and the existence of entire industries of crime prevention, management, and research effectively add meaning to the initial act, i.e. as crime, and how this then also reflects on the identity of the perpetrator:

Dressed properly and acting his part, the personification of authority, whether police-man, judge, or someone less notable, impress; by being impressive, he helps a bit to cast the subject in his deviant part ... In shocked discovery, the subject now concretely understands that there are serious people who really go around building their lives around his activities – stopping him, correcting him, devoted to him. They keep records on the course of his life, even develop theories about how he got to be that way. Pressed by such a display, the subject may begin to add meaning and gravity to his deviant activities.

(Matza 1969: 163–164)

40 *Studying terrorism*

Significantly, and in some sense similar to the mechanism specific to underground organizations, isolation from others and other meanings also helps solidify this identity, or effectively exclude others. Focused as it is on secondary deviance, this theory does not explain primary deviance. That is, external labeling can help us understand how individuals might persist in carrying out their terrorist activities, but not how and why they engaged in terrorism in the first place. If we were to think about the gradual nature of involvement in terrorism, it nevertheless remains important to consider the effects of external labeling. It can push in one direction a development which might have otherwise stopped, or which might have been initiated by random events. This is, however, only one piece of the puzzle.

Moving on to the next question on our list, *what* should, or has terrorism been a study of? Or in other words, what is it about individuals, groups, and states engaged in terrorism that we want to find out? One obvious aspect is the biography of individual terrorists, something that has been conceptualized in the literature as 'life stories' or 'careers.' While it might seem counter-intuitive at first, the concept of 'career' or 'occupation' is supported by various features of life as an activist: the length of involvement with terrorism; the quasi-employment relationship with an organization; the extent to which terror-related activities take up space in the person's public and private life; and the individual self-perception. In Horgan and Taylor's (1997) analysis of PIRA, we see how membership is a matter of long-term involvement and not just participation in some isolated terrorist acts. They also show how members are de facto 'employed' by the organization, in that they receive material benefits, for instance. Other features of organizational embedding, which are not unlike real-world employment, are specialization of labor, on-the-job training, or recruitment (see the following section on roles).

In terms of personal involvement, della Porta's (2012: 242) work on biographies of German and Italian left-wing terrorists reveals a particularly intense type of material and emotional commitment, a "24-hours-a-day" commitment, and a "lack of any time for 'thinking,' critically reflecting on the sense of the crimes the terrorists had carried out." Finally, in the first author's work dealing with Islamist radicalization in Europe, interview and court statements of individuals charged and sentenced on terrorism counts reveal a perception of self and of the activities they engaged in which can be adequately conceptualized as occupation, in the majority of cases as 'soldier' or 'combatant' but also things like 'journalist.' That is, these individuals did not see terrorism as something that just 'happened' to them, and for the most part did not see it as terrorism. Rather, they carried out their day-to-day activities in a very similar way to those involved by regular jobs. Furthermore, and different to della Porta's sample, these occupations were not always full time, but involved sometimes just part-time activities. This kind of involvement is in fact quite common for right-wing extremist individuals.

The analysis of Islamist 'occupations' also revealed another dimension, namely the specialization of labor. These individuals were involved in training and the acquisition of skills, and the skills they thus acquired or already had were then decisive for the kinds of concrete activities they later took up within the group or network. In an initial jihadi typology with four categories of cell members, Petter Nesser (2010) shows, among others, how particular skills or aptitudes correspond to the kinds of roles that the individuals then fulfill in the terror cell (see Box 3.2). This mechanism is also known from general organizational behavior theory and evidences a further parallel to 'regular' occupations.

Box 3.2 Jihadi cell member skills, aptitudes, and roles in Petter Nesser

The entrepreneurs: "The heads of the cells, the entrepreneurs, are critical for terrorist cells to coalesce and go operational. They proactively connect with jihadi networks, and they proactively recruit, socialize and train their cadre. Once a cell is consolidated, entrepreneurs are in charge of its operational activities. They also control the cells' external relations with the jihadi infrastructure, operational and ideological mentors."

The protégés "are similar to the entrepreneurs, but junior and inferior to them. They are typically second in command in cells ... Protégés tend to be very intelligent, well-educated and well-mannered persons, who excel in what they do, professionally, academically and socially. Through being educated, they might provide the cells with needed expertise (for example, bomb making or IT skills)."

The misfits "do not enjoy a high status within cells, and at times there have been serious controversies between misfits and other elements of a cell, including the leader. Some misfits have displayed violent tendencies and some have been convicted for acts of violence before they became involved with militants. Because they are physically fit, inclined to show violent tendencies, and familiar with criminal practices, the misfits are well suited for the execution of important practical tasks at the preparatory and operational level, such as being in charge of acquiring weapons and bomb making materials."

The drifters: "Possibly because of their 'volatile' characteristics and dubious devotions, drifters are typically not entrusted with the most important tasks in the group, and they might not be privy to details about the terrorist operation. However, they do fulfill important support functions for the group. At times, recruitment of drifters also seems to involve stronger elements of youth rebellion, search for adventure and lack of viable options."

(Nesser 2010: 92–95)

Not unlike regular firms, the larger and the more hierarchical the terrorist organization, the sharper the specialization and division of labor will be. Horgan and Taylor (1997) illustrate this for the case of the PIRA, a hierarchically organized organization, with a complex command and functional structure. They compare the IRA with accounts of ETA (Euskadi Ta Askatasuna), whose organizational table bears "remarkable similarities with the functional organizational chart of a large business" and conclude that the PIRA is quite similar, "an organization having numerous roles to fill, as in any large business, each role having specific responsibilities still allowing for accountability to 'same-level' peers or higher authorities" (Horgan and Taylor 1997: 4). The article illustrates not only the highly complex organizational structure of the PIRA, but also the variety of types of activity: security, operations, foreign operations, finance, training, engineering and research, intelligence, education, and publicity (ibid 10–18), as well as how individuals were trained for specific tasks, such as robbery, shooting, bombing, or intelligence-gathering. Roles and training can be also observed in the case of jihadism, although in this case there is no hierarchical organization but rather networks and cells. Furthermore, in both cases, prior qualities, skills, and aptitudes are relevant for the adoption of particular roles or as a precondition for joining. The PIRA would be for instance looking for qualities such as "dedication and commitment" (ibid: 22).

42 *Studying terrorism*

Apart from the broader dimensions of individual career and roles, some other, more concrete aspects of individual, group, and state terrorism have also captured scholars' attention, such as: the causes and motivations for terrorism; facilitators for terrorism, such as, for example, nowadays more prominently the Internet, but also means of communication and the media in general, means of transportation, technical innovations, or innovations in weaponry; terrorist activities around the actual attacks (procurement, logistics, recruitment, planning, etc.); the phases, mechanisms, or indeed interlinkages between terrorism and other forms of political violence (such as insurgencies and civil wars) or political protest; whether and to what extent terrorism 'works'; more descriptive questions dealing with the forms and manifestations of terrorism, in terms of ideology or *modus operandi*; and of course various aspects of counter-terrorism, which is a subject matter in itself. While all of these topics are relevant, the questions of motivation and process—why and how individuals engage in terrorism, have by far preoccupied the literature to the greatest extent.

The *when* question can be considered from two perspectives: the terrorist's and the researcher's timeline. From the subject's perspective, of interest is obviously the period of actual involvement in terrorism, starting with the moment of joining a group or an organization. Nowadays, the applicability of this reference point has somewhat decreased in significance, since the traditional hierarchical and closed groups have given way to other forms of organization, such as networks, cells, or even lone wolves. Considering this change on the ground, it still remains useful to consider the point of joining, whether it is a clearly identified group or a more or less confined community of like-minded people who share a cause and are willing to use violence against civilians in order to reach it. This initial phase of involvement in terrorism needs to be differentiated from 'radicalization'—a gradual evolution towards extreme ideas and behaviors which might or might not eventually involve terrorism. Usually radicalization precedes involvement in terrorism; however, there can also be cases of involvement in terrorism without the existence of a radical mindset. Similarly, the life of terrorist organizations has not been only studied at the stage of their actual involvement in terrorism, but also in their previous phases. Scholars of social movements and critical scholars have made a point of the fact that terrorism most of the time emerges during cycles of political contention and is thus a form of political violence rather than something *sui generis*.

The *when* of studying terrorism then also differs on the side of the researcher. Many terrorism articles are 'one hit wonders,' in that there is rarely something on terrorism before and after those particular articles in the author's publishing list. This is due to the fact that research on terrorism is very much empirics-led, and especially driven by the punctual occurrence of spectacular events. That means that at any particular point in time, most scholarship on terrorism will be dedicated to the group or phenomenon prominent at that time. Depending on their prominence, some will receive more attention than others, so scholarship will show regular peaks in the quantity of studies produced, such as is the case at the moment with Islamist terrorism. In this context there will be various disciplinary sources of expertise on the matter and centers of such expertise. In practice that means that, at the moment, work from any kind of discipline—from political science to religion or art, so long as it deals with jihadism, will be more frequently read than a similar article on, say, right-wing extremism. This is of course so, unless an intervening right-wing attack should occur, at which point expertise on the extreme right would be on the rise. Of no little importance in this equation are counter-terrorism-related interests which might at times supersede the mere empirical scale of relevance attached to the various phenomena.

Studying terrorism 43

Particular attention to the *where* question and to context in general can be very beneficial in terms of a deeper understanding of the phenomenon, but at the same time can also prevent broader generalizations. The *where* question can refer to the dimension of space—the region, country, and the political, historical, and cultural particularities of these regions or countries, but also to a social dimension—in which social context does terrorism arise? With the exception of the so-called lone wolves, terrorists usually act in a group, are bound in various social networks throughout their radicalization process, are usually located in a certain aggregation of individuals with a high degree of politicization, and are sometimes part of a larger social movement. Such social movements share to some extent the sense of grievance and the goals pursued, but not necessarily the means to achieve them. Della Porta (2012) argues that terror organizations should be understood as a subdivision of, and as originating in, social movements. She takes two core characteristics of social movements as "self-conscious groups" and expressing "claims of challengers" and finds that terror organizations are "small minorities within larger political subcultures or countercultures" (della Porta 2012: 237). Further, she argues that:

> They [left-wing underground] were founded by social movement activists – often as a result of splits in social movement organizations – as a by-product of those interactions between challengers and the opponents which constitute the essence of social movements … And not only did the militants perceive themselves as part of the social movement sector, the social movement activists (from whom the underground drew its new recruits) often recognized the militants as "comrades" – albeit as "comrades who were wrong."
>
> (della Porta 2012: 237)

In between the terror organization and the broader social movement lies a further type of community, which has been labeled and classified in various ways depending on disciplines and research foci. Common to all are the functions of operational support for the terrorist organization and of socialization into ideologies and types of behavior prior to joining such organizations. In a *modus operandi* approach, Horgan and Taylor (1997) differentiate in the case of the PIRA between active or operational membership, and the support network or non-operational membership. Whilst the former take part in actual terror attacks as part of the 'Active Service Units,' the latter fulfill other supporting roles such as hiding weapons or offering safehouses (ibid: 3). A more recent conceptualization of this supporting social context is that of 'radical milieu.' The connection and relationship between this radical milieu and the terrorist organization or cell are more ambiguous and loose. The terrorist organization or cell emerges from this milieu, with which it shares to a great deal the ideology and even in part ideas about the appropriate means of action. At the same time, as the group becomes more radicalized and turns toward terrorist action, the initial milieu begins to disavow it, though punctual instances of support can nevertheless occur. Finally, subculture is another concept which has become more prominent in recent years as an intermediary between terrorist groups and the broader social movement. The concept of 'subculture' originates from criminology and depicts certain subgroups in society which function according to their own rules and standards, rather than those of the mainstream. Traditionally, subcultures have been depicted as either criminal or aesthetic (such as the hippies or the mods, for instance), or as groups with particularities of music and style but also placed at the margin of some political movement or group (such as the skinheads and the neo-Nazis, for instance). More recently, some authors have found that subculture could also be usefully applied to actual terrorist or extremist groups, in

44 *Studying terrorism*

that these also promote a certain style and lifestyle and diverge from the mainstream system of norms and values (see Further reading for more on these concepts).

Finally, *where* can also refer to the positioning of the researcher himself/herself. In the previous chapter we discussed among others the adage 'where you stand is where you sit' to illustrate how institutions and states define terrorism depending on their own mission and interests. Individual authors, even if not necessarily ideological, are still, by virtue of their human nature, not entirely objective. One's own socialization and education can influence and attach labels to the objects of study. This is why, particularly in qualitative, interpretive studies, authors discuss their own subjectivity and possible biases.

The fifth, and arguably most complex question is *how* to go about researching terrorism. This is a question of theories and methods, i.e. what kinds of theories and methods are useful for the exploration and analysis of terrorism, terrorists, and terrorist groups? Given that the terrorism literature is not just rather large, but also very heterogeneous, reuniting theories from various disciplines, it is useful to organize it around three dimensions of analysis, *deterministic, intentional,* and *relational*. These three approaches should be understood as heuristic devices that can help classify and understand the underlying assumptions of theories at hand. The main criterion for their differentiation is the extent to which they emphasize agency vs. structure. 'Agency' refers to the capacity of individuals to act independently and make their own independent choices, whereas 'structure' is a more general depiction of all kinds of external factors which affect individual behavior. Some theories of terrorism prioritize structure over agency (deterministic approaches), and others emphasize agency over structure (intentional approaches). A third category (relational approaches) is a mix in that it acknowledges intentionality, but affords ideational structures an important determining role. Additionally, agency is always seen as formed by the relations in which it engages. These three dimensions should not be confused with a classification of levels of analysis of another order, namely the macro-, meso-, and micro-levels of analysis, which refer to the nature of the dependent and of the independent variable, respectively, namely terrorism, terrorist groups, terrorist individuals; and broader societal, political, or cultural factors, group mechanisms, and individual factors.

Deterministic approaches

Deterministic approaches, also known as the 'grievance' paradigm, work with the assumption that terrorism is caused by identifiable and measurable factors which exist *a priori* of such terrorist behavior, and which 'determine' it, i.e. cause it to happen. Depending on the disciplines involved, sociology and political science vs. psychology, these factors can be of a broader social, political, or cultural nature, such as poverty, regime type, ideology, or religion, usually depicted as 'root causes'; or can be of individual psychological nature, such as personality features. Alongside a vast array of structural causes, frustration is in fact the backbone of deterministic approaches. In spite of the prominence of large-N data, variables, and correlations, terms that rather sound like research in natural sciences, the human element had to be captured in some way, and this is where frustration comes in. That is, one needs to experience some level of discomfort with the given circumstances in order for one to be willing to change them in a violent manner.

The frustration-aggression hypothesis postulates that aggression is always a consequence of frustration, the latter occurring as a result of an interference with the pursuit of certain goals. Initially proposed in 1939 by John Dollard, Leonard William Doob, Neal Elgar Miller, Orval Hobart Mowrer, and Robert Richardson Sears, it has remained extremely influential until today and is, explicitly or implicitly, at the basis of many root-cause approaches to terrorism and political violence more broadly. For example, one of the major and often cited paradigmatic works on political violence is Ted Gurr's (1970) *Why Men Rebel*. Here, political violence is explained as driven by the "perceived discrepancy between value expectations and value capabilities" (ibid: 37), that is, between what people feel that they are entitled to and what they actually can achieve. In this case, Gurr also resorts to frustration and posits that the "primary source of the human capacity for violence" is indeed frustration (ibid: 36). This conundrum can be found also in the criminological strain theory and later the subcultural theory of status frustration. Strain theory, developed by sociologist Robert K. Merton, posits that crime occurs as one of the possible responses to the discrepancy between culturally defined goals and the institutionalized means available to obtain them. To this, criminologist Albert Cohen added the psychological element of frustration to explain the emergence of deviant subcultures (for more on this see Chapter 6).

Deterministic approaches are some of the most oft-invoked kinds of explanations in the terrorism literature and some of the most problematic ones at the same time. An obvious limitation is the ignorance of individual agency. That is, for both root causes and deterministic psychological theories, individuals and organizations are simply the object of broader social, political, or cultural forces, or personality specificities. If we look at individual case studies of leaders alone, however, it becomes clear how important individual agency is, not just for the understanding of individual behavior, but also as it impacts on organizational behavior. A second problem has to do with the lack of specificity of such causes. Most of the time, a lot more individuals and groups are affected by them than the ones who eventually engage in terrorism. Such causes thus appear as neither necessary, nor sufficient.

Intentional approaches

Intentional approaches prioritize agency over structure in explaining terrorism and generally explain individual and group involvement as a matter of gain. Studies in this tradition have been often labeled 'rational choice' or 'greed,' as opposed to 'grievance.' Such labels are not entirely accurate though, as, first, the kinds of gains that individuals and groups are assumed to anticipate are only rarely of a material nature; and second, the kind of rationality involved is not the classical economic one of profit maximization, but an 'everyday' one, or 'soft rationality' (see Box 3.3). This is the understanding under which rational choice theory in criminology, for example, works; the latter has been, as we shall see in Chapter 5, very influential on intentional approaches to individual involvement in terrorism.

Box 3.3 A weak rationality concept

Economist Herbert A. Simon (1978) elaborated on conceptualizations of rationality in economics which are different to the ones of utility maximization. He argued that "almost all human behavior has a large rational component, but only in terms of the broader everyday sense of rationality, not the economists' more specialized sense of maximization." He further pointed out that "Much economic literature (for example, the literature on comparative institutional analysis) uses weaker definitions of rationality extensively" (ibid: 2). The main features of this alternative rationality would be sufficiency and functionality, as opposed to necessity: "Behaviors are functional if they contribute to certain goals, where these goals may be the pleasure or satisfaction of an individual or the guarantee of food or shelter for the members of a society" (ibid: 3). Deducing function from observing behavior then "may demonstrate the sufficiency of a particular pattern for performing an essential function, but cannot demonstrate its necessity—cannot show that there may not be alternative, functionally equivalent, behavior patterns that would satisfy the same need" (ibid: 4). Interestingly, he suggests that functional reasoning might in fact also apply to explanations of pathological behavior in the psychoanalytic literature, whereby illness would be a solution to need, and thus perform, as it were, a function.

Not unlike 'regular' rational choice theories, the case of individual participation in violence poses a type of free rider dilemma. The free rider dilemma postulates that for goods that are public, i.e. which everyone would benefit from, such as, in this case, the gains of committing terrorism, there is no incentive to participate. This is because individual participation is not necessary in order for the individual to benefit from these gains. Participation in terrorism or the 'doing' of terrorism is furthermore associated with high *costs*, which in this case can mean imprisonment or death. That is, at first sight, there is little if any incentive to participate in a highly risky activity, especially considering the fact that the gains that might come out of it could theoretically be enjoyed by all, regardless of participation. Yet as we see that both individuals and organizations regularly do resort to terrorism, how can we explain this? There are two ways in which this dilemma can and has been resolved. One argues that individual participation might appear necessary to the person, from a subjective point of view. If we look at the testimonies of current or former terrorists, we get the distinctive impression that they believe that their own action will have an effect, that this action is absolutely necessary for the success of the overall undertaking, and that there are no other alternatives. A second explanation, which is more relevant for our discussion here, is that there *are* immediate gains from participation, but gains of an emotional nature or non-material benefits, such as belonging or status, or for the case of organizations, the show of power or recruitment.

Intentional approaches are also not without problems, especially from a positivist point of view. As opposed to classical rational choice/game theory approaches, such soft rationality approaches are not amenable to generally applicable explanations or laws. That does not mean that authors have not attempted to identify such laws, in particular with regard to the behavior of organizations, and some of them have indeed proved applicable to several cases. In general, however, due to the strong human element at the core of this approach, the most one could reasonably aim for is to establish commonalities, oftentimes limited to certain geographical areas or 'types' of terrorism. This is because individual wellbeing or organizational advantage are a matter of interpretation, which are forcefully different, depending on who makes them, the amount and kinds of information they have available, and the previous experiences that influence the ways interpretations or assumptions are made. The last two elements are in this sense parallels to the relational approach.

Relational approaches

Relational approaches, as the name says, do not focus on individuals or structures, but on relations—among individuals/organizations, and between individuals/organizations and the state. Since most of the scholarship in this approach stems from social movement research, it mostly deals with organizations, while some authors have attempted nevertheless to also include the individual level of analysis. As another consequence of this embedding in social movements research and their specific approach, studies here tend to be very much historical in nature and focused on specific cases which they describe in great detail. In terms of explanations, this approach prefers concepts such as 'process' and 'mechanism' to those of 'cause' and 'effect.' Importantly, scholars in this category see terrorism as a form of political violence rather than something *sui generis*. Furthermore and consequently, they see terrorism as emerging during various types of interactions between organizations and between organizations and the state. Typically, terrorism would occur towards the end of cycles of political violence and as a sign of failure of other, less extreme forms thereof. Again, here, agency is considered, yet the emphasis rather lies on these processes and mechanisms and on various elements of context that affect the nature of individual and organizational action. Similar to the determinist approaches, the ways in which these elements of context act in their turn, are of a rather cause and effect nature.

Apart from the work done in the tradition of social movement theory, there is a series of socio-psychological and criminological studies which follow most of the assumptions outlined here, and which in some ways parallel or complement these theories and concepts. Added to that, the *critical* literature, with respect to the question of causes of terrorism, has also placed itself in this relational approach. They also see terrorism as embedded in other forms of political violence and are additionally more skeptical about the labeling as 'terrorist' vs. something else or at all. They similarly see agency as embedded in structure and attempt to capture the interaction between the two. In terms of causation, instead of explaining violence by identifying regularities, they attempt to understand its meaning, either from the perspective of the ones who carry it out, or at a more abstract level. While there is some overlap here with social movement scholars, the latter differentiate themselves in that a search for regularities, even though in a softer form than 'laws,' still occurs.

Process

Asking the question 'how do individuals/organizations get involved in terrorism?' implies addressing the issue of involvement in terrorism as process. Process is usually defined as a series of actions that produce something or that lead to a particular result. The ways in which these actions hang together, the ways in which they emerge, and the sequence in time are different. In individual deterministic approaches, the phases of radicalization are usually lined up in a sequence of phases, where often one phase automatically leads to the other. Generally, these approaches to both individual and organizational terrorism have a relatively difficult time modeling process, due to the nature of their explanations as cause–effect. What we usually have here is a succession of phases with often obscure interphase transitions. Intentional and relational approaches also consider sequence in time, but the relationship between the factors or mechanisms involved there is not linear, but multi-dimensional or multi-level.

These three approaches are not only different in their assumptions, focus, and workings, but also concerning the types of *methods* they use. Given its strong positivistic nature, determinism easily lends itself to quantitative methods, where root causes can be operationalized and analyzed statistically. The kinds of studies performed here are therefore: large-N data ones, usually drawing on the various terrorism incident databases available and which aim to find correlations between the prevalence of one or more factors and terrorist incidents; or surveys, longitudinal large-N studies, or experiments. More recently, within the growing

48 *Studying terrorism*

literature on 'radicalization,' the root-causes approach has also been applied to individuals as units of analysis, so that in these cases the methodologies include middle-N data which is nevertheless analyzed quantitatively, or qualitative case studies. The other two approaches, given the impact of interpretation and context, are usually carried out through qualitative methods such as case studies, interviews, discourse analysis, or ethnographic methods. Depending on the discipline and focus, there are, however, methodological specificities and at times also quantitative elements. For example, social movement scholarship looking at the behavior of groups from a political process perspective (i.e. the interaction between them and the state) can engage in 'protest event' analysis, which is basically measuring the occurrence and intensity of protest events and relating them with other factors. Psychologists working with relational approaches engage in experiments to ascertain the occurrence of particular mechanisms. For example, experiments have shown that strong identification with the group reduces fear of death. This is a generally applicable mechanism, but one that can also help understand the apparently abnormal terrorist self-sacrifice. Critical scholars use a series of methods in their attempt to understand violence, such as ethnography, discourse analysis, feminist, or postcolonial methods.

The difference in approaches will of course also influence the kinds of *counter-terrorism* policies envisaged. If the assumption is that certain social, political, or cultural conditions lead to the emergence of terrorism, then policies might be directed towards eliminating those conditions. Examples of such policies are the promotion of human rights, fighting poverty, development aid, democracy promotion, etc. If intentional approaches are at the core of understanding how and why terrorism occurs, then policy would attempt to change the nature of incentives. That is, measures might be taken so that the use of terrorism ceases to offer the returns expected, or that the gain of peaceful means overcomes the ones of terrorism. Some examples of policies here are negotiations, but also repression, whereby the latter can influence motivation in either way. For the case of relational approaches, the kinds of measures would be either non-specific (if it is about general psychological mechanisms), or specific to particular contexts and points in time. Arguably, the last two approaches do not lend themselves to straightforward and generally applicable counter-terrorism measures. This might be one of the reasons why they are so seldom put into practice. Apart from the kinds of policies that can be analytically allocated to one of the three approaches, there are also of course others which operate on completely different premises, namely they do not (only) deter or influence in some way, but effectively eradicate the phenomenon as such—see, for example, military interventions. Here, from the very beginning, it is not considered necessary to address the *why* question in the first place and this, in turn, communicates something about the way terrorist groups and individuals are essentially seen, namely as incorrigible. This is one of the issues that is taken up by CTS scholars, who are from the very beginning not in search of the most effective way of countering terrorism, but rather see it as their mission to question these practices with regard to their assumptions and especially their consequences.

Summary

This chapter has introduced some of the main conceptual, theoretical, and methodological questions around the topic of terrorism and its study. Along the lines of the basic social science questions: who, what, when, where, and how, the chapter has dealt with:

* the issue of unit of analysis—who is a terrorist and what kinds of aspects do we in fact explore when we carry out research on terrorism?

Studying terrorism 49

- the points in time when behaviors can be meaningfully classified as terrorism, as well as the fluctuations in quantity of the literature, as influenced by events and political pressure;
- context in the broader socio-political and cultural sense, but also at the more basic human level;
- social environments that are connected to and often support terrorist organizations and groups;
- the three broad approaches to the explanation of individual and organizational motivation and process to get involved in terrorism.

Exercises

3.1 Compare and contrast biographies of IRA volunteers and those of al-Qaeda operatives with regard to types of careers, roles, and specializations. In what ways does the type of organizational structure influence these?

3.2 Is online terrorism training possible? Discuss Michael Kenney's (2010) article 'Beyond the Internet: *Mētis, Techne*, and the limitations of online artifacts for Islamist terrorists', *Terrorism and Political Violence*, 22(2), pp. 177–197. Can you think of examples that contradict his argument?

3.3 Try to identify in the literature various models of radicalization and assess their strengths and weaknesses.

References

della Porta, D. (2012). On individual motivations in underground political organizations. In J. Horgan and K. Braddock (eds) *Terrorism Studies: A Reader*, London, New York: Routledge, pp. 231–249.

Gurr, T. (1970). *Why Men Rebel*, Princeton NJ: Princeton University Press.

Horgan, J. and Taylor, M. (1997). The Provisional Irish Republican Army: Command and functional structure. *Terrorism and Political Violence*, 9(3), pp. 1–32.

Matza, D. (1969). *Becoming Deviant*, Englewood Cliffs, NJ: Prentice-Hall, Inc.

Nesser, P. (2010). Joining Jihadi Terrorist Cells in Europe. Exploring motivational aspects of recruitment and radicalization. In M. Ranstorp (ed.) *Understanding Violent Radicalisation. Terrorist and Jihadist Movements in Europe*, Abingdon, New York: Routledge, pp. 87–114.

Sciolino, E. (2002). Word for Word/Roots; Portrait of the Arab as a young radical, *The New York Times*, September 22.

Simon, H.A. (1978). Papers and Proceedings of the Ninetieth Annual Meeting of the American Economic Association, *The American Economic Review*, 68(2), pp. 1–16.

Further reading

English, R. (2016). *Does Terrorism Work? A History*, Oxford: Oxford University Press.

Falciola, L. (2015). A Bloodless Guerrilla Warfare: Why US white leftists renounced violence against people during the 1970s. *Terrorism and Political Violence*, 28(5), pp. 928–949.

Malthaner, S. (2014). Contextualizing Radicalization: The emergence of the "Sauerland-Group" from radical networks and the *Salafist* movement. *Studies in Conflict & Terrorism*, 37(8), pp. 638–653.

Zelinsky, A. and Shubik, M. (2009). Research Note: Terrorist groups as business firms: A new typological framework. *Terrorism and Political Violence*, 21(2), pp. 327–336.

4 Determining *individual* terrorism

In the previous chapter we differentiated approaches to the study of terrorism along three broad dimensions: deterministic, intentional, and relational. We made this differentiation depending on the extent to which various theories resort to agency, structure, or both, or the extent to which there is a case for individual or organizational choice. In this and the following five chapters, we apply these dimensions to individual and organizational involvement in terrorism. We further dissect these dimensions into two: the *why* and the *how*, namely the causes or motivations for individuals and organizations to get involved in terrorism, and the ways in which they do so, or in other words, the process of involvement in terrorism. Involvement in terrorism and radicalization more broadly have been generally acknowledged as occurring over time and thus unraveling in the form of a 'process.' Therefore, all approaches address process to some extent.

Deterministic approaches attempt to establish causal or quasi-causal relationships between individual engagement in terrorism on the one hand, and individual or environmental predisposing factors on the other. In this context, studies attempt to identify causes for terrorism or its 'determining variables.' This is by and large a logic of the type: A leads to B, where B is terrorism. Obviously, this type of thinking is very attractive for counter-terrorist efforts since, in order to do away with terrorism, it would suffice to identify and then eliminate its causes. Political science and sociological approaches look at broader social or political factors, also known in the terrorism literature as 'root causes,' while psychological approaches focus on personality characteristics and usually draw on psychoanalytical theories. All approaches attempt to identify variables which are *specific* to the environment or personality of terrorists and which can then be considered as *determining* their involvement. The following sections outline some of the more commonly used external and internal factors that presumably lead to individual involvement in terrorism: root causes, narcissism, and identity; and various types of deterministic processes of individual involvement as they have been developed within the literature on individual radicalization.

Relative deprivation

The effect of root causes on individual motivation has not been theorized directly, but rather through the intermediary of some psychological variables—in particular, those of *frustration* and *humiliation*. For example, in the context of material deprivation, the reason for engaging in terrorism would not be the fact that the individual does not have enough material resources, but the frustration or humiliation he/she experiences as a result. Relative deprivation is an older concept, which was initially used to explain political violence in general and has the element of frustration at its core. As outlined in the previous chapter, relative deprivation originally referred to the discrepancy between expectations and capabilities, between what groups are entitled to and what they can in fact achieve, or are allowed to achieve, in particular in relation to comparable groups. Adapted to the case of individual involvement in terrorism, relative deprivation was initially transposed on the individual and his/her disadvantaged position as a member of their group as compared to others. This has created some difficulties, as research has often shown how within both their communities and the broader society, terrorists in fact are often well educated and economically secure. In part as a solution to this problem, scholars have adapted their explanations by resorting to a second dimension, namely subjective perception. In these readings, individuals are not necessarily motivated by their personal and objective situations of relative deprivation, but by the ways they *perceive* these as applying to their *communities*. Michael King and Donald M. Taylor (2011: 610) argue that "It is the perception of deprivation, and not actual deprivation that will motivate a person to action." Drawing on insights from social psychology, and empirical studies testifying that "group-based feelings of injustice reliably predict collective action" they further posit that "it is the emotions elicited by the injustice—not only the cognitive awareness of the injustice— that predict collective action. Second, it is group-based relative deprivation, as opposed to personal deprivation, that predicts collective action" (ibid: 610). That is, individuals are moved by subjectively perceived situations of relative deprivation, which are, however, not their own but those of others with whom they identify.

Humiliation

Another root cause of individual involvement in terrorism theorized in the literature is humiliation. In her book *Terror in the Name of God: Why Religious Militants Kill* (2003), Jessica Stern presents several empirical case studies compiled on the basis of an elaborated fieldwork involving interviews with terrorists in various corners of the globe. For the case of Palestinian terrorism, she identifies humiliation as central. She does not define humiliation beforehand, but recognizes numerous variations of it as it comes up in conversations with her interview partners. Her findings show various kinds of humiliation, how this facilitates support for terrorist groups, and how terrorist organizations like Hamas take advantage of it. The first person she interviewed was General Osama al-Ali, an official of the Palestinian Authority, the Palestinian interim self-government that was established in 1994. The general was especially irritated about the non-compliance of the Israelis with the Oslo Accords. These are agreements signed between the government of Israel and the Palestine Liberation Organization (PLO) in 1993 and 1995, which were intended to start the Oslo Process, a peace process that should have culminated in a peace treaty between Palestine and Israel and the self-determination of the Palestinian people. What upset him were the military outposts of the Israel Defense Forces (IDF) and the greenhouses on the Israeli settlements that use an unfairly large amount of the water supply of the region. Six thousand Israeli settlers in the Gaza Strip used 70 percent of the water resources of Gaza, which they go at subsidized prices. While the Palestinians did not have enough bottled water for themselves, water was shipped to Israeli settlers via a pipeline. Moreover, the general noted: "they treat Palestinian workers [in the greenhouses] unfairly. They expose the workers to unsafe levels of dangerous pesticides, and the workers often end up with damaged lungs" and "The workers have no job security" (ibid: 36). The author states that Gaza Strip is the most overcrowded place on Earth, with three-quarters of the 1.2 million Palestinians living in an area of 147 square miles as refugees, half of them in camps, while Israel—under the Oslo accords—

52 *Determining* individual *terrorism*

retains 42 per cent of the land, mostly reserved for the 6,000 settlers who comprise 0.5 percent of the population in Gaza. While walking through the city she observed that the people living in Gaza Strip live totally different lives:

> The settlers live in a different world, which a passerby can glimpse through chain-linked fences and barbed-wire entanglements. A world with pristine white villas, gardens, and manicured lawns. The settlers burn the ancient olive groves to make room for their lawns and pools and consume, on average, five times as much water as their Palestinian neighbors.
>
> (Stern 2003: 37)

To the contrary, the Third-World style Palestinian land is characterized by sewage, rotting meat, uneven sidewalks covered with garbage, and a feeling of depression, humiliation, and despair. Stern's second interviewee, a renowned Palestinian lawyer, noted that Palestinians have totally been at the mercy of the Israeli Civil Administration, with exhausting wrestles with bureaucracy and often indifferent and hostile Israeli officials. A Palestinian student told the author that she was confronted with intense humiliation at the age of nine when a trip to Gaza took her and her family twenty hours instead of nine because the border crossing was made so difficult for them:

> The endless lines of other travelers and children, waiting for the unwelcoming and belligerent faces of their occupiers to place a simple stamp in their travel document giving them approval to return to their home; or to arbitrarily interrogate them; imprison them; or deny them entry.
>
> (Stern 2003: 38)

Humiliation was also taken up by Hamas leaders interviewed by Stern. One of them, Sheik Younis al-Astal, argued that it is in fact poverty and hopelessness that increase the support for groups like Hamas. When people's lives are characterized by deprivation, humiliation, and poverty, death and the prospect of paradise is more appealing to them. Ismail Abu Shanab, another Hamas leader, emphasized that it was the culmination of Palestinian frustration and suffering under occupation that led to the founding of the PLO, which subsequently established the Palestinian struggle. The Hamas leader noted that a very important element that increases the appeal of groups like Hamas is its social welfare activities and its lack of corruption. Another interviewee, Brigadier General Nizar Ammar of the Palestinian General Security organization, explained that, in fact, 60 percent of Hamas' budget is invested in social welfare, like the establishment of schools, youth clubs, mosques, orphanages, and clinics and that it also provides families of suicide bombers with lifetime annuities. Hamas itself benefits from the social investments as it is able to recruit its bombers directly from the sports clubs and schools. The importance of humiliation, poverty, and hopelessness for the recruitment of potential terrorists could be exemplified by the typical profile of a potential suicide bomber. The Hamas leader noted that these individuals were mostly mentally immature young individuals, often teenagers, unemployed and unable to work for the Palestinian Authority because of a lack of connections, without a girlfriend, without a meaning in life, and without any means to enjoy it. Such individuals often started to visit mosques more frequently. This in turn is used by Hamas members for recruitment. They are promised to become martyrs, heroes, and do good for their families as they are then provided with money and food by Hamas and a high social status by society. The high status of martyrs is illustrated by death notices, which are often announced like wedding announcements in Palestinian newspapers. Finally, Hassan Salameh, a 28-year old, and possibly most important Hamas leader imprisoned in an Israeli jail, interviewed by Stern, stated that he joined Hamas because he wanted to fight the Israeli government. His most important motivation was not only a religious one but the Israeli occupation, and the will to free the oppressed and humiliated Palestinians.

Jessica Stern refers in her accounts to instances of actual humiliation that had occurred to the individuals under investigation, or which they otherwise witnessed first-hand. Similar to the case of relative deprivation above, it has been noted that not all the individuals who eventually became involved in terrorism had actually experienced such humiliation themselves. For these cases, authors have proposed the idea of a transfer from the community onto the individual, so again this is the subjective experience of humiliation experienced by the broader community with which the individual identifies. The concept has been labeled by the French sociologist Farhad Khosrokhavar as 'humiliation by proxy.' Also, Marc Sageman has invoked humiliation as an initiator of the radicalization processes in his work on leaderless jihad (for both see Further reading).

Narcissism

Along with other psychoanalytical concepts, narcissism is a theme in terrorism studies which re-emerges time and time again, in spite of repeated rebuttal and criticism for being backward and impossible to falsify. This is also because, time and time again, cases of lone actors emerge who display symptoms of the narcissistic personality and which are often highly controversial (see an example in Box 4.1).

Box 4.1 The case of Anders Breivik

Norwegian right-wing terrorist, Anders Breivik, singularly carried out an attack on a summer camp for young center-left political activists in which 69 people were killed on 22 July, 2011. Before the rampage, Breivik had also detonated a car bomb in Oslo, killing eight people. Breivik's rationale behind the terrorist attacks was to protest against a 'Marxist Islamic takeover of Europe.' He held no remorse and described his actions as 'atrocious, but necessary' to defeat the Islamization of Western Europe and stop immigration. During his trial, Breivik was assessed twice by psychiatrists; the first assessment concluded that he had a psychotic disorder as he displayed grand delusions and paranoia that went further than the conspiracies of an Islamic conquest of Europe. For example, he believed that there was an ongoing ethnic cleansing in Norway and that he was in danger, but also had a responsibility to protect his fellow citizens. With this assessment, Breivik would be legally unaccountable. However, following protests from the media, politicians, and even Breivik himself, the defendant was re-evaluated. The results of the second evaluation stated that Breivik possessed the symptoms of severe narcissistic personality disorder and was a pathological liar. Contrary to the first assessment, Breivik was attested to be legally accountable and was subsequently sentenced to 21 years.

Psychoanalysis is built on the premise that human behavior is in many ways determined by unconscious factors which can be traced to the person's childhood. In the terrorism literature,

54 *Determining* individual *terrorism*

there is an initial pre-9/11 period where psychoanalytic approaches were explicitly named as such and traced back to Freudian and post-Freudian theories, in particular narcissism and identity theories. More recent studies neither acknowledge this theoretical origin, nor make use of its basic concepts, such as 'narcissistic injury,' for instance, but consider the respective causes and symptoms (e.g. broken families and lack of self-esteem) and formulate them as factors or steps in the radicalization process. Initial psychoanalytic approaches to the study of individual involvement in terrorism were based on systematic qualitative and clinical studies on left-wing terrorists in Germany, Italy, and the US in the 1970s and 1980s. No systematic exploration has been carried out since then; the 'second generation' of approaches has looked at limited samples, and has based their conclusions on either data sets of open-source individual characteristics, or interviews with terrorists.

Narcissism and in particular 'narcissistic injury' was, and continues to be, albeit not always identified as such, a very influential hypothesis in terrorism studies. Drawing on the work of Heinz Kohut (an Austrian-American psychoanalyst) who argued that narcissistic injury is the source of the most dangerous human aggression, Shaw (1986: 363) defines narcissistic injury as "any event interpreted by an individual as critically affecting his view of himself or self-esteem." Based on evidence from an extensive German study on left-wing terrorism, including biographical analyses of individual pathways, he argues that particular features or events, such as incomplete family structures, physical defects, failure in career or education, social conflict, and juvenile convictions acted in those cases as sources of narcissistic injuries in that they diverted these individuals from the 'normal' pathway of integration in society and affected their self-esteem. Terrorist activity and membership in a terrorist group compensated for this, as they offered the feeling of belonging to a community of like-minded people, as well as the opportunity to achieve. In this view, therefore, involvement in terrorism occurs as a result of personal failure or socio-environmental dysfunctions and as a restoration of self-esteem. Shaw's 'personal pathway model' is more complex, as he also includes elements of family socialization into particular ideologies and a macro-perspective on modern economic and political tensions where these 'political philosophies' tap in. Nevertheless, the core of the model, and the terrorist specificity in this sense, is the pattern of failure. It is important to cite this here more extensively, as this type of explanation appears in a great majority of current analyses of individual involvement in terrorism and extremism more broadly, although, again, without explicit reference to the concept of narcissistic injury:

> The personal pathway model suggests that terrorists come from a selected, at risk population, who have suffered from early damage to their self-esteem … As a group, they appear to have been unsuccessful in obtaining a desired traditional place in society, which has contributed to their frustration. Apparently membership in a terrorist group often provides a solution to the pressing personal needs of which the inability to achieve a desired niche in traditional society is the coup de grace. The terrorist identity offers the individual a role in society, albeit a negative one, which is commensurate with his or her prior expectations and sufficient to compensate for past losses. Group membership provides a sense of potency, an intense and close interpersonal environment, social status, potential access to wealth and a share in what may be a grandiose but noble social design.
> (Shaw 1986: 365–366)

More than a decade later, Jerrold Post (1998) also supported the theory of narcissism, but he laid a greater emphasis on the element of group belonging and 'splitting.' The latter concept was elaborated by psychoanalyst Otto Friedmann Kernberg (1970) in the following way:

the normal tension between actual self on the one hand, and ideal self and ideal object on the other, is eliminated by the building up of an inflated self concept within which the actual self and the ideal self and ideal object are confused. At the same time, the remnants of the unacceptable self images are repressed and projected onto external objects, which are devaluated.

(Kernberg 1970: 55–56)

Post argues that narcissistic injuries in childhood produce narcissistic wounds and an 'injured self,' which leads to splitting and externalization. The positive and negative parts of the self are split and the latter parts are projected on others, in this case the scapegoated enemy. Post takes the example of Hitler as a 'destructive charismatic' who:

projects the devaluated part of himself onto the interpersonal environment and then attacks and scapegoats the enemy without. Unable to face his own inadequacies, the individual with this personality style needs a target to blame and attack for his own inner weakness and inadequacies. Such people find the polarizing, absolutist rhetoric of terrorism extremely attractive. The statement "It's not us – it's them; they are the cause of our problems," provides a psychologically satisfying explanation for what has gone wrong in their lives. And a great deal has gone wrong in the lives of people who are drawn to the path of terrorism.

(Post 1998: 27–28)

In support of this, Post cites the same German study, where there was evidence of fragmented families and conflict, in particular with the parents, as well as criminal histories (ibid: 28). Joining a group is a solution for the split identity, "an attempt to consolidate a fragmented psychological identity, to resolve a split and be at one with oneself and with society, and, most importantly, to belong" (ibid: 31). Post also goes further than the confines of the individual psychological level of analysis and projects his model at the social and political macro-level. Nationalist-separatist terrorists are "loyal to parents who are disloyal to their regime; they are carrying on the mission of their parents, who were wounded by the establishment"; the anarchic-ideologues are "disloyal to their parents' generation, which is identified with the establishment" (ibid: 30). Right-wing terrorism is not included here and it is also rather difficult to classify, as actors here often but not always come from families with (neo-)Nazi heritage (see Box 4.2).

Box 4.2 The Nuclei Armati Rivoluzionari in Italy

The Nuclei Armati Rivoluzionari (NAR Armed Revolutionary Core) was Italy's most violent right-wing organization active from 1977 to 1988. The organization had a fluid and weak hierarchical structure and encouraged the use of its name to claim any attacks with a revolutionary character. Ideologically, the organization was neo-fascist but not explicitly anti-Communist and occasionally also collaborated with left-wing groups, yet it sought to unite all anti-state groups. Its ideas regarding the shape of a future Italian state were not clear. The group mainly supported itself through robberies of arms depots. They usually did not carry out mass-casualty attacks but claimed responsibility for Italy's worst terror attacks: the train bombings in Bologna in 1980 which killed 85 people and wounded 200. They mostly used firearms and grenades for

56 *Determining* individual *terrorism*

raids or to kill people such as law enforcement officers, left-wing militants, or journalists. Their second deadliest attack was the killing of two police officers in Rome in 1981. One of its leaders was Giuseppe Valerio (Giuvsa) Fioravanti, a former Italian child TV-star born in 1958; his father was a television presenter. In order to protect him from escalating violence his parents sent him to the US, where he studied for a year. After he came back to Italy he made his last film. In 1977 he was charged with possession of a pistol. Subsequently, Fioravanti abandoned his studies and joined a paratroop unit of the Italian army where he was frequently punished for disciplinary infractions, and was even sentenced to several months in a military prison for leaving his post when hand grenades were stolen while he was on guard duty. He eventually leaves the army and dedicates his activities to militancy, making a point out of not obeying his parents, unlike others in his generation.

As mentioned before, while not explicitly making reference to narcissism, several contemporary empirical studies infer the types of symptoms and causes pertaining to this theory. In particular, the German literature on right-wing extremism but also the Anglo-American literature on jihadism use indicators relating to early socialization, such as broken families or failed educational paths, in an overall frame of 'failure.' These elements partly overlap with relative deprivation and subcultural accounts (see Chapter 6 for more on subculture), the common denominator being a worse-off situation by comparison, accompanied by frustration, and a lack of self-esteem.

Identity

Identity as a psychoanalytical concept, developed by Erik Homburger Erikson (a German American developmental psychologist and psychoanalyst) in his psychosocial lifecycle model, was taken up in terrorism studies in the interpretation that an incomplete or lacking identity can be supplemented by membership in a terrorist organization and identification with a cause. For Erikson, the concept of identity is a reflection of the social and familial setting of an individual (Erikson and Erikson 1998). Crenshaw (1986: 391–394) drawing on Erikson, argues that the successful development of an identity, "which is found in a collectivity and rooted in one's ethnic, national, or family past" (ibid: 391), is essential to the integrity and continuity of one's personality. The concept of personality in turn is based on the assumption that personality is developed by a child through cumulative developmental stages (called turning points). This might result in the matured integration of the individual's personality or in the persistence of unresolved conflicts which might come up in later life. Of importance for a vital personality is basic trust. Early failures to develop trust or autonomy handicap the adolescent's search for a positive identity in later life which might lead to an extreme identity confusion or to the formation of a negative identity. In the process of identity formation individuals seek meaning and a sense of completeness and have the need to have faith in something or someone. Ideologies then often serve as guardians of identity. A crisis of identity, when an individual finds self-definition difficult and suffers from ambiguity, fragmentation, and contradiction, may mean the adolescent becomes susceptible to 'totalism' or to totalistic collective identities that promise certainty.

Again in a 'diluted' version, the identity argument was absorbed within the homegrown radicalization research in the form of an identity crisis among young Muslims in the West

Determining individual *terrorism*   57

due to discrimination, lack of integration, and dual identity (King and Taylor 2011). This was argued based on the assumption that the particular characteristics of a social group can say something about individual propensity to engage in terrorism: "linking identity issues to radicalization makes intuitive sense. Not only do second and third generation immigrants face discrimination based on their identities, but they also must manage a mainstream Western identity with their heritage identity, to arrive at some internalized and coherent identity" (ibid: 611). This focus on identity and the fact that it has been applied in relation to Muslims and Islamist radicalization, but not other groups and other kinds of radicalization, has attracted some critique along the lines of stigmatization and false relations of causality.

Orla Lynch (2013) argues that since 9/11 and the attacks in Madrid and London in 2004 and 2005 respectively, homegrown radicalization has become closely associated with (male) Muslim youth. This is due to the widespread assumption that Muslim youths struggle with their Western and Islamic identity. Lynch argues that in the case of UK Muslims, there has been a shift in perceptions of this group from an ethnic minority community to a national security concern. In the light of such a narrative, Lynch conducted a study with the aim of understanding how these constructions impacted on Muslim youth in the UK after the July 7, 2005 terrorist attacks in London. Lynch found that British Muslims do not reject British values and norms, but rather try to incorporate a British identity through their faith:

> Equally for the youths in this study, an increase in religiosity or in the use of religious symbols does not equate with a rejection of notions of Britishness, but represents an increased security in one's identity and the ability to successfully incorporate multiple elements of one's self into their expressed or developed identity.
>
> (Lynch 2013: 257)

Lynch acknowledges that the results of this study cannot be generalized and applied to the entire Muslim community in the UK, however, she argues that this very fact demonstrates that assumptions regarding Muslims that emanate from the radicalization discourse can also not be generalized.

Deterministic approaches and their critics

Deterministic approaches to the explanation of individual involvement in terrorism have attracted a series of critique points of an empirical and methodological nature. The most dominant critique has been the so-called specificity problem. Another formulation of this would be to say that deterministic explanations are neither necessary nor sufficient. In essence, the specificity problem subsumes two observations: on the one hand, not all individuals affected by factors supposedly leading to involvement in terrorism also become terrorists. This aspect is rather obvious if we think for instance about the overwhelming majority of individuals affected by relative deprivation or an identity crisis and who do not become terrorists. On the other hand, the biographies of actual terrorists more often than not reveal a completely different picture in terms of background characteristics. As mentioned above, authors have attempted to solve this problem through the transposition of determining factors onto the community that individuals are deemed to represent. This, however, might in fact only prolong the problem, since it still remains unclear why certain individuals would take it upon themselves to fix or avenge their community and not others. This kind of critique is made possible by the nature of the causal explanation which is 'cause and effect,' and which, additionally, assumes necessary and sufficient causality and the incidence of singular causes.

58 *Determining* individual *terrorism*

To overcome this and to allow for the capturing of more empirical variance, some authors have proposed aggregations of causes which would be individually not necessary but sufficient. This kind of solution has been also proposed at the meso- and macro-levels (see Chapter 7) and basically means that the incidence of any one factor or combination of factors would suffice to make the theory applicable. Matching this approach is the method of qualitative comparative analysis (QCA; see Further reading). Another approach has been to develop typologies and argue that certain causes or sets of causes are applicable to certain type of terrorists, but not others (see, for example, the typology by Nesser in the previous chapter).

By far, the most ardent critique has, however, been aimed specifically at the psychoanalytical approaches. Contemporary psychologists John Horgan and Andrew Silke in particular, but also social movement scholar Donatella della Porta, have identified a series of methodologically weak points of the approach. Andrew Silke (1998) coined in his study 'Cheshire-Cat Logic: The recurring theme of terrorist abnormality in psychological research' the phrase 'Cheshire cat logic' to denote the kinds of inferences linking abnormal behavior to psychological abnormality, also known as the 'attribution error' (see Box 4.3). Just as the cat assumes Alice must be mad because "we're all mad here," Silke argues that some scholars go on to assume that people who do mad things, i.e. terror attacks, must be mad, or at least have some sort of personality disorder. The author refers to three main identities that are regularly attributed to terrorists by scholars, namely "The Terrorist as Psychopath", "The Terrorist as Narcissist," and "The Terrorist as Paranoid," but also personalities with mixed paranoid and antisocial traits. Yet the author argues that these classifications are mainly the result of an attribution error, where expectations about the personality of an individual are based on what the individual does. Terrorism provokes extreme perceptions which easily influence the considerations of the actors that commit violence. The author notes that misconceptions and prejudices are rooted in the amorality of terrorist acts. In fact, some scholars only provide anecdotal evidence and often base their conclusions purely on secondary sources like terrorist autobiographies or media interviews. To the contrary, scholars who did have access to the individuals in question and conducted interviews arrived at opposite conclusions (see Further reading). Pearce, who stressed the importance of sociopathy in terrorism, in one case even based his findings on an individual having tattoos, and David G. Hubbard based his findings on a physical disorder. He interviewed 80 imprisoned terrorists in 11 countries and found that 90 percent of them had defective vestibular functions causing poor balance and coordination. The scholar linked this deficiency to antisocial behavior aimed at gaining attention and the inability to relate to people. Hubbard never released descriptions of the data he used and his study has never been replicated. These kinds of explanations have important implications for the adoption of relevant policies. When terrorists, for example, are perceived to be irrational and mentally ill, no policies that consider a reasonable response from these individuals will be created. This in turn might prolong campaigns of violence and exacerbate the search for proper counter-terrorism strategies.

Another methodological weakness of psychoanalytical studies is sampling bias, namely the fact that they only captured cases of imprisoned individuals. Indeed, in the case of imprisoned individuals, it is quite likely that things that 'went wrong' in their childhood and early socialization will be found. This, however, does not suffice to establish a direct causal link between precisely these factors and involvement in terrorism. Additionally, it could thus be argued that the effects of imprisonment, rather than biographic events and features, could similarly have created the appearance of narcissistic symptoms. Shaw (1986: 362) himself admits that "The Baader-Meinhof terrorists held in West German prisons were disabled cognitively by such conditions sufficiently to delay their trial. Thus it is hard to tell whether certain adaptations were related to the person becoming a terrorist or a result of the events which followed." Ideally, one would need to supplement the results of psychoanalytical studies with data on the effects of terrorist socialization processes. This is, however, where psychoanalysis, as an approach primarily dealing with the effects of childhood experiences, reaches its limits.

Box 4.3 History repeats itself

Neither narcissism nor identity crises are instances of mental illness or 'pathology.' Both Shaw and contemporary psychologists agree that terrorists are not mentally insane. Before introducing his narcissistic injury hypothesis, Shaw (1986) in fact presented an elaborated critique of psycho*pathological* approaches to the explanation of individual involvement in terrorism, in particular antisocial personality, narcissistic personality disorder, thanatos or the death instinct. Empirically, he argues, primary data testify to the contrary: the systematic studies on left-wing terrorists in the 1970s in Germany, Italy, and the US all found no evidence of psychopathology (ibid: 360). Even more interesting, however, are the rest of the arguments he brings forth as a critique of psychopathological approaches, since they are in essence the same as those that contemporary psychologists use to critique narcissism. First, the attribution error:

> the basic human tendency to attribute stable personality attributes to people who are disliked who do things we do not approve of. Conversely, when people who are liked do bad things, we tend to rationalize their acts as primarily the result of environmental circumstances. Not only are negative personality attributes inferred from the acts of people who are disliked, but we are more likely to ignore other types of background information about their acts and endorse more extreme forms of punishment for their actions.
>
> (ibid: 361)

A related fallacy is the conflation of symptoms and cause, i.e. just because particular acts are socially deviant, it does not mean that so is their cause: "social deviance, per se, cannot be the sole basis for diagnostic conclusions" (ibid: 361). Finally, he notes the same issues of data sampling and data validity: first, the interviewees were imprisoned, and second, particular experiences specific to terrorist lives might have created the appearance of pathology:

> The dramatic pressures of the terrorist occupation create their own forms of psychological adjustment. Conflict with authorities, social isolation or the assumption of false identities may create adaptive paranoid traits. The extreme conditions which give rise to terrorist activity, such as refugee camps, may also create forms of adaptation easily interpreted as psychopathology. If examined in prison, the conditions of sensory deprivation, and other effects, may be sufficient to produce depressive symptomatology.
>
> (ibid: 362)

As we have seen, there are some methodological issues inherent to psychoanalytical approaches in general and their application in the case of terrorism in particular. At the same

60 *Determining* individual *terrorism*

time, empirical indications of narcissism in concrete cases would suggest that the abandonment of these theories might be premature. Their usage in concrete cases of individual involvement in terrorism would, however, need to involve a deeper reading and a more systematic application of the original theories. With respect to the diagnosis of narcissist personality, the original theoretician lists a series of concrete features: "Chronically cold parental figures with covert but intense aggression"; possession of "some inherent quality which could have objectively aroused the envy or admiration of others," being the only child and being showed off as "objects of art" (Kernberg 1970: 58–59). We can see how these key features for the diagnosis of narcissistic personalities are hardly present in terrorism analyses. What we have there instead is rather broad constructs such as broken families or juvenile criminality. The theoretical formulation from which the identity hypothesis originates is also different in that identity crisis is not an occurrence specific to certain individuals or groups, but a step occurring during the adolescence phase of all life-courses. Furthermore, the adoption of certain ideologies at this stage is also a generally applicable mechanism that pertains to identity formation, while ideologies can be of various natures and not just militant (see below). A central question to ask here, therefore, would be why and how the move towards an extreme ideology occurs (rather than something else) in this life stage, rather than whether or not someone has an identity crisis:

> adolescence harbors some sensitive, if fleeting, sense of existence as well as a sometimes passionate interest in ideological values of all kinds – religious, political, intellectual – including, at times, an ideology of adjustment to the time's patterns of adjustment and success … As it transfers the need for guidance from parental figures to mentors and leaders, fidelity eagerly accepts their ideological mediatorship – whether the ideology is one implicit in a "way of life" or militantly explicit one.
>
> … I would then consider adolescence the life stage wide open both cognitively and emotionally for new ideological imageries apt to marshal the fantasies and energies of the new generation. Depending on the historical moment, this will alternatively confirm or protest the existing order or promise a future one, more radical or more traditional, and thus help to overcome identity confusion.
>
> (Erikson and Erikson 1998: 73, 93)

Deterministic processes

All three approaches agree that involvement in terrorism is a process, in the sense that it does not occur all of a sudden, but over a longer period of time. The content of this process is, however, different, with deterministic approaches trying to identify phases and transitions between these phases; intentional approaches rather outlining the seamless nature of individual evolution towards involvement; and finally relational approaches emphasizing interaction—among individuals, between individuals and the organization, between individuals and the state. Quite a few deterministic models have been proposed to explain individual Islamist homegrown radicalization in the West. King and Taylor (2011) summarize and evaluate some of the most influential ones. The models are quite diverse, with some sourced in social movement theory, such as the one by Wiktorowicz; an empirical descriptive model (the NYPD); and the rest psychological. Common to all, however, is an initial situation of grievance of some sort—thus their classification here under determinism. The authors classify these models under social psychology, a field looking at individuals in their

Determining individual *terrorism* 61

social environment, and justify their choice based on the fact that others are too general. The excluded models are in fact the intentional and relational ones.

Borum (2003) argues that in order to develop an effective counter-terrorism strategy, one must focus on the behavioral processes of individuals. Borum explains that radicalization happens in a four-step process. First, the individual feels a sense of injustice, which is often born out of social and economic deprivation. Second, due to this inequality, the individual feels resentful towards society. Third, this leads to blaming a specific target group, such as the West or minorities. The final step is demonizing the target and thus legitimizing violence against the target.

Wiktorowicz (2005) identifies four sub-processes that increase the probability of an individual joining a terrorist organization. The first is a 'cognitive opening' born out of certain preconditions such as identity or personal crisis. A cognitive opening can then encourage individuals to look towards alternative ideas and world views, which may include religious seeking. Radical groups target these potential recruits within pre-existing social environments or during public events by framing their ideology as one that 'makes sense' and is attractive to the seeker. Wiktorowicz emphasizes that all three conditions outlined are crucial preconditions for the fourth and final process—socialization. This is where the individual embraces the ideology, values, and constructed identity of the group.

For Moghaddam (2005), the pathway towards conducting a terrorist act can be explained by using the metaphor of a 'narrowing staircase,' where the final step on this staircase results in carrying out an act of violence. The ground floor is where the majority of people occupy— the psychological perception of frustration and injustice. It is important to note that Moghaddam emphasizes "the fundamental importance of *perceived* deprivation" (ibid: 163). This is an attempt to solve the specificity problem, as perceptions are subjective and therefore individuals respond to their (perceived) frustrations differently. According to the model, those who feel mistreated climb to the first floor to seek solutions to their grievances. The second floor represents 'displacement of aggression' onto out-groups such as the West. This step can be encouraged by affiliating with certain extremist groups. The third floor is 'moral engagement' with the goals of a terrorist organization, where behavior that would appear immoral by an external group is normalized. The fourth floor is reached once an individual is within a terrorist organization and perceives the organization as wholly legitimate. The fifth and final floor is the terrorist act. Moghaddam concludes that security practitioners should therefore focus on preventive measures and turn their attention to those on the ground floor rather than those individuals who are already at the top-end of the staircase.

Based on five US-based homegrown terrorist case studies and using the same radicalization model that was applied to a study of the 9/11 Hamburg cell individuals, Silber and Bhatt (2007) argue that there are four distinct phases of the radicalization model: pre-radicalization, self-identification, indoctrination, and 'jihadization.' Not all individuals who begin this process pass through all of these stages, but individuals who do are quite likely to carry out a terrorist attack. These case studies show that these individuals were largely ordinary, 'unremarkable' people. However, a crisis or catalyst then leads the individual to a self-identification phase, where they begin to search for an ideology and find like-minded people who share this outlook. The indoctrination phase intensifies these beliefs—usually with the help of an influential spiritual leader. The final phase of jihadization is where the individuals accept their duty to participate in jihad.

Writing about the development of terror networks in the 21st century, Sageman (2008) argues that there is a four-step process through which Muslim youth become radicalized.

62 *Determining* individual *terrorism*

First, certain alarming events such as the West's interference in the Middle East can trigger moral outrage. Second, this outrage is interpreted and framed through a specific ideology of good vs. evil. Third, such outrage resonates with personal experiences of frustration and through personal social networks and/or Internet communications individuals are able to identify others who share these frustrations and outrage. Finally, this anger is acted upon in the form of terrorist acts. Sageman's model is based on his thesis of 'leaderless jihad,' whereby terrorist groups such as al-Qaeda no longer authorize and coordinate terrorist attacks, but rather act as an ideological inspiration for local independent groups.

Turning now to the critique points of these models, the first obvious observation is that they all start with a moment of crisis. That is, it is assumed that certain individuals who are otherwise following a regular life path, experience a moment of crisis which then derails them from this original path towards a deviant one and in the direction of radical Islam. There is indeed research on sects which evidences that religious conversion can occur as a result of a personal crisis, such as a near-death experience. The problem is, however, that the kinds of crisis supposedly experienced by radicalizing individuals are not of such a dramatic nature, but rather mundane events. With regard to the second element of this argument, assuming that events such as losing a job or being discriminated against have an effect on the subsequent phases of someone's life, there is no apparent necessity justifying a turn towards religion rather than something else. Additionally, as we shall see in the following chapter, most individuals either cannot pinpoint such an initial trigger, or when they do, it is apparent that it functions as a *post-factum* rationalization. Thus, this questions a basic assumption of these models, which is that something must have gone wrong in these individuals' lives for them to consider involvement in terrorism. Indeed, as the newer interpretations of relative deprivation also seem to suggest, militancy for the cause of a group does not necessarily require that individuals themselves need to have been affected by grievance. It then remains open of course how this identification with a group's cause occurs, in particular in cases where there is no ethnic, religious, or other link observable.

A final important point to make is the still unclear nature of the relationships between the phases of radicalization. In most cases, the phases of the process seem to just describe states, without any particular determining link between them. In others, there seems to be interaction, such as in Sageman's model, where moral outrage at the situation of other people can also emerge from personal experiences, both of which can then confirm the perception that there is a war against Islam. Apart from this and the link between crisis and religious seeking mentioned earlier, there are no recognizable connection points between the phases, such as for instance between fighting an unfair treatment and displacement of aggression. This indicates two possibilities: either there is need for additional research into these intermediary mechanisms, or we need to allow for elements of chance as well, such as, for example, for the case of contact with radical Islam.

Summary

This chapter has introduced the deterministic approach to individual motivation to engage in terrorism and has dealt with:

- factors or 'causes' which can be either external or internal to the individual, the role of which are to differentiate 'regular' individuals from the ones prone to become terrorists;
- three theories: relative deprivation, narcissism, and identity crisis;

Determining individual *terrorism* 63

- various models of individual involvement in terrorism which work on a deterministic basis;
- the specificity critique: being very specific about the kinds of qualities people vulnerable to becoming terrorists should possess invites critique in the form of exceptions to the rule.

Exercises

4.1 In light of the narcissism theory, examine the case of Anders Behring Breivik, responsible for 77 victims in a double attack in Oslo and on the island of Utøya on July 22, 2011.
4.2 Compare the socio-economic characteristics of IS recruits with those of previous organizations. Is there more support in this case for deterministic theories?
4.3 Compare the motivations of jihadis and of left-wing terrorists from the perspective of grievance transfer from the community onto the individual.

References

Borum, R. (2003). Understanding the Terrorist Mindset, *FBI Law Enforcement Bulletin*, July, pp. 7–10.

Crenshaw, M. (1986). The Psychology of Political Terrorism. In M.G. Hermann (ed.) *Political Psychology: Contemporary Problems and Issues*, London: Jossey-Bass, pp. 379–413.

Erikson, E.H. and Erikson, J.M. (1998). *The Life Cycle Completed*, New York: W.W. Norton.

Kernberg, O.F. (1970). Factors in the Psychoanalytic Treatment of Narcissistic Personalities. *Journal of the American Psychoanalytic Association*, 18(1), pp. 51–85.

King, M. and Taylor, D.M. (2011). The Radicalization of Homegrown Jihadists: A review of theoretical models and social psychological evidence. *Terrorism and Political Violence*, 23(4), pp. 602–622.

Lynch, O. (2013). British Muslim Youth: Radicalisation, terrorism and the construction of the "other". *Critical Studies on Terrorism*, 6(2), pp. 241–261.

Moghaddam, F.M. (2005). The Staircase to Terrorism: A psychological exploration, *American Psychologist*, 60(2), pp. 161–169.

Post, J.M. (1998). Terrorist Psycho-logic: Terrorist behavior as a product of psychological forces. In W. Reich (ed.) *Origins of Terrorism: Psychologies, Ideologies, Theologies, States of Mind*, Washington, DC: Woodrow Wilson Center Press, pp. 25–40.

Sageman, M. (2008). *Leaderless Jihad: Terror Networks in the Twenty-First Century*, Philadelphia: University of Pennsylvania Press.

Shaw, E.D. (1986). Political Terrorists: Dangers of diagnosis and an alternative to the psychopathology model. *International Journal of Law and Psychiatry*, 8, pp. 359–366.

Silber, M.D. and Bhatt, A. (2007). *Radicalization in the West: The Homegrown Threat*, New York: NYPD Intelligence Division.

Silke, A. (1998). Cheshire-cat Logic: The recurring theme of terrorist abnormality in psychological research. *Psychology, Crime & Law*, 4(1), pp. 51–69.

Stanford University (2017). Armed Revolutionary Nuclei. [Online]. Available from: http://web. stanford.edu/group/mappingmilitants/cgi-bin/groups/view/259 [Accessed April 16, 2017].

Stern, J. (2003). *Terror in the Name of God: Why Religious Militants Kill*, New York: HarperCollins.

Wiktorowicz, Q. (2005). *Radical Islam Rising: Muslim Extremism in the West*, Oxford: Rowman & Littlefield.

64 *Determining* individual *terrorism*

Further reading

Hubbard, D. (1978). Terrorism and Protest. *Legal Medical Quaterly*, 2, pp. 188–197.

Khosrokhavar, F. (2016). *Inside Jihadism. Understanding Jihadi Movements Worldwide*, Abingdon: Routledge.

Knutson, J.N. (1981). Social and Psychodynamic Pressures Toward a Negative Identity: The case of an American revolutionary terrorist. In Y. Alexander and J.M. Gleason (eds), *Behavioral and Quantitative Pespectives on Terrorism*, Elmsford, NY: Pergamon Press, pp. 105–150.

Marx, A., Rihoux, B. and Ragin, C. (2014). The Origins, Development, and Application of Qualitative Comparative Analysis: The first 25 years. *European Political Science Review*, 6(1), pp. 115–142.

Pantucci, R. (2011). What Have We Learned about Lone Wolves from Anders Behring Breivik? *Perspectives on Terrorism*, 5(5–6), pp. 27–42.

Pearce, K.I. (1977). Police negotiations. *Canadian Psychiatric Association Journal*, 22, pp. 171–174.

Rihoux, B. (2006). Qualitative Comparative Analysis (QCA) and Related Systematic Comparative Methods: Recent advances and remaining challenges for social science research. *International Sociology*, 21(5), pp. 679–706.

Silke, A. (2008). Holy Warriors: Exploring the psychological processes of jihadi radicalisation. *European Journal of Criminology*, 5(1), pp. 99–123.

Victoroff, J. (2005). The Mind of the Terrorist: A review and critique of psychological approaches. *Journal of Conflict Resolution*, 49(1), pp. 3–42.

5 Choosing *individual* terrorism

The previous chapter walked you through a series of deterministic theories and models of individual involvement in terrorism. We now do the same for intentional approaches and present some influential psychological models, trace them back to broader psychological and criminological theories, and show their limitations. Following this, we introduce and discuss two further approaches which function in principle with the same intentional logic, but go beyond the strict psychology of terrorism by integrating elements from other disciplines.

Intentional approaches to the study of terrorism have largely emerged as a critique to the existing deterministic approaches and their claim to identify characteristics specific to terrorists. As early as 1988, Max Taylor noted the following:

> Very many people share the kinds of attributes that can be identified. The reasons for this may be that there are, perhaps, no special causes of terrorism, in the sense of a common class of explanations, as there probably are no "special" causes for many complex forms of behavior.
>
> (Taylor 1988: 139)

Intentional approaches usually focus on the individual considered as an autonomous and (relatively) free actor. That is, the point of inquiry is not to identify some personality features, biographical dysfunctions or features of economic deprivation which would determine involvement, but decision-making processes and motivations for engaging in various types of behavior. They also look at the individual's environment and at process, yet from a more actor-centered perspective. In particular, they examine individual behavior and how it unfolds in various contexts and phases. In this case, the rationale behind individual involvement in terrorism is the idea of gain. Individuals make conscious choices on the basis of an expectation of gain, usually in non-material terms. The kinds of gain that individuals might expect have been conceptualized as selective incentives or 'lures' that reinforce and sustain behavior. They function therefore as a feedback loop—individuals receive positive feedback to their actions in the form of such selective incentives or lures, so that they then go on to commit those or related actions. When thinking about individual motivation in terms of gain, it is important to remember that we are not dealing with gain in an economic sense, as maximization of profit, but rather with an 'everyday' type of rationality. Furthermore, because involvement is seen as a gradual *process*, the main focus of investigation here is particular decisions along this process, which are made on the basis of an expectation of gain. Intentional approaches draw on psychological and criminological theories, as well as some select branches of social movement theory.

Rational choice

Max Taylor and John Horgan are two prominent psychologists who early on delineated the contours of the first quasi-rational choice approach to involvement in terrorism. In his book *The Terrorist*, Taylor (1988) begins by comparing terrorism with other areas of psychological inquiry, and draws analogies with crime in terms of the process of involvement. Taylor then builds on the basic assumption made in the criminological rational choice approach as formulated by Derek B. Cornish and Ronald V. Clarke in *The Reasoning Criminal* (1986), namely that "the offender benefits from his criminal choices, and that this benefit is the determining factor in his commission of crime" (Taylor 1988: 181). As Taylor further points out, this benefit does not necessarily need to be of a material nature as an individual "also gains excitement from his activity, status amongst his peer group, and confirms his membership of that marginalized group" (ibid: 181). Here, the key terms for the analysis of terrorist behavior are the 'situation' and the anticipated feedback from the environment: "The factors contributing to both the 'involvement' and the 'event' processes can be conceptualized in environmental terms as various psychological stimuli that either 'set the occasion' for the terrorist act or terminate it" (ibid: 183). In making this argument, Taylor draws on behaviorism and the work of Burrhus Frederic Skinner. The behavioral approach, as explained by Taylor:

> is characterized by an emphasis on the relationship between the relevant consequences of behavior and events associated with those consequences. The important consequence to behavior is reward, or reinforcement. Behavior which is followed by reinforcement tends to have an increased probability of occurrence. Many things can act as reinforcers to us – social approval, gaining status, financial gain, food, and so forth. Specific reinforcers are mainly personal but there are broad classes of reinforcers (like those mentioned earlier) which are largely universal.
>
> (Taylor 1988: 201)

In *The Psychology of Terrorism*, Horgan (2005) builds on Taylor's work in that he also draws on the rational choice theory in criminology, focuses on individual *choices* rather than *features*, and on the anticipated consequences of acts as incentives for behavior. These form decisions which are taken during the process of involvement in terrorism. Apart from the obvious core mechanism to explain individual behavior, another important element that Horgan borrows from criminology is the *distinction between committing a crime and committing specific criminal offences*, for which different types of decisions are made. He additionally lays more emphasis on the process nature of involvement and consequently points out the *plurality* of decisions along this process (ibid: 81). His focus is therefore on "factors that maintain involvement and sustain behavior, and eventually contribute to the commission of acts of terrorism" (ibid: 82) and "behavior reinforcers that illustrate the attractiveness of pursuing particular avenues of activity that become accessible or obvious for the individual at any stage of the process" (ibid: 99). These lures, or "positive features of increased engagement for the individual terrorist," can be "the rapid acquisition of some sort of skill or skills, an increased sense of empowerment, purpose and self-importance, an increased sense of control ... a tangible sense of acceptance within the group, and in combination with this, the acquisition of real status within the broader community" (ibid: 105). In line with the idea of progression in time and the multiplicity of decision-making processes, lures vary in each case and have different subjective importance attached; he notes that "each and every one of these factors can be brought to influence the individual at any stage of his or her involvement" (ibid: 105). Different to deterministic approaches, the incidence of these lures *is not* to compensate for previous lack or failure:

> Again, it is important that we do not interpret these supportive qualities as indicative of some sort of pre-existing deficiencies in personality or indicative of some disorder but of behaviour reinforcers that illustrate the attractiveness of pursuing particular avenues of activity that become accessible or obvious for the individual at any stage of the process.
>
> (Horgan 2005: 99)

In relation to status, Horgan identifies that when the source of approval is not just within the small activist group, but also in the *broader community* this can add significant value: "there is also an accompanying sense of status and excitement for the individual faced with the knowledge of the significance of the role within the broader community" (ibid: 93). The community context and the kinds and degree of support they might gain are clearly variable. At one extreme, in the case of nationalist-separatist groups, where there is broader approval in society for the militant organization, joining such a group might in fact be considered as a 'rite of passage' towards a consolidated identity within the community. Palestine is an often-cited example of how role models and approval from the social environment play a decisive role in motivating young people to become suicide bombers (see Box 5.1).

Box 5.1 Heroic role models and community approval: The case of Middle Eastern terrorists in Israel

In a study by Post et al. (2003), the authors carried out semi-structured interviews with 35 Middle Eastern terrorists: 21 Islamic terrorists and 14 secular terrorists. The authors' findings regarding recruitment suggested that boyhood heroes were just as important for the religious and secular terrorists. For example, the religious terrorists noted important figures for them such as the Prophet and Abdullah Azzam, and the secular terrorists found influence in Che Guevara or Fidel Castro (ibid: 172). Post et al. additionally observed that the social environment was a 'major influence' for the terrorists. The mentality of 'everyone was joining' and strong community approval from both religious and secular groups played a prevalent role in the decision to join a terrorist group. Many of the terrorists were recruited by friends or acquaintances rather than family members. Sixty-four percent of the secular terrorist group members and 43 percent of the Islamist terrorist group members claimed that the group they joined was very active in their communities, with involvement in mosques and youth and community clubs. Less than 10 percent from each group reported that they came from communities that were not particularly active in the struggle (ibid: 173). Post et al. further noted that:

> There is a heightened sense of the heroic associated with fallen group members as the community supports and rallies around families of the dead or incarcerated members. Most interviewees reported not only enhanced social status for the families of fallen or incarcerated members, but financial and material support from the organization and community for these families as well.
>
> (Post et al. 2003: 175)

68 *Choosing* individual *terrorism*

> 'Success' in the eyes of the community was not seen through academic or economic achievements, but rather through fighting for 'the cause.' This in turn encouraged individuals within the terrorist group to be 'successful' and provided some kind of rationale and validation for their actions (ibid: 175).

The Psychology of Terrorism is also so far the most complex and comprehensive account of the *process* of involvement in terrorism. Horgan divides his process model of terrorism into three sub-processes: 'becoming a terrorist,' which refers to the process of becoming involved in doing terrorism, 'being a terrorist,' which examines what is going on after involvement, including the commission of terrorist offences, and 'disengaging from terrorism.' Different to deterministic models, which focus primarily on the cognitive aspect (indeed, radicalization there is primarily understood as a shift in attitudes and beliefs), this model aims to explain *behavior*. In Horgan's words, his model is looking at "identifiable behaviours and their antecedents, expected consequences and outcomes that are associated with terrorism" (Horgan 2005: 80). In spite of the division into three phases, the model is furthermore conceived as a process of incremental involvement. Seamless transitions occur not only between phases, but also at the beginning of the overall process. The latter observation is based on comparisons with joining social movements, or what he calls 'lower risk organizations,' and on the somewhat blurry borders of terrorist organizations, whereby it is not always clear what is and what is not already part of the organization. See Box 5.2 for an illustrative citation on this concept of seamless transition.

Box 5.2 On the seamless transition to terrorism in Horgan

In Italy, Alison Jamieson's interviews with former Red Brigades (RB) member, Adriana Faranda, are exceptionally revealing, providing us with unusually lucid accounts of involvement. Jamieson tells us that Faranda became engaged in politics around 1968 as a student in Rome. When Jamieson said to Faranda that she once heard her describe her involvement as almost 'necessary,' Faranda replied:

> Things are never quite clear as that. Countless others lived in Rome at the same time as me: kids of my age who weren't as involved as me, either in the political struggles or in the choices of the successive years. I suppose really it was the way I experienced the events of that time, my own personal stand-point on the problems, the crises, the hopes and the expectation that we had as well as what was happening outside which determined that particular path ... there were lots of little steps which led to where I ended up ... it wasn't a major leap in the true sense of the word. It was just another stage ... it was a choice.
>
> (Hogan 2005: 98)

At the beginning of the process there is again mention of an initial catalyst or trigger, which nonetheless is not as dramatic as in the deterministic models, and is further biographically and psychologically contextualized. Horgan allows for the impact of certain events, such as personal victimization or communal identification with the victimized, but argues that they are only significant in the context of previous experiences such as demonstrations and emotional responsiveness, whereby involvement in terrorism is perceived as a reaction in self-defense against an enemy. Additionally, he lists and elaborates on several caveats questioning the actual significance, or even relevance of such initial triggering events. One aspect is selective memory, where such events might be recalled more vividly than the 'small steps' of the initial involvement, although the latter might have played a more important role. A second aspect relates to the post-factum individual, subjective rationalization of past experiences, where again such events might be afforded a causal effect. A further objection to the importance of such initial events is the impact of membership in terrorist organizations and in prison, an aspect that was also mentioned in the context of the critique to psychoanalytical theories. In this case, Horgan argues that such arguments might in fact not be possible—in the sense that individuals would not possess the ability to articulate them, had they not been already politicized and effectively integrated in an organization:

> sometimes it can be difficult, if not completely impossible, to tell when self-accounts of involvement in terrorism derive from the individual's own sense of truth or some sort of commonly shared or acquired "truth" that might develop from being involved in terrorism over time. While it may be plausible, certainly given what might appear bona fide personal accounts, to assume that such "fraternalistic over egoistic" goals exist from the outset, it is more likely that this reflects a learning quality incurred from continuous involvement.
>
> (Horgan 2005: 89)

During the period of membership, or the process of 'being a terrorist,' the group is afforded a major role in sustaining involvement and supporting the commission of acts of violence. Horgan outlines in detail the kinds of operational activities that take place at this stage and in particular the ones surrounding a terrorist event (see Box 5.3).

Box 5.3 The four stages of a terrorist event in Horgan

Decision and search:
target and means identification
surveillance and evaluation of the risk

Pre-terrorism:
identification and selection of appropriate personnel
training requirements—general preparation and specific target
design, construction and manufacturing
device testing and preparation

Event execution:
logistic demands of assembling device and manpower
surveillance and security of the operation
dynamics of the event: context, escape routes
securing weapons after attack

Post-event activity and strategic analysis:
situational factors affecting the escape of the individuals
destruction of evidence
post-event evaluation feeding into the post-event stage

(Hogan 2005: 110–120)

70 *Choosing* individual *terrorism*

Rational choice and beyond: Interpretative frameworks

The two models introduced thus far have explicitly focused on behavior, assumed benefit as the major driver of involvement, and operationalized it in the context of interactions with the social environment. However, not entirely clarified remain the questions of how individuals end up in such communities in the first place, how ideas about what status is, for example, form in the first place, and how individuals adopt them. In classical cases such as the IRA or Palestinian terrorism, where the community as a whole is involved in the broader conflict and is to a large extent sympathetic to terrorist acts, such questions are irrelevant. Yet thinking about involvement in Islamist terrorism in Europe, for example, where there is a broad choice of communities and ideas, the orientation towards Islamist terrorism involves a change of social environment and involves a change in world view, and this requires an explanation. Deterministic approaches explain these changes as a matter of sudden occurrence and on the background of some crisis. This kind of explanation would not be useful here, as it conflicts with the idea of gradual change and with the 'rationality' of behavior.

Obviously, the main problem of the intentional approaches outlined so far emerges from its defining worth: the assumption of normality. Here, individuals are assumed to be no different to other regular people in terms of socio-demographic characteristics or personality. Furthermore, the basic mechanism of motivation based on expected gain is also in principle nothing specific to terrorists. It is, however, also here that the problem lies: why would people decide for lures in the context of terrorism rather than something else? Why look for a status as a terrorist rather than another type of status? Or why follow particular role models and not others? This is especially important since these theories do not work with the mechanism of status-frustration—individuals looking for an alternative source of status in terror organizations because they were not able to obtain it in other ways.

Filling these gaps requires going outside individual psychology and looking at the interaction between people—the social, as well as the role of ideology. The model developed by Daniela Pisoiu (2012) to explain Islamist radicalization in Europe combines rational choice in the psychology of terrorism with elements from social movement theory, and in particular framing theory. Following the grounded theory (GT) methodology (see Box 5.4), and a mix of data sources including trial notes, case files, and interviews, this model emerged from the empirical data around a 'core' category identified as the Islamist radical occupational change process. The main drivers for motivation in this case are similar to the ones proposed by the models above with regard to their underlying mechanism, namely feedback from the social environment. Rather than empirical examples of selective incentives, here we have a set of three abstract categories: standing, recognition, and reward. Furthermore, the concept of 'interpretative frameworks' is key, as these world views shape the nature of these motivational categories.

Box 5.4 Grounded theory

Grounded theory was developed by sociologists Barney Glaser and Anselm Strauss in the 1960s as a methodology to 'discover' theory straight from data by systematically applying a set of methods. The methodology was originally developed as an alternative and a reaction to the dominant methodological paradigm at the time, namely hypothesis testing which, in the opinion of the authors, prevented the emergence of new theory to explain social phenomena. Twenty years later, the two original authors took slightly different paths, in that Strauss allowed for the consideration of previous theoretical knowledge in the form of guiding principles for analysis, while Glaser insisted on the original idea of proceeding to the analysis of the data in a theory-free fashion. Both approaches work with the basic analysis technique of 'coding,' among others. The code "conceptualizes the underlying pattern of a set of empirical indicators within the data. ... Coding gets the analyst off the empirical level by fracturing the data, then conceptually grouping it into codes that then become the theory which explains what is happening in the data" (Glaser 1978: 55). Both use open coding and a second type of coding which aims to establish relationships between the codes, yet differ with regard to the nature and shape of the coding scheme. A third variation of GT was introduced in the 2000s by Catherine Charmaz, who proposed a constructivist reading of GT, in that positivist concepts such as 'causality' and 'objectivity' were relativized in favor of 'interpretation' and 'subjectivity' of both the author and subjects. This implied also a relaxation of the systematic nature of the methods applied.

Standing, recognition, and reward are at a higher level of abstraction than selective incentives. They are "components of the overall motivation or criteria according to which decisions to engage, stay and act orientate, and concretize in specific selective inventives at specific times along the process" (Pisoiu 2012: 85). Standing refers to "a position of prestige and superiority relative to, and as a reflection of, the social surrounding, based on commonly shared values as to what standing should constitute ... these values are: *courage, altruism, power* and *specialized knowledge*" (ibid: 86). Recognition is "the perceived *approval* and *support* of actions and activities by the social surrounding, again based on a commonly shared apprehension of what is valuable and acceptable" (ibid: 94). Finally, reward "refers to the idea of making a difference, doing something valuable to impact and change a given situation seen as unfair," in this case perceived oppression and injustice affecting Muslims worldwide (ibid: 87).

In line with the assumption of this approach, these kinds of categories are not specific to Islamist terrorism or terrorism in general. As she explains:

> The fact that standing might be associated with being a mujahid is traced to the fact that, within a certain worldview, heroism is a value, and one associated with the activities involved in being a mujahid, such as defending the global community of Muslims or a particular Muslim community against "occupation". In other groups, standing will concretise into something completely different.
>
> (Pisoiu 2012: 85)

From this emerges the relevance of 'radical interpretative frameworks'—a concept similar to that of 'frames' (see Chapter 6).

These occupational categories are therefore "present in other types of occupation as well, so that choosing the radical Islamist occupation is in effect a process during which they are gradually conceived differently from other occupations, a function of different conceptualizations of what is valuable" (ibid: 84). The Islamist radical occupational change *process* implies that individuals undergo a change from regular to 'radical' activities. Therefore, the author emphasizes, the process of radicalization is not a *sui generis* one but a variation of a general process of occupational change which might result in a radical, activist, or Islamist

72 *Choosing* individual *terrorism*

occupation. This is also in line with a fundamental assumption in GT with respect to social processes in general. One of the founders, Barney Glaser, has made a point out of the general applicability of the categories in general and social processes in particular that GT should produce, based on the observation of everyday activities. He notes that:

> If he were to study whore houses, which it safely can be said are generally considered deviant, from the point of view that the fact of their deviance is the most important thing about them, sociologically, he would likely miss the more general relevant fact that sociologically – in terms of structure, function, organization, and process – they are similar to barber shops, beauty salons, garages, and so forth; all are *servicing operations*.
>
> (Glaser 1978: 104–105)

The process leading to an occupational change towards becoming a jihadi involves several mechanisms capturing the interaction between ideas and behavior and more broadly how they become more exclusive, more rigid, and more autonomous from 'regular' or previous ones. For example, 'rules directed redesigning' is a mechanism involving "the redefinition and re-organisation of most or all areas of life according to new precepts" (Pisoiu 2012: 61) and which often involves mentoring. Within this mechanism:

> behavioral patterns were projected in opposition to the "Western lifestyle", particularly with regard to family relations, leisure and what has been branded as "consumerism". All areas of life were regulated: social life, eating, drinking and sleeping habits, the range of friends, places of work and leisure. Certain activities were stopped altogether – such as working in a restaurant that serves pork, because they involved actions or behavior forbidden by the new rules. There also intervened completely new domains of life, such as praying, fasting or going to the mosque on a regular basis, along with new habits such as wearing beard and religious clothes, opting for an Islamic marriage, referring to religious authorities for permission to do certain things or, indeed, starting to perceive jihad as a religious duty.
>
> (Pisoiu 2012: 62)

The process also entails several phases which illustrate the relationship to the new 'occupation'—from the initial steps, to an increasingly exclusive and intense focus, to it becoming a profession—a sub-process involving the acquisition and practice of skills as well as specialization.

Rational choice and beyond: Situations

A further branch of scholars working within what we have deemed 'intentional' approaches has looked beyond individual subjectivity to understand how this may interact with the 'situation' where terrorists might act. This way of looking at terrorism has much in common with the idea of 'opportunities' from social movements, as it similarly posits that motivation is not sufficient to explain action, the occasion to do so would also be necessary. Consequently, the particular focus of such approaches is the *terrorist act per se rather than the process of radicalization*—remember the differentiation between involvement in crime and involvement in criminal acts which we signalled earlier. Situational approaches draw again on criminological theories, in particular situational action theory (SAT), but also other concepts such as that of 'affordance' (see Further reading).

Per-Olof H. Wikström and Noémie Bouhana (2017) propose in their work, *Analyzing Radicalization and Terrorism: A Situational Action Theory*, SAT, which derives from criminological theories, as being especially useful for the explanation of terrorism and radicalization. This is a theory of moral action and crime causation that draws on social and behavioral sciences. SAT explains how acts of crime or terrorism arise from an interaction of a person's propensity to crime and his or her exposure to terrorism-promoting environments. The theory proposes that people commit acts of terrorism because 1) they find that it is a normally acceptable alternative, or 2) they fail to adhere to personal morals (i.e. do not exercise self-control or are deterred). The first set of basic assumptions of SAT is that humans are rule-guided creatures and that society, the social order, is based on shared rules of conduct which influence individuals to respond to frictions and their expression of desires. SAT defines acts as moral actions (guided by value-based rules of conduct) in response to particular motivations in particular circumstances. A second set of basic assumptions is that people are the source of their actions, meaning that they decide what to do, but that this is dependent on situational circumstances. This means that the action chosen by an individual is the result of a person–environment interaction. The key element in this action process is the motivation, the moral filter as well as the presence of controls (self-control, deterrence). Processes of *social and self-selection* create interactions that cause situations to which people respond, whether in committing acts of crime or not. *Social selection* refers to rules and social forces that influence people to participate in certain actions. For example, the exposure to certain social groups potentially affects the chance of exposure to radicalizing context and hence the possibility to become radicalized. This might help to explain why members of a particular terrorist cell or group share socio-demographic characteristics. However, radicalizing settings displace over time (as a result of counter-terrorist activity). *Self-selection* refers to the preferences of people with regard to certain choices within the constraints of rules and social forces. Moral education (instruction, observation, and trial and error) and cognitive nurturing (the neurological constitution and the exercise of neurological capabilities) help to understand why people become vulnerable to radicalization. SAT does not contest individual rationality, but argues that individuals are primarily rule-guided actors.

Silvia Bunge (2004) carried out a review on cognitive neuroscientific research to assess how rules are learned, stored, and retrieved from the brain. Bunge concluded that learning new rules does indeed have a critical impact on how people behave and interact with others; however, at the time of writing, the author established that yet more research was required to fully determine how individuals retrieve and use rules for behavior (Bunge 2004: 575–576). This, in a sense, brings rational choice somewhat to its limits, as the choice does not appear to be as free as thought. A clear parallel can also be drawn to relational approaches, where behavior also appears directed after a certain point in time completely by ideology (see Chapter 6).

It is apparent that, first of all, SAT attempts to address a similar problem of rational choice theories as occupational choice theory above, namely: why would individuals make choice A as opposed to choice B, given that both could be beneficial? Occupational choice attempted to solve this problem by resorting to interpretative frames and the ways in which they shape the nature and the type of incentives. SAT introduces morality as a shaper of choices. Fundamentally, however, the two theories are different, as the former still holds to the rational choice nature of the 'choice'; frames only shape options, and only indirectly influence choice. The second introduced determinism, in that the choice itself, not just the options, is also shaped by morality—of the individual and that of the environment.

74 *Choosing* individual *terrorism*

Box 5.5 SAT in action

A longitudinal study on youth and crime carried out by Wikström et al. (2012) was one of the first studies to utilize SAT. This study is referred to as the Peterborough Adolescent and Young Adult Development Study (PADS+). The authors used data from approximately 700 young people in the UK town of Peterborough and made use of questionnaires and psychometric tests to determine the effects of social environment and personality on police-recorded and self-reported crime. Wikström et al. (2012) tested crime propensity (the level of morality combined with the ability to exercise self-control) and "criminogenic exposure" (environments with "poor collective efficacy" and/or city or local centers outside school or the home, where young people are unsupervized) (ibid: 117–155). The authors contend that the most innovative aspect of their methodology was the use of a "space-time budget" in conjunction with a small area community survey and more traditional data on individual characteristics. The space-time budget methodology measures participants' experiences by gauging:

> (1) which settings they take part in, and (2) the circumstances under which they encounter those settings, from which we can analyse (3) their activity fields – the constellation of settings to which they are exposed during a specific time period, including how much time they spend in each of those settings.
>
> (Wikström et al. 2012: 67)

This type of methodology is especially apt for SAT, as it allows researchers to examine how exposure to different settings, as well as how much time is spent in these settings, influences individual behavior (ibid: 68). Wikström et al. found, among other things, that there was a strong correlation between an individual's crime propensity and their involvement in crime; and there was a strong correlation between 'criminogenic exposure' and crime involvement. This became even stronger when considering peer crime involvement. The results confirm many of the assumptions made by SAT that an individual's interaction with their environment is an important step to understanding criminal behavior (ibid: 406). The authors assert that: "young people with a low crime propensity are largely situationally resistant to criminogenic influences while young people with a high crime propensity are particularly situationally vulnerable" (ibid: 158).

SAT has also been suggested as a way to prevent terrorist offences, but not necessarily prevent radicalization. For example, Graeme Newman (2014) suggests that the same principles applied to situational crime prevention can be applied to counter-terrorism. As such, Newman (ibid: 4855) presents three basic principles that play a key role when analyzing terrorism from a situational perspective: opportunity, rational choice, and intervention. The first two principles assume that a terrorist acts according to rational choice and that the conditions for attack are advantageous for the terrorist. The intervention principle involves two procedures for pinpointing the key weaknesses in planning a terrorist attack: first, the series of events leading up to the decision to attack should be carefully determined; and second, the opportunity structure should be assessed carefully to expose any vulnerable conditions that could be exploited by terrorists. Following such an assessment, appropriate security measures can be enforced (ibid: 4855–4856). In order to identify opportunity structures available to terrorists, Newman suggests that there are four pillars of terrorist opportunity: targets, weapons, tools, and facilitating conditions (ibid: 4856). Terrorist targets are usually iconic areas or buildings where many people gather. The idea here is to cause as many casualties as possible to targets which are of vital and symbolic value to the enemy. Terrorists additionally seek to use undetectable, multi-purpose, and reliable weapons to carry out their operations. Tools are also important in planning and executing attacks. Such tools include, mobile phones and the Internet to communicate and research targets, transport organized in advance, money, documents, maps, etc. Finally, facilitating conditions such as the appeal of carrying out an attack, personal rewards, and relative ease, contribute to enabling terrorist actions (ibid: 4856–4859). Thus, having identified these opportunity structures and the possible means of intervention, Newman suggests a number of techniques to prevent attacks. Such measures include: protecting targets and restricting weapons sales to increase the effort of carrying out an attack; investing in additional surveillance measures and community policing to increase the risk inherent to carrying out an attack; improving first response systems to minimize casualties and avoiding overreaction to attacks to reduce rewards; reducing provocations by working closely with migrant communities; and finally, removing excuses by aiming to win hearts and minds and countering terrorist propaganda (ibid: 4861–4862). This approach essentially aims to 'bridge the gap' between academic knowledge on the causes of terrorism and practical responses to prevent an attack (ibid: 4863). In other words, the core belief of advocates of the situational approach to terrorism is that attacks could be prevented by manipulating the opportunity structure available to potential terrorists.

Summary

From an intentional perspective, this chapter has offered insights into why individuals choose to engage in acts of terrorism. It has put forward:

- two psychological models drawing on rational choice and working with the assumption that individual motivation is a gain, which is shaped by the social environment;
- a further intentional model which resorts to social movement concepts to explain how change towards radical world views and social environments occurs;
- a third approach focusing on properties of the situation in which choices are made, as well as sets of rules that influence it.

Exercises

5.1 Do you think individual terrorism can be explained predominantly through intentional approaches? Support your answer by referring to a terrorist biography.
5.2 Compare and contrast deterministic and intentional approaches to individual involvement in terrorism. Which one do you find more convincing and why?
5.3 Examine the *quest for significance theory* and identify intentional and deterministic elements.

76 *Choosing* individual *terrorism*

References

Bunge, S.A. (2004). How We Use Rules to Select Actions: A review of evidence from cognitive neuroscience. *Cognitive, Affective, and Behavioral Neuroscience*, 4(4), pp. 564–579.

Cornish, D.B. and Clarke, R.V. (1986). *The Reasoning Criminal*. New York: Springer-Verlag.

Glaser, B. (1978). *Advances in the Methodology of Grounded Theory. Theoretical Sensitivity*. Mill Valley: The Sociology Press.

Horgan, J. (2005). *The Psychology of Terrorism*. London, New York: Routledge.

Newman, G.R. (2014). Situational Approaches to Terrorism. In *Encyclopedia of Criminology and Criminal Justice*. New York: Springer, pp. 4853–4864.

Pisoiu, D. (2012). *Islamist Radicalisation in Europe. An Occupational Change Process*. Abingdon/ New York: Routledge.

Post, J., Sprinzak, E. and Denny, L. (2003). The Terrorists in their Own Words: Interviews with 35 incarcerated Middle Eastern terrorists. *Terrorism and Political Violence*, 15(1), pp. 171–184.

Taylor, M. (1988). *The Terrorist*. London: Brassey's Defence Publishers Ltd.

Wikström, P.-O.H. and Bouhana, N. (2017). Analyzing Radicalization and Terrorism: A Situational Action Theory. In Gary LaFree and Joshua D. Freilich (eds) *The Handbook of the Criminology of Terrorism*. West Sussex: John Wiley & Sons, pp. 175–186.

Wikström, P-O H., Oberwittler, D., Treiber, K. and Hardie, B. (2012). *Breaking Rules: The Social and Situational Dynamics of Young People's Urban Crime*. Oxford: Oxford University Press.

Further reading

Atran, S. (2003). Genesis of Suicide Terrorism. *Science*, 299(7), pp. 1534–1539.

Charmaz, K. (2006). *Constructing Grounded Theory: A Practical Guide Through Qualitative Analysis*. London: Sage Publications.

Kruglanski, A.W., Chen, X., Dechesne, M., Fishman, S. and Orehek, E. (2009). Fully Committed: Suicide bombers' motivation and the quest for personal significance. *Political Psychology*, 30(3), pp. 331–357.

Kruglanski, A.W., Gelfand, M.J., Bélanger, J.J., Sheveland, A., Hetiarachchi, M. and Gunaratna, R. (2014). The Psychology of Radicalization and Deradicalization: How significance quest impacts violent extremism. *Advances in Political Psychology*, 35(1), pp. 69–93.

Schils, N. and Pauwels, L. (2014). Explaining Violent Extremism for Subgroups by Gender and Immigrant Background, Using SAT as a Framework. *Journal of Strategic Security*, 7(3), pp. 27–47.

Taylor, M. and Currie, P.M. (2012). *Terrorism and Affordance: New Directions in Terrorism Studies*. London, New York: Bloomsbury.

6 Relational *individual* terrorism

This chapter deals with a series of theories and models stemming from social movement research, criminology, social psychology, and CTS which all aim to explain individual involvement in terrorism (and/or extremism) *as a matter of interaction* with other individuals, the group as a whole, and/or the state. On a structure vs. agency axis, these theories are somewhere in the middle; while they consider individual preferences and choices, as well as gradual progression in time, they eventually conceptualize individual behavior as a result of either group pressure or of the norms and values adopted. In this chapter, social relations and especially norms and values play a primary role.

Individuals in social movements

Similar to intentional approaches, relational approaches to social movements have also emerged as a critique to deterministic approaches, especially those drawing on psycho-analytical theories. Della Porta (2012), for example, has particularly scrutinized and contradicted their basic assumptions with respect to how experiences during childhood and in the family supposedly affected individuals' evolution towards terrorism. She juxtaposed research results on left-wing terrorists in Italy, which contradict both the family dysfunction and the supposed oppositional political orientation of the 'anarchic-ideologues,' as expected from Post's model (see Chapter 4):

> past research has found no sign of any typical pattern in the primary socialization of militants, no sign of particular family problems or of an authoritarian upbringing. On the contrary, Passerini's subjects, for example, remembered their childhood as serene and happy. My research among Italian militants confirms Passerini's findings: 85% of a total of 29 former militants described their family atmosphere as 'good' or 'very good'. Moreover, the interviews indicate that, far from conflicting with the values of their parents the radical commitment of the young activists often reflected a continuity with the political traditions of their families ... In fact, more than half of the militants of left-wing underground organizations grew up in left-wing families.
>
> (della Porta 2012: 233–234)

According to della Porta, one of the main reasons for these contradictions is down to measurement. She calls prisons and underground organizations 'total institutions' and argues that the black and white picture specific to terrorists might in fact have its origin there, rather than in a period predating involvement: "Even in the few cases in which militants have been given personality tests, the subjects were individuals who had passed through two 'total

78 *Relational* individual *terrorism*

institutions' – the clandestine organizations and the prison system – which had influenced their personalities" (ibid: 233).

Similar to intentional approaches, relational approaches to social movements reject the idea that terrorists were in any way special at the beginning of their involvement. On the contrary, they also make a point of showing their normality. Furthermore, the ways in which individuals join terrorist groups—or rather gravitate towards them—is rather inconspicuous, very much like the idea of 'small steps' we saw in the previous chapter. For relational approaches, what happens *during* involvement is most important. Again, similar to intentional approaches, progression in time is considered. With some exceptions, when analyzing individual motivations, these authors usually emphasize factors and mechanisms that have an impact *during* the period of involvement rather than personality or environmental features prior to involvement; they are also sensitive to the fact that motivation might change over time. Second and different to both approaches above, the lens of analysis is situated at the meso-level, whereby involvement occurs as part of an interactive dynamic between the group and the individual, and between the state and the individual. Clearly, the fact that radicalization is a process rather than a sudden change of state has become mainstream; what distinguishes these scholars from the rest, however, is the emphasis on this interaction. That is, individual motivation in this context cannot be understood outside the individual's interactions with the group and with the state. A third characteristic here is the emphasis on the cognitive dimension: beliefs, norms, and values which *shape motivation* in time. Importantly, these cognitive elements are not innate, nor 'subconscious,' but are *adopted and become normalized in the course of these interactions*. Once internalized, however, they act as *determinants of action*, in the same way in which structural features do. This is a major difference from intentional approaches, which maintain a rather high degree of autonomy. Whilst the authors here begin with an assumption of intentionality of involvement, the conscious nature of behavior fades away once indoctrination is completed. This can be traced to two major fields of inquiry: social movement theory in sociology, in particular 'contentious politics' and 'framing theory'; and subcultural theories of deviant behavior in criminology. Both emphasize learning processes, where particular norms and values are adopted. In terms of individual acts, however, both revert to normative determinism.

The focus of social movement theory is on groups (or movements) rather than individuals; this is, however, not a psychological but a political science/sociological lens. Social movement scholars try to explain how groups evolve from protest to violence and eventually also terrorism. Some scholars have additionally also specifically looked at individuals, however, and demonstrated how individual motivation is shaped by their interactions with the group, with the state, and with other actors in the political arena. Della Porta's (2012) study on left-wing terrorism in Germany and Italy in the 1970s and Wiktorowicz's (2005) study on the Islamist Al Muhajiroun group in the UK (see also Chapter 4) are both good examples of this approach. In their accounts, individual motivation is shaped by the socialization processes and the features specific to these particular types of organizations, and emerges as a direct result of the internalization of alternative norms and values. Given the different branches of social movement theory they use—contentious politics vs. framing theory and rational choice—the source of these norms and values are collective identity and ideology vs. a redefinition of self-interest.

Della Porta's (2012) overall approach is that underground organizations are a special type of social movement, displaying essentially similar processes—in particular the formation of collective identities and new cultures (ibid: 244). These have a direct impact on individual motivations: "the real transformation in individual motivations begins within the terrorist organizations"; "The experience inside the terrorist organizations was then what shaped their dispositions" (ibid: 241). Norms and values are the decisive element, and they are shaped by two features of terrorist organizations: their underground nature and their ideology. In turn, the underground nature means control over members, including their private lives, and isolation from alternative channels of communication. The result of this total commitment is the lack of critical thinking, subordination of the individual to the collective and to the cause, and a loss of the sense of reality.

> In social movements as in the underground, activists construct "new" cultures, and commitment transforms the individual's private life. Social movements also produce collective identities to which the members willingly subordinate their own identities or roles ... Collective identities and the activists' motivations to participate are enforced by the integration of the individual into a movement counterculture built on alternative value systems and social structures. Activism in the social movement organizations strongly influences the 'lenses' through which reality is perceived, information is selected, and motivations are produced.
>
> (della Porta 2012: 244)

Adding to this is the nature of ideology, which frames the collective as an elitist, exclusive, and vanguard community (ibid: 243). Putting these two together, the overall argument is that the special nature of these organizations creates a particular rapport to absolutist ideas, which is total acceptance and reflection in private life, including individual acts, which then reflect a soldier's identity:

> the individual's value systems and perceptions of the external world became those of the group, and his or her motivational structure was transformed. By internalizing the group's rigid ideological systems, characterized by extreme elitism and 'absolute' enmity, the militants accepted the definition of the situation as a war. This militaristic outlook in turn shaped their perceptions and motivations.
>
> (della Porta 2012: 245)

Wiktorowicz (2005) also emphasizes the socialization factor, but explains individual motivations not as a reflection of a particular type of identity, but as a rational choice, pursuant to a change in the definition of self-interest, which becomes spiritual salvation. Furthermore, the adoption of alternative norms and values does not occur as a result of processes and features inherent to underground organizations (isolation and absolutist ideology), but through the mobilizing rhetoric of movement entrepreneurs. Framing theory has outlined a series of framing and resonance mechanisms. Out of these, Wiktorowicz emphasizes the resonance element of 'authority of the frame articulator,' in this case, that of the religious scholar and ideologue Omar Bakri, whose credibility draws on reputation, charisma, character, and personality. (ibid: 26) Having internalized these alternative norms and values, individuals orient their choices accordingly. Their choices are not guided by the pursuit of some common good, but by mere self-interest, which, however, has been redefined as a consequence of this indoctrination. For Wiktorowicz, rationality is shaped by ideology and, moreover, limited to the pursuit of one goal only—spiritual salvation:

> Rather than seeing their own interest as material or political, individuals come to see their dominant self-interest in "spiritual terms" – saving their souls on Judgment Day. It

80 *Relational* individual *terrorism*

is not simply that activists are socialized to believe in the inherent goodness of civic virtue; instead, they are socialized to believe that social activism and civil obligations are necessary vehicles to ensure salvation. Socialization redefines self-interest, and helping produce the collective good is a means, not an end, toward fulfilling individual spiritual goals ... Activists engage in actions for the collective good because that is what is necessary to protect spiritual self-interest. In this sense, even seemingly altruistic behavior can be understood as the rational pursuit of self-interest.

(Wiktorowicz 2005: 28)

Importantly, rational choice in this case is not a matter of anticipated reward (see the behavioral reinforcers argument in Chapter 5), but one of cognitive restructuring. That is, individuals effectively function in an alternative system, which alters the very nature of preferences. Furthermore and also different to the intentional rational choice approaches, individual agency is reduced to one choice only—salvation or damnation:

the ideology provides a heuristic device for those interested in the hereafter. Socialization, or what activists term *tarbyia* ('culturing' Muslims in proposed Islamic beliefs and practices), is intended to inculcate both interest in salvation as well as ideologically sanctioned strategies for reaching Paradise. In the case of radical Islamic groups, audiences are 'cultured' to believe that true believers must engage in (or at least support) violence because this kind of activism is divine order: particular forms of activism are proscribed as fulfilling God's will. Just as importantly, the ideology posits things like arrest and death as benefits rather than risks, glorified sources of honor and pride.

(Wiktorowicz 2005: 29)

Although in essence a rational choice approach, Pisoiu's (2012) model also involves a redefinition of essentially rational choice incentives, by their 'situation' within interpretative frameworks. They are similar but in a number of ways different to 'frames' and 'collective beliefs':

As opposed to collective action frames, interpretative frameworks are more inclusive; they are not limited to the prognostic, diagnostic and motivational functions in relation to an issue, but include general and specific meanings, norms and values. In this sense, they are more similar to collective beliefs, with the difference being that interpretative frameworks are not stable and limited to any "social environment", but are in continuous evolution, relative to individuals and groups and therefore with numerous overlapping levels.

(Pisoiu 2012: 109–110)

She elaborates on how these frameworks emerge, are learned and legitimized and the role social contacts play. Furthermore, she analyzes mechanisms through which these frameworks become exclusivist and absolute and how that leads individuals to engage in violent activities. Radical interpretative frameworks emerge in her study as a layer of interpretative frameworks with a certain degree of absolutism. They draw on ideas of conflict, oppression, aggression, injustice, and self-defense, and include a concrete enemy and war reality (for example, like the US or the West and the war in Iraq). Pisoiu argues that grievances are strategically constructed in order to motivate action like, for example, retaliation or resistance, conceptualized as self-defense. The establishment of an Islamic state with regulations based on the Koran and divine law would stop injustice and sufferance.

Pisoiu suggests two ways through which radical interpretative frameworks can be adopted. These are learning ways of doing and thinking, and forming ways of doing and thinking (i.e. within a group). The first draws on framing theory (see Box 6.1) and occurs through various mechanisms such as the authority of the frame articulator or empirical credibility. The study shows that this is often facilitated by religious nescience of some individuals which renders religious speeches even more credible and convincing. The more credible these sources are, the more legitimization is attached to them and the more likely it is that the framework will be accepted. Forming as the second way of doing and thinking occurs through discussions on current events and the cementation of attitudes towards these issues. Arguably, such discussions take place nowadays more and more online. With relation to it is that framework exclusivizing and how that interacts with social isolation, there are clear parallels with the work of della Porta (2012). Personal and ideational reference points for alternative views vanish and with them the tolerance for these alternative views and perspectives. The outside world is then increasingly rejected socially and politically because of a parallel moral system and an incompatibility with these values and world views. Importantly, an implication of such a radical parallel moral system is the legitimization of jihad as armed battle against occupiers, self-defense, or resistance.

Box 6.1 Frames and framing

The main features of framing theory have been skillfully presented by Benford and Snow (2000) in their work *Framing Processes and Social Movements: An Overview and Assessment.* They denote framing as:

> an active, processual phenomenon that implies agency and contention at the level of reality construction. It is active in the sense that something is being done, and processual in the sense of a dynamic, evolving process. It entails agency in the sense that what is evolving is the work of social movement organizations or movement activists. And it is contentious in the sense that it involves the generation of interpretive frames that not only differ from existing ones but that may also challenge them. The resultant products of this framing activity are referred to as "collective action frames."
>
> (Benford and Snow 2000: 614)

Following Goffman, the authors note that frames are schemata of interpretations that allow individuals to locate, perceive, identify, and label occurrences in the world. They render events meaningful and guide action, mobilize adherents and antagonists, and garner support. The authors note three different core framing tasks: 1) diagnostic framing which is the problem identification; 2) The prognostic framing which is the articulation of a proposed solution (a plan of attack—importantly, these two core framing tasks constrain each other); 3) The motivational framing which is the call to arms, the engaging in collective action as such. There are several features of collective action frames such as, for example, problem identification and direction of attribution. This means the identification of a certain problem that lies at the core of the framing and the way frames address certain social groups. The larger the types of social groups addressed with the frames, the greater the mobilization capacity of the frame. Second, frames can be differentiated along the following characteristics: exclusive, rigid, inelastic, and restricted, or to the contrary, inclusive, open, elastic, and elaborated. The more inclusive and flexible collective action frames are, the more likely they become master frames. Third, frames can be differentiated along their scope. Master frames are broad in their scope and reflect also the orientations and activities of other movements, whereas organizational frames are movement specific and do not have utility for other social movement organizations. Finally, the last feature is the resonance of frames. This relates to the effectiveness or the potency to mobilize and is essential when analyzing the effect of framing. Factors for resonance are the credibility of a frame as well as its relative salience. Credibility is a function of three factors: 1) frame consistency which is the congruency of the beliefs, claims, and the actions of a social movement organization. There should be no contradictions between its words and deeds; 2) Empirical credibility which is the fit between the framings and the events in the real world. The more culturally believable the evidence, the more credible the frame and the higher its appeal; 3) The credibility of the frame articulators or the claim-makers. This refers to the status and knowledge of the articulators about the issue. The more credible the articulators, the more plausible and resonant are the frames and their persuasiveness. Salience has three dimensions: 1) the centrality of beliefs, values and ideas. The higher the centrality, meaning the more essential the beliefs, values, and ideas for the targets of mobilization, the easier the mobilization; 2) Experimental commensurability. When framings of social movement organizations are resonant with the everyday personal experiences of the targets, the easier the mobilization is; 3) Narrative fidelity or the cultural resonance; the greater the cultural resonance of the frames, the greater the prospect of mobilization.

Social movement approaches to explaining individual involvement in terrorism are of course looking at process *par excellence*. These scholars underline socialization in particular environments—underground, radical, or otherwise, which have an effect on the ways individuals perceive and interpret reality. Individual involvement in terrorism is here understood as an interaction with members of the group, of the broader counterculture, other groups, and the state. A further marked difference of this approach to deterministic and intentional approaches is to focus on the continuities of attitudes and behaviors. Horgan's model in the previous chapter also talked about a seamless transition towards involvement in terrorism. In this case, however, more concrete links and continuities are drawn between life as a terrorist in a terrorist cell or the 'underground,' and life before and after that. Elements of militancy, ideological thinking, or violent behavior are thus identified also prior and post involvement per se, at clearly lower levels of intensity, but still with an effect on, or as a residue of involvement in terrorism. As mentioned in the first chapter, at the group level terrorist undergrounds are not seen as isolated units of analysis, but as off-shoots or variations of broader protest movements. Consequently, the social origins of the militants are those of the protest movements from which they were recruited, so that "future terrorists can be described as small minorities within larger political subcultures of countercultures" (ibid: 12). In relation to these initial countercultures, terrorist groups are seen as a matter of difference in degree, a gradual evolution towards (more radical) violence.

Relational individual *terrorism*   83

The representative model we are looking at here is the one developed by della Porta (1995) for the case of left-wing German and Italian terrorism in the 1970s. A suitable candidate would have also been the one advanced by Wiktorowicz, since elements of social movement theory are also taken into consideration in this case and the core mechanism that acts on individual behavior is in the end the effect of adopted norms and values. For the purposes of *process*, as opposed to *motivation*, however, we decided to keep it in the deterministic category, because of the limited elaboration on the transition between phases and the limited emphasis on gradual evolution, as opposed to sudden transformations (see the important role that 'crisis' and 'cognitive opening' play in his model).

In her monograph, della Porta aimed to combine three levels of analysis: macro, meso, and micro. This concerns not only the kinds of units of analysis that she is looking at, but also the kinds of theories and mechanisms used as an explanation. This means that for individuals and their evolution towards, through, and out of the 'underground,' individual, group, and higher-level variables are invoked. Although not explicitly structured as such, individual processes of involvement in terrorism could be divided in four broad stages: *involvement in countercultures*; *joining the underground group*; *being in the underground*; and *involvement in acts of violence*. Note the gradual approach to process and the different-iation of acts of violence vs. broader involvement, both of which are similar to intentional approaches. However, emphasizing continuity with previous forms of involvement is specific to these relational approaches. Della Porta noticed that all the members of the terrorist groups she examined were previously active in various types of left-wing organi-zations and were more broadly embedded in these political countercultures. Joining these organizations occurred as a matter of friendship and kinship relations. Counterculture involved similar music, lifestyle, and language, as well as the formation of affective ties, but also the formation of political attitudes. Here, additional social networks and alternative value systems emerged and through partly violent interactions with the state, its image as violent and unfair emerged; this was a stepping stone towards the legitimization of violence. This in effect laid the foundations for the later commitment to militancy, as well as a normal-ization of the use of violence:

> by exposing the activists to vital formative experiences, the political and social activities in which they participated helped to create distinctive political countercultures. The members of these countercultures shared two characteristics: a strong political identity, that is, political commitment was an essential constituent of their personality, and a political socialization to violence, that is, their political ideology and activities did not exclude the use of physical violence.
>
> (della Porta 1995: 149)

The next step, *joining the underground group*—or for some, going underground *together*—also occurs on the basis of existing social networks. Recruitment on the basis of existing social networks or 'affective networks' works due to both the low social cost imposed by the transition and the existence of strong affective ties. As a specificity here, it appears that for recruitment in the underground, the ties need to be stronger than for recruitment in non-militant groups, as there needs to be trust among the members, given the situation of illegality and risk. Apart from social networks, going underground occurred also as a reaction to an event, such as the victimization of a friend or the risk of arrest. The transition is, however, also marked by a series of elements of continuity: in the previous political countercultures, there was already contact with violence, martial skills, and structures of

84 *Relational* individual *terrorism*

violence, as small groups were formed, from which recruitment to the underground then took place. Additionally, violent confrontations created a perception of politics as a 'battle,' a perception of violence as being a natural component of 'doing politics'; in other words, violence became part and parcel of the emerging alternative system of norms and values.

In the underground, della Porta describes two types of dynamics: cognitive and affective. At this stage, the freedom fighter identity solidifies, mainly as a reaction to exaggerated state reactions (secondary deviance; see Chapter 1). Additionally, an own, separate sense of reality develops—the reality of a war—on the background of group isolation from alternative sources of information and under the influence of the ideology. Affectively, solidarity among members increases, first of all due to the situation of danger with which they are all confronted, but also due to the developing sense of responsibility for the others. Strong affective ties are in turn needed for the adoption of new values, the new reality, and the new identity, similar to primary socialization. The ones who do not fit the new construct are eliminated. With increasing danger and isolation, emotional intensity increases as well. The nature of underground groups as 'greedy institutions,' small and illegal, involves the need for coherence among members. This further demands total commitment to ideas and to each other, exclusivity of ideas and social contacts, and eventually the loss of individual identity. All aspects of private life become a group matter, while individual life becomes politicized and politics becomes a totalistic experience where 'everything is political.' This then increases even more the material and emotional involvement as a 'community of the armed struggle.' At the same time, in an argument similar to the intentional approach, the group also offers a series of benefits, things that, della Porta argues, individuals were seeking at that age: adventure, action, utopianism, energy, autonomy, openness, experimentation, and answers to the search for identity and fidelity. Similarly, being in the group also enables the experience of love, solidarity, self-transformation, success experiences, excitement, and party.

According to della Porta, individual *engagement in acts of violence* occurs primarily as derived from the acquired norms, values, and ideology, which includes the depersonalization of the enemy, a self-perception as hero, and a perception of the situation as war. An important role is also played here by a specific element of political and historical context: the broader perception in the counterculture that the state was a continuation of the Nazi regime, and was therefore illegitimate. Sustaining, or perhaps 'making' acts of violence 'possible' were previous experiences: first, the practice of (lower-level) political violence in which the members had already been socialized and the symbolic value of it as empowerment; and second, the experience of a 'violent' and 'unfair' state, of police brutality, and the defensive use of violence.

In the context of Islamist terrorism, the work of Marc Sageman also entails elements of process which are very much resonant with social movement research, in particular the importance of social bonds for joining jihadi groups and socialization in the new ideology. His recent 2016 book, *Misunderstanding Terrorism* (see Further reading), also makes reference to social movement scholarship, but focuses in its central model on socio-psychological theories, in particular social identity (for more on this see below). In his earlier book, *Understanding Terror Networks*, Sageman analyzed data based on the biographies of 172 terrorists (Sageman 2004: vii) and found that no single profile fitted members of the global Salafi jihad movement, however, they tended to be young men from middle-class, educated, and religious backgrounds (ibid: 96). With regard to joining the jihad, Sageman rejects the "common notions of recruitment and brainwashing," and instead argues that joining occurs along a "three-pronged process: social affiliation with the jihad accomplished through friendship, kinship, and discipleship; progressive intensification of beliefs and faith leading

Relational individual *terrorism* 85

to acceptance of the global jihad ideology; and formal acceptance to the jihad through the encounter of a link to the jihad" (ibid: 135). Sageman stresses the importance of *social bonds* and contends that whilst factors such as relative deprivation, religion, and ideology are also important, it is more likely that social and emotional support as well as a common identity are instrumental in the process of joining jihadi groups (ibid: 135). This conclusion is supported by the fact that 78 percent of the sample were found to be cut off from their social and cultural origins at the time of joining the movement (ibid: 92–93). Working or studying abroad as expatriates, these individuals sought like-minded companions with a similar background. For many of these Muslims in Western countries the mosque was a natural place to look for companionship, despite the fact that many of them were not necessarily particularly devout believers beforehand. Friendships were based on a shared sense of loneliness, alienation, and resentment towards their host societies, and they developed a common collective identity based on religious ties (ibid: 97). As the relationships intensified, their religious beliefs became increasingly extreme along with the resolve to connect with a group who shared their sentiments. In other words, they were a 'bunch of guys' who sought out jihad together (ibid: 97–98).

Individuals as subcultural deviants

A second type of relational approach bears resemblances with concepts and processes in social movements yet draws on the concept of deviant subculture in criminology. Simon Cottee (2011) draws on subcultural theory, in particular Albert Cohen's *Delinquent Boys: The Culture of the Gang* (1955) (see Box 6.2), and reframes Sageman's 'bunch of guys' thesis through this prism. Specifically, Cottee looks towards Sageman's work on 'third wave' jihadis, which was developed in his 2008 book *Leaderless Jihad: Terror Networks in the Twenty-First Century*. The third wave is unlike the terrorists studied in *Understanding Terror Networks*; there is no central network with physical headquarters, but rather informal networks that are largely facilitated by the Internet (Sageman 2008: 48–50). Sageman refers to this wave as "wannabe terrorists" (ibid: 79), and suggests that in contrast to their predecessors, they are typically from lower-class backgrounds, younger, less educated, more Westernized and less religious (ibid: 50–58). In light of Sageman's findings, Cottee seeks to expand on this work and apply Cohen's theory on delinquency. Cohen's core argument is: delinquency occurs in accordance with the norms and values of a subculture which "takes its norms from the larger culture but turns them upside down" (Cohen 1955: 28). Cottee makes the argument that the jihadi subculture is similar to the delinquent one in that it is "unmistakably negativistic, malicious and non-utilitarian" and that Cohen's theory "offers a promising conceptual vocabulary for making sense of Sageman's central empirical findings on Al Qaeda's third-wave" (Cottee 2011: 738).

Box 6.2 *Delinquent Boys: The Culture of the Gang* (1955)

Albert Cohen's work focuses on the theory of delinquent subcultures in the case of juvenile American gangs. Cohen's central argument is that delinquent gang behavior is a collective protest against middle-class norms and values. Namely, members of these gangs are likely to come from lower-class backgrounds where social conditions have largely prohibited them from reaching middle-class goals. For Cohen, the delinquent subculture exists as a consequence of socialization within inner-city

> environments and the disadvantaged position of lower-class males in the societal structure. Within this structure, individuals are more likely to underachieve in school and have a lack of discipline at home. Therefore, these youths lack the basic skills to achieve social and economic success in the current structures which they live in (Cohen 1955: 115). In other words, these youths experience "status frustration." As a result, they are likely to join a delinquent gang, which, contrary to mainstream society, provides a status and criteria that individuals are able to meet. The subculture of the delinquent gang is antithetical to mainstream culture, and as Cohen notes: "The delinquent's conduct is right by the standards of his subculture precisely because it is wrong by the norms of the larger cultures" (ibid: 28).

In Cottee's (2011: 738) account, the jihadi solution is a reaction to status frustration and identity confusion, which emerge from a series of social strains: poverty, lack of education, discrimination in the labor market, cultural uprootedness, enmity, and exclusion. Second- and third-generation Muslim immigrants tend to feel torn between two very different cultures—the more conservative one of their parents, and the liberal, secular Western societies which they were brought up. In this way, the global jihadi movement offers alternative norms and a lifestyle that run contrary to more dominant 'Western' values in which typically third-wave jihadis have been raised (ibid: 738). Cottee theorizes that "third wave jihadism can be described as a collective solution, devised by young westernised Muslim males, to resolve their twin problems of status-frustration and identity-confusion" (ibid: 738). The 'cumulative weight' of societal rejection and identity crisis becomes intolerable and jihad offers an attractive alternative. The jihadi subculture offers status criteria that are easier to achieve than more traditional 'Western' status criteria. The jihadi subcultural style is specifically formulated as a rejection of mainstream Western society and as a result, individuals that form part of this movement are able to retaliate against their source of status frustration and identity conflict (ibid: 738). Cottee explains:

> the ideology of the global Salafi jihad is not only strongly critical of American foreign policy; it is also resolutely opposed to the defining political and cultural values of Western secular society. It is anti-democracy. It abhors the ethos of materialism, which it sees as soulless and corrupting. It assails sexual freedom, which it castigates as "promiscuity" or "licence." It scorns its lack of martial vigor. It rejects notions of gender, sexual and religious equality. In place of these values, the global jihadi subculture stresses the primacy of fortitude of faith over material success; it extols the principle of manly honor and individual sacrifice; and it glorifies death and celebrates killing. Like the values of the delinquent subculture, jihadi values serve to vehemently rebuke and indeed mock those of the dominant order.
>
> (Cottee 2011: 738)

Beyond the classical approach to subculture which conceives of it as 'deviance' and draws on the criminological delinquency literature, there is another approach to subculture which focuses more on the aesthetics and looks at subcultures as manifestations of resistance. Some additional readings are proposed for a direct contrast with the less-intentional, deviant approach to political violence (see Further reading).

Individuals in groups

The relational theories surveyed so far emerging from social movement scholarship and from criminology have proposed a series of concepts—such as the role of social networks in joining, for example, which they have inferred empirically from the analysis of actual individual biographies. Social psychology has developed in parallel a series of concepts which parallel or confirm them. Psychologists Clark McCauley and Sophia Moskalenko list and support with evidence from existing socio-psychological research in their article *Mechanisms of Political Radicalization: Pathways Toward Terrorism* (2008) a series of radicalization mechanisms at several levels of analysis: individual, group, and mass levels. Interesting for our discussion here are the ones which look at individuals in groups, namely: joining a radical group—the slippery slope; joining a radical group—the power of love; extremity shift in like-minded groups; extreme cohesion under isolation and threat. They are particularly interesting because they provide socio-psychological concepts and evidence for the mechanisms described in social movement research with regard to: the gradual nature of joining, the supportive role of social networks in joining; the coherence and exclusivity of ideas in the underground. The authors in fact even explicitly reference della Porta's work in their article and provide illustrative citations for their arguments.

McCauley and Moskalenko (2008: 420) translate the gradual nature of joining in socio-psychological terms as the "power of step-by-step self-persuasion through one's own behavior." They furthermore note that "Hundreds of experiments have shown a strong tendency for self-justification after an individual does something stupid or sleazy" (ibid: 420). In other words, people would generally tend to confirm, repeat, and find justifications for immoral or otherwise 'bad' behavior. This has been explained through the dissonance theory which "understands this tendency as an effort to reduce the inconsistency between positive self-image and bad behavior" (ibid: 420), as well as through a series of experiments (see Box 6.3). In other words, it appears easier to find justifications for bad behavior rather than admit a wrongdoing. With regard to the role of social networks, McCauley and Moskalenko (2008) focus on a particular aspect of it, namely affective ties, which they label the 'power of love.' They also notice a rather logical rationale for why such ties are relevant in joining groups, namely the necessity of trusting the people who join anew: "No terrorist wants to try to recruit someone who might betray the terrorists to the authorities. In practice, this means recruiting from the network of friends, lovers, and family" (ibid: 421). No psychological construct is provided here as evidence for a rather straightforward mechanism.

Box 6.3 Cognitive dissonance theory

Cognitive dissonance theory was developed by social psychologist Leon Festinger in 1957. It is a counter-intuitive social psychology theory, also called an 'action-opinion theory.' It proposes that beliefs and attitudes are influenced by actions. As the general assumption is that it is the other way around, namely that actions are normally influenced by beliefs and attitudes, the theory is labeled as being counter-intuitive. The cognitive dissonance theory addresses this discrepancy with the human tendency to rationalize. The theory is based on three fundamental assumptions: first, that humans are sensitive to inconsistencies between actions and beliefs. If one acts in a way that is not in line with his beliefs, attitudes, and opinions, it is recognized. Second, the recognition of the violation of beliefs, attitudes, and opinions will cause

> dissonance which most people want to resolve because they are averse to its effects. Third, the dissonance will be resolved in one of three ways: a) through a change in beliefs, but this is somehow difficult in case the beliefs are fundamental and important. Moreover, beliefs and attitudes are rather stable and are not changed easily; b) Through a change in actions, meaning that one promises him/herself to never resort to a certain action again. However, some actions are beneficial and one might try to get rid of the bad feelings associated with the inconsistency of actions and beliefs. The most common method to deal with such a problem is c) to rationalize an action. This means to change its perception, to think about the action in a different manner and context, to reconceptualize it post-hoc and thereby get rid of anguished feelings (Festinger 1957).

In relation to increasingly extreme opinions, Clark McCauley and Sophia Moskalenko (2008: 422) refer to the mechanism of "group polarization," "group extremity shift," or "risky shift." They argue that group opinions regarding risky behavior and politics tend to shift towards the majority opinion held by members of the group. For example, if the majority of the members favor high risk taking, the opinion of the whole group will shift towards "increased extremity" on this issue (ibid: 422). The authors point to two explanations of group polarization rooted in social psychology: *relevant arguments theory* and *social comparison theory* (see also Brown 1986). Relevant arguments theory posits that "a culturally determined pool of arguments favors one side of the issue more than the other side" (McCauley and Moskalenko 2008: 422). Members of the group present their arguments, which tend to lean in one direction, and as a result the individual is "rationally persuaded" by the disproportionate representation of arguments in favor of one particular side (ibid: 422). Social comparison theory suggests that opinions have social values attributed to them. Therefore individuals feel pressure to share certain opinions—especially the opinions that are held by the majority of group members. Moreover, members that hold more extreme interpretations of the majority opinion tend to be afforded more respect and admiration from other group members, and as a consequence they attain a higher status within the group (ibid: 422). McCauley and Moskalenko (2008: 422) go on to argue that in turn: "This extra status translates into more influence and less change during group discussion, whereas individuals less extreme than average in the group-favored direction have less influence and change more." As there is too much pressure attached to failing to support the group-favored opinion and the most influential group member(s) harbors more extreme views, the average opinion becomes more extreme (ibid: 422). McCauley and Moskalenko (2008: 422) indicate that, for the case of the US group, the Weather Underground (or the Weathermen), "Within-group competition for the status of being 'most radical' moved the group to terrorism."

Group cohesion is a related mechanism in that it also in effect offers an explanation for why individuals in a group tend to agree. Here, it is argued that groups which are isolated tend to achieve an even higher degree of cohesion, precisely due to their isolation. Drawing on group dynamics theory, they start off with the "value of the social reality" of a group, which is illustrated with questions such as: "What is good and what is evil? What is worth working for, worth dying for? What does it mean that I am going to die?" (ibid: 423). In isolated groups, individuals can only derive answers to such questions and certainty about their answers from the other members of the group; this means in turn that there is pressure to have this certainty in the group, which can only be given if people agree:

The social reality value of a group is weak to the extent that members belong to other groups with competing standards of value. Conversely, the social reality value of a group is strong when members are cut off from other groups. This principle is the foundation of many powerful forms of group-focused persuasion, including cult recruiting and thought reform or brainwashing. When cohesion is very high, as when an individual's social world has contracted to just the few friends in his combat group or his terrorist cell, the social reality value of the group is maximized. The group's consensus about value and morality acquires enormous power, including the power to justify and even require violence against those who threaten the group.

(McCauley and Moskalenko 2008: 423)

It appears that social psychology sees certainty as something of a fundamental need for people in general; on the reverse, they appear to see extremist groups as something that can provide this certainty. Some authors have in fact argued that lack of certainty is a factor that can lead to people joining extremist groups. This, incidentally, would be an additional item to the approaches here which could explain why certain people join certain groups (and not others). Building on social identity theory and self-categorization theory, Michael A. Hogg has proposed the uncertainty reduction hypothesis (see Further reading) which he then applied to extremism (Hogg and Adelman 2013). This theory is based on the assumption that self-uncertainty (i.e. feeling that one does not know how to behave, what to think etc.) motivates behaviors that aim to reduce self-uncertainty. One of the ways to reduce self-uncertainty is to identify with a group. Joining a group provides the individual with a feeling of identification and belonging, as well as direction regarding how to act and behave (Hogg and Adelman 2013: 438–439). Under uncertainty, individuals not only seek out cohesive and united groups, but also seek out leadership that exhibits direction, clarity, and authority. Under these conditions individuals may seek rather authoritarian leadership qualities, and groups structured in terms of hierarchy and roles—which tend to be characteristic of extremist groups (ibid: 445). Hogg and Adelman tested the relevance of uncertainty-identity theory on a number of empirical case studies, including one conducted at an Australian university and results from a two-year study in Israel and the Palestinian Territories. The Australian university study was conducted at a time when students were facing increasing uncertainty as public funding was being cut and the (unpopular) idea of fee increases was being set in motion. Participants were shown videos of two different protest groups—one with an extreme hierarchical structure and one with a more moderate informal structure—and another video where students expressed high or low uncertainty regarding their educational future. After watching the videos, the participants were asked questions to determine uncertainty levels concerning their future, as well as to what extent they identified with the two groups shown in the first video, and whether they would intend to engage in certain behaviors on behalf of these groups. The case study in Israel and the Palestinian Territories was intended to extend on the previous study and fully explore the idea of why individuals support extremist groups. Specifically, this study aimed to ascertain to what extent strong national identity interacts with aspects of self-uncertainty and how this may influence extreme actions. The authors measured strength of national identity amongst Israelis and Palestinians, levels of (self-)uncertainty, and whether certain conflict behaviors could ever be justified (ibid: 442–445). From these two studies, Hogg and Adelman found that feelings of uncertainty had the potential to lead to the following:

90 *Relational* individual *terrorism*

(1) strengthen identification with highly entitative or extreme groups, (2) enhance intentions to behave in more extreme group-serving ways and to support extreme measures to protect and promote one's group, (3) enhance the desire for ingroup leadership per se, such that even relatively less ingroup prototypical leaders become a viable leadership option, and (4) build a preference for strong, hierarchy-based, autocratic leadership.

(Hogg and Adelman 2013: 447)

Given these findings, the authors additionally sought to examine why some individuals in extremist groups choose to engage in violence, whilst other members do not (ibid: 447). Based on original ideas from Goldman and Hogg (2013), the authors suggest that individuals who feel that their membership in a group is uncertain (i.e. that they are not core members), attempt to reduce such uncertainty by resorting to extremes on behalf of the group. This works when the groups themselves are likely to embrace and accept extreme behaviors (Hogg and Adelman 2013: 447–448). In sum, Hogg and Adelman (2013) argue that: "Self-categorization as a group member reduces this type of uncertainty very effectively because it transforms self-conception so that it is governed by a group prototype that defines the self and prescribes perceptions, attitudes, feelings, and behaviors, and describes how others view and treat you" (ibid: 449). But the conduction of violence can also stem from a violation of certain group norms. Hogg et al. (2010) argue in their article 'Religion in the Face of Uncertainty: An uncertainty-identity theory account of religiousness', that religions provide well-developed ancient and nonmalleable ideologies and world views as well as normative practices with regard to everyday life choices and behavioral routines that often conflict with modern society. These world views are grounded in consensus circumscribed by group membership. A strong religious identification of an individual and the assumption that the world view of the in-group and the associated practices are superior and more absolutely moral than those of other groups, can create ethnocentrism with in-group protective and promotive behavior with regard to their religious identity and associated values and practices. This behavior can become extreme and result in domination and even violence (against other groups or modernity in general). The potential conflicts of violence with other ideological tenets are then often justified and legitimized with reference to the sacred (ibid: 76–77).

Individuals and power

Investigations of individual involvement in terrorism often rely on interviews as a means to gain a deeper understanding of the circumstances and mechanisms unfolding along the radicalization process, and to access the individual subjective perspective in the process. Interviews were also the main source of information for Charlotte Heath-Kelly's (2013) study *Politics of Violence: Militancy, International Politics, Killing in the Name*, yet a realization during fieldwork and later the post-structuralist theoretical and methodological background, led her to a different research focus and a different take on the interpretation of these interviews. She realized that former EOKA (Ethniki Organosis Kyprion Agoniston/ National Organization of Cypriot Fighters) members in Cyprus narrated their experiences in a completely different manner than former members of the Red Brigades in Italy. The former had little difficulty explaining why and how they joined, and this story blended with the overall story of the political struggle for national liberation. The latter had difficulties explaining their militant path. In both cases it could be assumed that what we learned in the previous chapter applies: namely the perceived normality of joining in the immediate social

Relational individual *terrorism* 91

environment where 'everyone was joining.' The difference between the two cases is, of course, that EOKA was successful and the Red Brigades were not; and this has implications for the ways involvement is narrated. Heath-Kelly ends up looking at the boomerang effects of involvement rather than at the 'causes' of it, and thus at something that had been thus far ignored by the typical scholarship on individual involvement in terrorism, and something that can only be processed by using post-structuralist theories and methods. Being successful or not in the militant struggle meant being successful in imposing their own world view or not, which in turn rendered coherence to the narratives, or not.

Heath-Kelly thus goes beyond actual involvement to the systemic level to illustrate how violence affects power, how the result of the struggle affects the relationships of power. The nature of the individual narratives become a consequence thereof and become illustrations of that rather than evidence for behavior or thoughts. The study then investigates the effects of violence on power, or, in other words, the politics of violence. The underlying logic is that the militant struggle establishes a certain political authority (or not), which then has an effect on language, subjectivity, memory, and politics. This, she convincingly argues, is something that had been hitherto ignored by the terrorism scholarship. This kind of investigation and findings link to a series of established critical concepts, and in particular the writings of Foucault, Derrida, Benjamin, and Žižek. For example, Heath-Kelly argues with regard to the subjectivity of the EOKA militants:

> Moving to consider the types of power configuration which produced these deployments of continuous subjectivity, it is useful to note, as Foucault has argued, that discourse should be understood as the conditions which make something sayable. Discourse is what regulates and structures the production of statements and meaning … not the words themselves. The discourse which situates the narration of "the fighter" is the mass of political practices which have taken place in the Republic of Cyprus since independence, from the institution of memorials and museums to the struggle to the contestations over meanings.
>
> (Heath-Kelly 2013: 127)

Heath-Kelly's work concerns itself not with the why and the how of militancy, but rather of 'with what consequences' and the 'how possible' of the narrative. These are questions that preoccupy critical scholars also with regard to other topics, not least counter-terrorism (see Chapter 13).

Summary

This chapter has outlined relational approaches to individual terrorism and dealt with:

- how individuals interact with their environment and what effects this has on joining terrorist groups or engaging in political violence;
- models of individual involvement drawing on social movement, criminological, and socio-psychological theories;
- the particular role of social networks in joining and staying on, of norms and values in committing terrorist acts;
- how groups and leaders can influence the ways individuals think and act;
- post-structuralist approaches on individual involvement in terrorism.

Exercises

6.1   What are the key features of relational approaches to individual terrorism? How does this approach differ to intentional and deterministic approaches?

6.2   To what extent do you agree that individual motivation cannot be explained without looking towards the interactions between individuals and the state, and individuals and groups? Explain your answer.

6.3   Explore the role of leadership on individual involvement by referring to Hogg (2000) in Further reading. How does that confirm, complement, or contradict the role of ideology?

References

Benford, R.D. and Snow, D.A. (2000). Framing Processes and Social Movements: An overview and assessment. *Annual Review of Sociology*, 26, pp. 611–639.

Brown, R. (1986). *Social Psychology: The Second Edition*. New York: Free Press.

Cohen, A.K. (1955). *Delinquent Boys: The Culture of the Gang*. New York: The Free Press.

Cottee, S. (2011). Jihadism as a Subcultural Response to Social Strain: Extending Marc Sageman's "Bunch of Guys" thesis. *Terrorism and Political Violence*, 23(5), pp. 730–751.

della Porta, D. (1995). *Social Movements, Political Violence, and the State. A Comparative Analysis of Italy and Germany*. Cambridge: Cambridge University Press.

della Porta, D. (2012). On Individual Motivations in Underground Political Organizations. In J. Horgan and K. Braddock (eds) *Terrorism Studies: A Reader*. London, New York: Routledge, pp. 231–249.

Festinger, L. (1957). *A Theory of Cognitive Dissonance*. Evanston, IL: Row & Peterson.

Goldman, L. and Hogg, M.A. (2013). *Going to Extremes for One's Group: The Role of Proto-typicality and Group Acceptance*. Manuscript submitted for publication. Claremont Graduate University.

Heath-Kelly, C. (2013). *Politics of Violence: Militancy, International Politics, Killing in the Name*. Abingdon: Routledge.

Hogg, M.A. and Adelmann, J. (2013). Uncertainty-Identity Theory: Extreme groups, radical behaviour, and authoritarian leadership. *Journal of Social Issues*, 69, pp. 436–454.

Hogg, M.A., Adelman, J.R. and Blagg, R.D. (2010). Religion in the Face of Uncertainty: An uncertainty-identity theory account of religiousness. *Personality and Social Psychology Review*, 14(1), pp. 72–83.

McCauley, C. and Moskalenko, S. (2008). Mechanisms of Political Radicalization: Pathways toward terrorism. *Terrorism and Political Violence*, 20, pp. 415–433.

Pisoiu, D. (2012). *Islamist Radicalisation in Europe. An Occupational Change Process*. Abingdon/NewYork: Routledge.

Sageman, M. (2004). *Understanding Terror Networks*. Philadelphia: University of Pennsylvania Press.

Sageman, M. (2008). *Leaderless Jihad: Terror Networks in the Twenty-First Century*. Philadelphia, PA: University of Pennsylvania Press.

Wiktorowicz, Q. (2005). *Radical Islam Rising. Muslim Extremism in the West*. London: Rowman & Littlefield Publishers, Inc.

Further reading

Crone, M. (2014). Religion and Violence: Governing Muslim militancy through aesthetic assemblages. *Millennium Journal of International Studies*, 43(1), pp. 291–307.

Hemmingsen, A.S. (2015). Viewing Jihadism as a Counterculture: Potential and limitations. *Behavioral Sciences of Terrorism and Political Aggression*, 7(1), pp. 3–17.

Hogg, M.A. (2000). Subjective Uncertainty Reduction through Self-categorization: A motivational theory of social identity processes. *European Review of Social Psychology*, 11(1), pp. 223–255.

Pisoiu, D. (2015). Subcultural Theory Applied to Jihadi and Right-Wing Radicalization in Germany. *Terrorism and Political Violence*, 27(1), pp. 9–28.

Sageman, M. (2016). *Misunderstanding Terrorism*. Philadelphia, PA: University of Pennsylvania Press.

7 Determining *organizational* terrorism

Deterministic approaches identify the so-called *root causes* of terrorism, variables of a higher order which would necessarily and in general be responsible for the emergence of terrorism in various countries and regions around the world and at various points in time. Furthermore, given the pronounced structural nature of this approach, organizational agency does not play a role here. That said, most analyses do make reference to organizations, if only to assign labels and classify terrorist acts in data sets. This chapter starts off with the classification of root causes of terrorism in structural, facilitator, motivational, and triggering causes and discusses studies which have tested some of the root causes included there.

In essence, the root causes approach is not much different to what has been otherwise labeled as 'structural' approaches to the explanation of terrorism. The expression 'root causes' has, however, been more prominently used in recent years and has been the focus of definitional, theoretical, empirical, and critical reflection. On 11 March 2004, an al-Qaeda inspired terrorist cell killed 191 and injured nearly 2,000 in several coordinated bombings on the commuter train system of Madrid. As an almost premonition of what was to happen less than a year later, a conference held in Oslo in 2003 on the root causes of terrorism concluded with a collection of essays covering terrorisms of various types of ideological orientations and in various geographical locations. The book, edited by Tore Bjørgo, appeared two years later and was entitled *Root Causes of Terrorism: Myths, Reality, and Ways Forward.*

In its introduction and conclusion, Bjørgo engages in a very useful discussion of generally acknowledged truths and critical points of the root causes approach. He also introduces a classification of root causes into *preconditions* and *precipitants*. Preconditions "set the stage for terrorism in the long run, whereas precipitants are the specific events or phenomena that immediately precede or trigger the outbreak of terrorism" (Bjørgo 2005a: 3). These are then further differentiated along four categories: structural causes, facilitator or accelerator causes, motivational causes, and triggering causes (to be discussed further below). Bjørgo also lists some general observations on the root causes approach: first, the reason behind the interest in root causes emerges naturally from counter-terrorism considerations, namely, combating the causes of terrorism, rather than its symptoms or consequences. To illustrate this, he compares terrorism with a mosquito infestation, in which case it is preferable to drain the swamps where they breed rather than killing individual insects. The conditions for this to work are, however, first, that there are causes and mechanisms available to intervention and change; they need to be specific and have a direct causal relationship to the problem. Later on in the conclusion, and under the influence of concrete cases of root causes analyses, this latter condition seems to be toned down, as Bjørgo notes that preconditions produce "a

Determining organizational *terrorism*   95

wide range of social outcomes of which terrorism is only one" (Bjørgo 2005b: 258). Second, there is no single cause of terrorism, but several factors, whose combination and respective weight might differ by case. Third, root causes operate in the initial phases of terrorist activity, while in later phases there might be other causes for the *continuation* of terrorism.

Importantly, a series of 'common wisdom' causes of terrorism are discarded, namely: poverty, regime type, state sponsorship, Islam, and insanity. The connection between terrorism and poverty could be discarded both at the macro level and at the micro level. The kinds of people who join or support terrorism are usually not among the poorest members of their societies, but rather average or above average in terms of both income and education. At the macro level, no correlation could be established between the level of terrorism and that of poverty, or in other words, terrorism does not occur in the poorest countries of the world (see Box 7.1). State sponsorship has also been discarded as a root cause of terrorism and formulated as an 'enabling factor' because usually it is the terrorists who approach governments asking for financial or other types of support. At the same time, Bjørgo acknowledges that there are instances where states control an organization completely—a case for intermediary factors. The reason why Islam is not considered a root cause of terrorism is because motivation is usually political, such as foreign occupation or the domination of one group over another.

Box 7.1 Poverty, education, and terrorism

The most often-cited study on the connection between terrorism and poverty is the one by Alan B. Krueger and Jitka Maleckova (2003) called 'Education, Poverty and Terrorism: Is there a Causal Connection?' The two academics first analyze opinion polls in the West Bank and the Gaza Strip collected by the Palestinian Center for Policy and Survey Research. The poll questioned 1,357 Palestinians aged 18 or older between 19 and 24 December 2001. The data, which included questions related to the use of terrorism, could be broken down by occupation and employment status and by educational attainment. There it could be seen that for questions such as "are there any circumstances under which you would justify the use of terrorism to achieve political goals?", or support for attacks against Israeli targets, the numbers in fact increased with the level of employment or education. Overall, the distribution was such that the higher the education or the level of employment, the more support for violence there was, or as the authors put it, the results "offer no evidence that more highly educated individuals are less supportive of violent attacks against Israeli targets than those who are illiterate or poorly educated" (ibid: 125). A second data set contained biographical information on 129 deceased members of Hezbollah's military wing. As compared to the Lebanese population of similar age, these individuals had higher income levels and were significantly better educated. The results thus showed that "poverty is inversely related with the likelihood that someone becomes a Hezbollah fighter, and education is positively related with the likelihood that someone becomes a Hezbollah fighter" (ibid: 133). A further analysis of a data set on Palestinian suicide bombers showed that "individuals who carried out suicide bomb attacks for these organizations are less likely to come from impoverished families and are much more likely to have completed high school and attended college than the general Palestinian population" (ibid: 135). The final analysis was at the macro level and looked at the country of origin of perpetrators of

> significant international terrorist incidents between 1997 and 2002 as recorded by the Department of State. The results showed an inverse relationship between gross domestic product (GDP) and the number of terrorists coming from any one country. When a control for civil liberties was introduced though, the effect of income became statistically insignificant.

That poverty does not lead to terrorism seems to be in the meantime a broadly acknowledged fact (see also the study by Abadie 2006, in Further reading). The relationship between education and terrorism, however, is not so clear-cut. Looking back on several decades of terrorist profiles, it is safe to say that terrorism is not an outcome of a lack of education; if anything, and as Krueger and Maleckova (2003) show, terrorists may well be highly educated. This, however, might be exactly the problem, if certain other conditions are present. Newer studies seem to confirm the fact that not lack of education, but education combined with lack of opportunities might in fact correlate with terrorism. Formulated this way, this hypothesis resembles in essence relative deprivation (addressed in Chapter 4), insofar as they both refer to a discrepancy between (perceived) potential and opportunities to fulfill it.

Diego Gambetta and Steffen Hertog (2016) combined both of these variables in their study *Engineers of Jihad: The Curious Connection Between Violent Extremism and Education*. They put together data sets on the level and type of education of five categories of Islamist activists. First, three large and diffuse groups: militant individuals born and active in Muslim countries during peacetime; militants born or raised in Western states; and non-violent Islamists from Muslim countries. Second, data sets of two more specific groups: Islamist extremists in Iran prior to the Revolution and Islamist extremists from around the globe who defected and abandoned violent politics. They focused on small groups rather than on full-blown insurgencies and therefore did not include Boko Haram in Nigeria, the al-Shabaab (The Youth) in Somalia, the Taliban in Afghanistan, or the Islamic State of Iraq and Syria (ISIS). They also collected educational data on nine types of right- and left-wing extremists active before and after World War II: early Nazi and Italian fascist movements, neo-Nazis in Germany as well as Austria, US and Russian white supremacists, members of the Spartakusbund, the Red Army Faction, and the Red Brigades as well as on anarchists active worldwide. In total, they collected biographical data on over 4,000 individuals.

On the one hand, the study revives the theory of relative deprivation and frustrated expectations as an explanation for why people join extremist movements. The proportion of graduates reflects shifts in economic opportunity of their regions of origin. In the West and in much of Asia, where they had the opportunity to pursue a career, there is no overrepresentation of graduates in violent Islamist radical groups. Yet, the authors found a significant overrepresentation of graduates, especially with elite universities, in the MENA (Middle East and North Africa) region (except Saudi Arabia). There, in fact, many highly educated individuals joined violent Islamist radical groups from the 1970s onwards. The authors ascribe this to a halt in economic development because of failing economies, cronyism, and corruption from the 1970s to the 1980s. This created obstacles for the careers of graduates and resulted in unmet expectations and unjust deprivation with respect to their social status. The reason why engineers were especially affected by economical crises is that their employment often depends on state-sponsored projects. In times of crisis, states cut budgets, which in turn affects engineers. Also, they often came from the middle classes which are especially affected in times of crisis.

However, the authors suggest that relative deprivation does not suffice as an explanation for why engineers join violent Islamist radical groups as many high-level jihadi had wealthy backgrounds. Moreover, in the West and South Asia, where people did face social deprivation to the same extent, such engineers also joined such groups. In fact, of 485 Western jihadis, 28.5 percent were engineers. This phenomenon is explained by the momentum that the movement has gained in the meantime. Gambetta and Hertog found evidence that engineers in general are more likely to join violent groups than non-violent ones, that they prefer religious groups to secular groups, and that they are less prone to defect from Islamist groups. This has nothing to do with relative deprivation. Engineers are overrepresented in vastly different social and economic contexts, across many different radical groups, and they predominate in small cells of self-starters in the West. The authors emphasize that it is not network connections that explain this phenomenon, and that concepts of social movement theory cannot explain it either. Also, it is not the preference of recruiters to approach engineers that provides an explanation. It is rather the engineers' own willingness to join radical groups; their personal traits make them prone to join radical violent groups.

Structural causes

In the following we take Bjørgo's categories of root causes and discuss them by making reference to various studies which have tested their incidence. As we are talking about macro-level variables impacting on terrorism in general, such studies are usually quantitative. The *structural causes* that Bjørgo lists are: "demographic imbalances, globalization, rapid modernization, transitional societies, increasing individualism with rootlessness and atomization, relative deprivation, class structure, etc" (Bjørgo 2005a: 3). These are causes which affect people's lives in ways they may or may not comprehend, at a rather abstract macro level.

With respect to *demographic imbalances*, two studies have produced interesting findings. Valerie M. Hudson and Andrea Den Boer (2002) have found in their study on China and India, 'A Surplus of Men, a Deficit of Peace: Security and Sex Ratios in Asia's Largest States', that there is a correlation between sectarian and ethnic violence and a high sex ratio. A high sex ratio means a surplus of males in a society due to 'offspring sex selection' (e.g. sex-selective abortion and female infanticide). Focusing on the impact of demographic imbalances, they examine the historical cases of China and Portugal and compare them to the now largest Asian countries with demographic imbalances, China and India. Based on their study, they suggest that societies with a sex ratio of 120:100 are inherently unstable. Drawing on existing theories, they argue that this is because single males without the prospect of finding a woman mostly come from lower socio-economic classes, are often unemployed or underemployed, and have only few ties to communities; as a consequence, they seek fulfillment through violence and try to capture resources to compete with others. Moreover, due to their unmarried status, they have higher serum testosterone levels which correlates with the abuse of alcohol, trouble with the law, and rebellion. Another study looking at demographic variables is Henrik Urdal's 'A Clash of Generations? Youth Bulges and Political Violence' (2006). The author analyzes in his cross-national statistical study whether youth bulges—i.e. a large proportion of people aged 15–24 relative to the adult population in a country—might increase internal political violence such as armed conflict, terrorism, and riots. He uses data on internal armed conflict for the period 1950–2000, as well as data on terrorism and rioting for the period 1984–1995, and finds that a large share of young people is indeed associated with the forms of violence noted above. Additionally, strongly autocratic states with a youth bulge seem to be more affected by the risk of conflict.

98 *Determining* organizational *terrorism*

Referring to the *Arab Human Development Report* of 2002 of the United Nations, he furthermore emphasizes that increasing higher education in connection with widespread economic stagnation might trigger terrorist activity in Arab countries because well-educated young people are frustrated over the lack of occupational opportunities. This confirms the study on the engineers of jihad mentioned above.

The *lack of democracy, civil liberties and the rule of law* have also been named as root causes of terrorism, but in this case the relationship is not simple. Indeed, the most democratic and the most totalitarian of states usually do not produce terrorism. Nevertheless, there is a widespread assumption that people would rebel against undemocratic states; and that, by contrast, the insertion of democracy would prevent or stop terrorism. In the background of the threat posed by al-Qaeda, the Bush administration at the time had set out to conduct a War on Terror. The underlying assumption of this campaign was precisely this inverse relationship between terrorism and democracy. Concretely, the reasoning was that a democratic Middle Eastern country would stop producing terrorism; and that once a country turned democratic—in this case Iraq—others would follow. This reasoning was based on 'democratic peace theory,' which in essence argued that democracies do not go to war with each other (see also Box 7.2). The problem is of course that this theory refers to ready-made democracies, and not to democracies 'in the making' (see also Freeman 2008, also discussed below). Indeed, precisely this period of transition towards democracy appears to be particularly prone to violence and terrorism.

Box 7.2 Democratic peace theory

Following the German philosopher Immanuel Kant and his work *Perpetual Peace: A Philosophical Sketch* of 1795 there is a common perception among some politicians and scholars of Western liberal democratic states that anarchy can be overcome through the principle of democratic peace, as democratic countries are less war-prone and hardly ever wage war against each other. Democratic peace theory has been advocated and revised in the present age by neoliberals like Robert O. Keohane and Joseph S. Nye. Kant provides an explanation for this pattern in his first definitive article about peace among nations where he claims that the constitution of every state should be republican because under such a civil constitution it is the citizens who legally decide whether a state should wage a war or not. As citizens have to fully pay the costs of war they are more likely to vote against it. This implies that if the whole international political system consisted of democratic states, the struggle for power and anarchy could be diminished. This assumption is often used by liberals to legitimize interventions in non-democratic states in order to democratize them. However, Beate Jahn (2005), a critic of liberal internationalism, argues in her study, 'Kant, Mill, and Illiberal Legacies in International Affairs', that this behavior does not indicate a pacifist body of thought but in fact rather points to the persuasion of imperialistic intentions. The promotion and forced implementation of liberal thought abroad can be seen as hidden imperialism and the intervention in sovereignty displays the non-application of the normative constraint of non-militarism to non-liberal states (ibid: 178–182). However, democratic peace theory has been widely acknowledged among many scholars, such as through the work of Michael W. Doyle who further laid out its philosophical and theoretical basis in the 1980s. According to some scholars such as Jack S. Levy, democratic peace theory is even acknowledged as the closest thing we have to an empirical law in the discipline of international relations.

The national context of each country also seems relevant for the relationship between democracy and terrorism. In his study 'Democracy, Al Qaeda, and the Causes of Terrorism: A Strategic Analysis of US Policy', Michael Freeman' (2008) takes up the scenario of a country affected by terrorism and inquires whether the introduction of democracy would help prevent it. Drawing on previous studies and statements of bin Laden, he inquires whether the spread of democracy could undermine the motivations of global Salafi jihad groups to resort to terrorism. The underlying assumption in his study is that there are various economic, social, political, and military problems in Middle Eastern countries that provoke frustrations and humiliations and in turn encourage people to turn to violence and terrorism. He parallels Bjørgo in identifying preconditions and precipitants of terrorism and names *permissive issues*: failures of modernization as economic cause (e.g. the failure of Western modern ideologies to improve the societies of Middle Eastern states) and authoritarianism as political cause (e.g. corrupt regimes and the inability to participate politically); and *immediate issues*: occupation as a military cause (e.g. meaning the support and deployment of American troops on the Arabian Peninsula and Western support for Israel), and threats to the Islamic identity as a cultural cause (e.g. meaning the spread of the Western lifestyle and its perception as a threat to identity). He stresses that the variables used by him are not factors causing people to follow jihadism, but they create grievances for which the Salafist ideology seems to be a cure. The author conceptualizes democracy as "the embodiment of the notions of equality, liberty, and the rule of law through the combination of norms, institutions, procedures, and/or outcomes" (ibid: 43). Drawing on arguments of proponents of the spread of democracy, who argue that democracy enhances peaceful secession, fosters tolerance as well as economic growth, and creates legitimate governments, Freeman takes each of the permissive and immediate issues individually and shows how democracy fails to address them, mostly because of the intervening function of the Salafi ideology.

In military terms, al-Qaeda as a Salafi jihadi group, for example, does not simply aim to obtain autonomy as a minor religious group in Saudi Arabia for which of course democracy would provide valuable instruments, but also aims to change the regime as a whole because of the fact that it is supported and influenced by Western states. The adoption of democratic means like elections might therefore not be perceived as a viable mechanism. With regard to cultural causes, it is argued that global Salafi jihadi groups might perceive Islamic identities, values, and beliefs (religion) as already under threat from Western ideas and lifestyles. Therefore, democratization as a Western concept imposed on Islamic cultures might rather lead to an even stricter and devout form of Islam which ensures that faith, identity, and behavior are intertwined. Unlike modernists, secularists, and even traditionalists, fundamentalists regard democracy as totally incompatible with Islam as it introduces values such as "individual liberty, tolerance, openness, secularism, and culture-less materialism" (ibid: 49). This would be the complete opposite of Muslim values such as "social justice, spirituality, and communal values" (ibid: 49). With respect to economic causes, the author states that modern ideologies like capitalism and liberalism that culminated in modernization, urbanization, and globalization in the West were not successful in improving Middle Eastern societies. To the contrary, countries in this region still suffer from corruption and unemployment. This is evidenced by other scholars who find that democracy (which is based on modern ideologies) does not necessarily create economic growth. Yet looking at Western countries, wealth is exactly what people in the Middle East expect from capitalism and liberalism. As a result, unmet economic expectations increase frustration and violence. Salafist groups use these unmet expectations of modern ideologies to promote the abandonment of these Western concepts and to vote for the application of Sharia law. However,

100 *Determining* organizational *terrorism*

although unmet expectations trigger frustration, the author admits, by referring to other scholars, that the relationship between economic factors and Salafi terrorism is not salient and seems to be weak, meaning that it does not necessarily lead to Salafi terrorism. Finally, democracy might also fail to combat political causes. For Salafist groups, democratic values such as secularism, sovereignty, nationalism, rights for women, and constitutionalism directly oppose their political values. Freeman concludes that the success of democracy depends heavily on what people perceive as the source of political legitimacy. In his opinion, combatting the spread of Salafist ideology might be a better strategy than spreading democracy to alter the dynamics of the four factors mentioned and hence to combat the causes of terrorism.

Another root cause of terrorism has been named as *rapid modernization*, which seems to correlate with ideological terrorism. A popular example here is, again, the case of Middle Eastern countries with the effect of oil-related welfare, the sudden change from tribal to high-tech societies, the breakdown of traditional norms and their replacement with radical ideologies. Lutz and Lutz (2014) analyze in their quantitative study, 'Economic, Social and Political Globalization and Terrorism', the potential correlation of economic, social, and political globalization with terrorism in sub-Saharan African countries. Drawing on earlier studies, they argue that the international cultural, military, political, and social interconnectedness of communities brings dissimilar groups into closer proximity, that economic globalization creates tensions for local societies and economies, and increases the level of inequalities. Furthermore, market capitalism undermines local economies. This in turn creates grievances of certain groups within a society which might in turn oppose their governments and political systems, potentially weakening state authority and paving the way for terrorist activities. The authors use the Global Terrorism Database of 2012 with data on incidents, fatalities, and injuries resulting from terrorist attacks for the years 1970–2010, as well as a database on globalization for the same period.

In the 1970s and more so in the 1980s, the authors find a correlation between terrorism incidents and globalization. It was especially higher economic globalization (measured in financial flows, trade, and international transactions) that was linked with terrorist attacks, whereas social globalization (measured in information flows, foreign citizens, and personal contacts with the world) was less frequently linked. It is therefore argued that globalization had negative effects on the societies mentioned above. However, political globalization (measured in the number of embassies in a country, membership of international organizations, international treaties, and participation in UN peacekeeping provisions) was not at all linked with terrorist incidents in this time period. Later on, however, empirical data point to a certain threshold regarding the level of globalization in the 1990s. The more globalized the countries were by the 1990s, the more terrorist incidents took place. To the contrary, from the 1990s onwards, it was the less globalized countries that experienced the higher number of attacks. The social and political indices were not statistically significant. The effect of economic globalization persisted during the first decade of the 21st century. Economically less-connected countries were still experiencing more terrorist attacks, but lower order social and political globalization was henceforth linked with a higher number of fatalities and terrorist incidents respectively at a statistically significant level. The authors argue that this was because globalization affected different groups of society in different ways, which is why different targets for their attacks were chosen in the countries under scrutiny. Following Rapoport and his concept of terrorist waves, the authors conclude that terrorist attacks in the 1970s and 1980s might have been conducted by new left-wing groups who criticized the negative effects of global capitalism followed by a religious wave in the 1990s and the first decade of the 21st century. From this time period onwards it was rather global jihadi groups who resorted to violence because of cultural and religious motives such as challenges to their religious beliefs. It can therefore be concluded that ideology seems to be an intervening variable and that globalization and terrorism are somehow intertwined, albeit often out of different reasons for different groups.

Facilitator, motivational, and triggering causes

Facilitator or accelerator causes make terrorism possible or attractive, without being prime movers. Bjørgo mentions some explicitly as facilitator causes, while others could be easily interpreted as such. Some examples here are failed or weak states, due to the power vacuum, or very liberal democracies, both offering the opportunity of safe havens and bases for training and logistics. James A. Piazza (2008) analyzed in his cross-national time-series regression analysis of 197 countries from 1973–2003, *Incubators of Terror: Do Failed and Failing States Promote Transnational Terrorism?*, if failing states are more prone to host terrorist groups, if nationals of such states are more likely to commit transnational attacks, and if such states are more likely to be affected by transnational terror attacks. He found that states that are experiencing intense failures (according to the 2006 Failed State Index) are significantly more likely to be affected by terror attacks and produce nationals who commit terror attacks in other countries.

Some other examples of facilitating causes would be historical antecedents of political violence, civil wars, revolution, dictatorships, or occupation, because they involve a normalization of violence or increased credibility for the construction of grievance and victimhood, as well as socialization into "cultural value systems that celebrate martyrdom, revenge and hatred of other ethnic or national groups" (ibid: 259). Religion as a facilitating cause has been analyzed by Peter S. Henne (2012) in his quantitative study, 'The Ancient Fire: Religion and Suicide Terrorism'. He investigates a potential link between religion and terrorism and analyzes religious groups, non-religious groups, and unknown groups. Because of possible differences among the types of religious groups, he subdivides religious groups further into ethno-religious groups and fundamentalist groups. Ethno-religious groups are groups that have 'religious' and 'nationalist-separatist' ideologies. Fundamentalist groups are groups whose only motivating ideology is 'religious.' In his study, religious ideology is measured by the importance of religion in the grievances of a group and the means by which the actions of a group are justified. This is based on the ideological categories in the Terrorist Organization Profiles (TOP) of the National Consortium for the Study of Terrorism and Responses to Terrorism in the US. In fact, the majority of the attacks under scrutiny were conducted by religious groups and among these religious groups, fundamentalist groups were responsible for the highest number of deaths by suicide attacks. However, he emphasizes, it is not a feature of the Islamic religion as such but rather of ideologies based on religion in general that intensifies the violence of terrorist groups.

Another cluster of facilitator causes points to technological innovation in communications, transportation, and weapons. As we shall see in Chapter 12 on terrorism in time and space, innovation in weaponry has over the years been crucial in giving terrorist organizations some edge vis-à-vis the government. Transportations and communications have also always played a role and have become particularly obvious in the case of al-Qaeda and their 9/11 attacks, but also more recently with the rise of the IS and their extremely professional use of online technologies. Gabriel Weimann has researched the relationship between terrorism and communications for a long time. In his most recent book *Terrorism in*

102   *Determining* organizational *terrorism*

Cyberspace: *The Next Generation* (2015) he explains how the Internet and other forms of electronic communication might act as a facilitator or accelerator of terrorism. According to the author, the Internet is frequently used for psychological warfare, for instance to spread threats or announce attacks. As it overcomes editorial selection, it furthermore serves as a tool for propaganda to garner publicity. The dissemination of online magazines like the al-Qaeda-produced magazine *Inspire*, or the *Encyclopedia of Jihad* as well as the *Al-Battar Training Camp*—to name just a few—potentially allows the indoctrination of interested people by online self-radicalization and by training them in the production of arms. Moreover, some terrorist groups, like the IS, use the Internet extensively to recruit and mobilize their members via social media such as Facebook and Twitter and by roaming online chat rooms. But the Internet is also of special use for gathering data on potential targets. In this respect Google Earth proved to be a useful tool for Hamas to conduct attacks on Israeli towns. Finally, also fundraising as well as the planning and coordination of attacks are rendered possible online. The usage of proxy servers and encryption technology facilitates clandestine peer-to-peer communication and the planning and execution of projects. This was used extensively by al-Qaeda for the 9/11 terror attacks.

Motivational causes refer to the actual grievances that people experience at a personal level, motivating them to act. We do not dwell on these as they are better dealt with by theories working on the individual level of analysis. *Triggering* causes are direct precipitators of terrorist acts, momentous or provocative events, a political calamity, an outrageous act committed by the enemy, or some other event that calls for revenge and action. This can include peace talks which might motivate opponents of political compromise to undermine negotiations and discredit moderates (Bjørgo: 3–4). They are not direct causes of terrorism as such, but act in the background of underlying factors as a 'last drop.' A rather well-known example of such a triggering cause is the killing of the student Benno Ohnesorg in Germany in the 1960s (see Box 7.3).

Box 7.3 The case of Benno Ohnesorg

On 2 June 1967, a group of students of the social German student union demonstrated peacefully against the official visit of the Shah of Persia to West Berlin because of his dictatorial politics and human rights abuses in his country. The protesters were assaulted by both the German police corps and Persian secret service agents. As the situation heated up and got more violent, one of the protesters, 27-year-old newly married Benno Ohnesorg observed the rounding up of a group of protesters by police officers in a nearby street and followed them to check whether the police officers would hurt the students. In the course of the incident Benno Ohnesorg was ultimately shot dead by the police officer Karl-Heinz Kurras who—as was later revealed in 2009—himself was a member of the Ministry for State Security of the German Democratic Republic and who was embroiled afterwards in conflicting reports about the incident. This police officer was later discharged from murder charges, which led to the interpretation of the incident as a conspiracy of the state against the protest movement. The murder of a peaceful student protester by a police officer triggered the condemnation of the state and its officials as Nazi fascists and the politicization of the movement. According to the most influential historical account, this was the cornerstone, the precipitating cause or trigger event, for the formation of terrorist groups in Germany in the 1970s with the aim of counteracting state violence. The incident

> furthermore constituted the myth of the formation of the 'movement of 68,' the priming of red terror in Germany. Before that incident, socialist students protested peacefully, mainly for more participation in university committees or against the war in Vietnam and global inequality. But after the incident their activities got more violent. In fact, the date of the murder of the peaceful protester against arbitrary state violence Benno Ohnesorg acted as the eponym of the left-wing extremist terror group 2 June Movement. Moreover, it also had an impact on the formation of the RAF. One of its founding members was Gudrun Ensslin who witnessed the murder of Benno Ohnesorg.
>
> (Aust 2009)

Sustaining factors

The sustaining factors of terrorism are often different from those that provoked it in the first place because terrorists might change their purpose, their goals, or their motivations. However, they are still working in the same deterministic logic. Bjørgo (2005) lists various factors as potentially sustaining the occurrence of terrorist activity. Reprisals by the state, for example, often do not work against non-state terrorism. They often outdo each other because every side wants revenge to satisfy their constituencies. Terrorists often provoke the state to overreact in order to gain more supporters. Also, the main objectives might change in the course of time or lead to a prolonged fight when a group wants to release imprisoned comrades or sustain its members economically. Furthermore, criminal activities are often profitable and the need of terrorist groups to finance their political and terrorist campaigns leads them to continue their actions, sometimes even after they realize that their political cause is lost. Finally, for some terrorists, going back to mainstream society is not a viable alternative as they would face imprisonment or death (Bjørgo 2005b: 260–261).

Critical issues

The root causes approach clearly has the advantage of offering relatively easy and straightforward solutions for counter-terrorism. In principle, it would suffice to identify the causes of terrorism and then set out to eliminate them. As we have seen, however, the relationship between such causes and terrorism is not that straightforward. We have, on the one side, intervening variables, such as ideology, and on the other regional differences; what might act as root cause in one country, might not do so in another. These aspects in their turn raise some questions with regard to the objectivity of these root cause variables, which is precisely the 'pride' of this approach. It appears that the mere presence of root causes is not sufficient; what is also needed is the subjective interpretation of them as such. Apart from this aspect, Bjørgo himself lists a series of other critiques, such as:

- there is in fact a high diversity of groups and causes;
- the more general the causes, the less directly they are related to terrorism, since they can lead to terrorism, but also to something else, such as is the case of the media, modernization and globalization processes, which also have positive effects;
- the fact that some causes are in fact too broad and too remote from the actual acts of terrorism, which makes it difficult to show causality and induce change;

104 *Determining* organizational *terrorism*

- terrorists are considered here as "passive objects" of social, economic or psychological force;
- in some cases, terrorism does not directly emerge out of some root causes, but is the escalation of other existing conflicts (Bjørgo 2005: 2–3);
- dealing with root causes might not mean eradicating terrorism, because "terrorism is often sustained for reasons other than those which produced it" (Bjørgo 2005b: 261).

Process

As we have already seen in the chapters on individuals, deterministic approaches have a hard time with the idea of *process* because it is dynamic and also because it involves at least a small amount of individual agency to push this dynamic forward, whereas relationships of the type cause–effect are rather static and do not involve agency. Also similar to the case of individuals, in order to combine the core causal mechanisms of deterministic approaches with progression in time, the conceptualization of process here involves a *series* of cause–effect relationships.

As an example of a more processual take on root causes, Mohammad (2005) proposes for the case of terrorism in the Middle East a multi-dimensional methodology with two levels of causation: four independent variables (socio-economic situation, literacy rate, democracy, and extremism), and two intervening variables (perceived American political bias and double standards, and Israeli occupation and politics in Palestine). At the first level, numbers show a relatively high per capita income, low unemployment rates, and high levels of literacy in Kuwait, Saudi Arabia, UAE, Bahrain, Qatar, and Oman, whereas the countries at the bottom of the scale are Iraq, Yemen, the North African states, Sudan, Iraq, and Palestine and these show the opposite. These differences are of course problematic if the variables are supposed to correlate with terrorism in the whole of the Middle East. Also problematic are differences within the same country, such as in the case of Jordan, for instance, which has one of the lowest levels of per capita income, unemployment in the middle range, but the highest literacy rate. Despite the regional predominance of terrorism over the years, Palestine overall does not rank lowest and it has a relatively low unemployment rate. Finally, in order to make valid assessments on the role of these factors in determining terrorism, comparison with other regions and countries of the world would have been necessary. While these have been, as it were, absolute indicators, a measure of relative deprivation also appears in the text:

> Regardless of their level of economic well-being, all Arab societies experience a certain degree of social and economic injustice. In the vast majority of these countries, a feeling of inequality is felt among the general population. Even in the richest countries, such as Kuwait, there is a general perception of economic inequality whereby a large portion of the national wealth is believed to be enjoyed by a small elite at the expense of the majority.
>
> (Mohammad 2005: 107–108)

This might have been a sensible pathway to further investigate, especially given the importance afforded to relative deprivation in processes of individual involvement in terrorism. The author dismisses it, however, because terrorists themselves in Kuwait, Egypt, and Saudi Arabia do not refer to economic factors but to foreign policies. While this might be true, this kind of argument is hardly suitable for deterministic approaches, since it refers to individual subjectivity. Indeed, no terrorist would argue that their struggle is motivated by the fact that they are jobless or illiterate, but would always put forward political or social grievances. Again, this is not to say that subjectivity does not matter, or to dismiss intentional approaches, it is only to point out paradigmatic limits.

The following two indicators are less controversial and fairly consistent throughout the region. Concerning democracy, as the author points out, except for Lebanon, all the others score between 0 and 1 on the Polity III democracy scale, and there is generally a lack of political pluralism, free press, and political tolerance. Interestingly, increased democratization in Kuwait and Jordan did not reduce terrorism activity. This is consistent with the broader observation in the literature that socio-revolutionary terrorism tends to occur in transitional countries, whereas ethno-nationalist terrorism occurs in all regime types.

The last independent variable of Mohammad's study is the increase in the role of Islamic extremist groups, which is clearly observable in all the countries of the region, thus not necessitating evidence as to its existence. What is interesting to know though, and Mohammad does satisfy this curiosity, is the explanation for the rise of such groups and their popularity. This is, according to the author, the use of religious rhetoric; the offer of an alternative to the government which is at the same time also the only alternative, given the lack of democracy and pluralism; the offer of an explanation for the defeat by Israel, in spite of superior population and resources, which is that Muslims have departed from the true path of Allah; the failure of socialist and nationalist regimes in the region; and the victories of Islamist groups against the Russian army and the Israeli forces in Lebanon:

> The Israeli defeat of the Arabs in 1967 and the burning of the Holy Mosque in 1969 were both events that were seen to have occurred under and, by implication, as a result of a secular form of government. By contrast, the defeat of both the Russians in Afghanistan and the Israelis in south Lebanon was seen as a direct result of the power of the emerging Islamic movement ... Islam has been operationalized as an episodic discourse to diagnose and treat the political, economic and social defects of the Middle East.
>
> (Mohammad 2005: 111)

Given the inconsistencies in some of the independent variables outlined above, the author goes ahead and adds a second layer of causation: the American bias and double standard and the Israeli occupation, as the ways how Islamic activists rationalize their violence. We see here again the problematic insertion of agency and subjective assessments which rather point towards an intentional kind of approach. Supporting this initial impression is the further *strategic* rationale according to which these second layer variables work. Mohammad argues that terrorism emerges given the "absence of other means of expression, the imbalance in direct confrontations, and the wish to maintain mutual deterrents," as well as a religious rationality of divine gains (ibid: 112).

The last part of the chapter turns more 'rational' than the usual rational choice approaches we have witnessed so far. Mohammad describes the relationship between terror groups and the state and specifically Palestinian groups and the Israeli state as a 'zero-sum game,' where it is not possible to have a win–win situation, and a gain for a party is necessarily a loss for the other, making violence the only possible option. In this constellation, the core logic of action is retaliation, tit for tat, which necessarily leads to increasing violence in what could be depicted as a spiral of violence: "As the cycle of violence escalates, retaliation is designed to deliver greater impact than the action committed by the opponent's prior action" (ibid: 114). This leads to "even more technologically advanced and dangerous methods of deterrence and

106 *Determining* organizational *terrorism*

retaliation" on the side of the state, while Islamic groups, not being able to match this, resort to "non-conventional weapons," implicitly, as a matter of compensation for the strategic disadvantage (ibid: 114). Targeted assassination therefore "cannot be expected to bring about an end to the Palestinian struggle against Israel. Rather, it will bring about a further escalation of the cycle of violence" (ibid: 114) with increasing casualties, and an increasing distance between the parties, with diminishing opportunities for exit and negotiations.

Summary

This chapter has introduced the deterministic approach to organizational terrorism. It has dealt with:

- underlying structural root causes like poverty, inequality, lack of political freedom, and education etc. as agitators for organizational terrorism, as well as motivators, facilitator, and trigger causes;
- various studies which have empirically tested some of the root causes;
- some critical points outlined in the study of root causes of terrorism;
- an approach to modeling root causes in a more complex fashion than simple cause–effect.

Exercises

7.1 Compare and contrast the political, social, and economic situation of the countries where the Islamic State and the IRA emerged and formulate six variables in terms of preconditional root causes.
7.2 Analyze to what extent the Internet as a facilitator and accelerator has an impact on IS radicalization, communication, organization, and information.
7.3 In some accounts, explaining terrorism through root causes runs the risk of justifying it. What is your opinion?

References

Aust, S. (2009). Die verirrte Kugel. [online]. Available from: www.nzz.ch/die-verirrte-kugel-1.2647691 [Accessed 9 November 2016].
Bjørgo, T. (2005a). Introduction, in Bjørgo, T. (ed.), *Root Causes of Terrorism: Myths, Reality, and Ways Forward*, London/New York: Routledge, pp. 1–15.
Bjørgo, T. (2005b). Conclusions, in Bjørgo, T. (ed.), *Root Causes of Terrorism: Myths, Reality, and Ways Forward*, London/New York: Routledge, pp. 256–264.
Freeman, M. (2008). Democracy, Al Qaeda, and the Causes of Terrorism: A Strategic Analysis of U.S. Policy. *Studies in Conflict & Terrorism*, 31(1), pp. 40–59.
Gambetta, D. and Hertog, S. (2016). *Engineers of Jihad: The Curious Connection Between Violent Extremisms and Education.* Princeton/New Jersey: Princeton University Press.
Henne, P.S. (2012). The Ancient Fire: Religion and Suicide Terrorism. *Terrorism and Political Violence*, 24, pp. 38–60.
Hudson, V.M. and Den Boer, A. (2002). A Surplus of Men, a Deficit of Peace: Security and Sex Ratios in Asia's Largest States. *International Security*, 26(4), Spring, pp. 5–38.
Jahn B. (2005). Kant, Mill, and Illiberal Legacies in International Affairs. *International Organization*, 59(1), pp. 177–207.
Krueger, A.B. and Maleckova, J. (2003). Education, Poverty and Terrorism: Is there a Causal Connection? *Journal of Economic Perspectives*, 17(4), Fall, pp 119–144.

Lutz, B.J. and Lutz, J. (2014). Economic, Social and Political Globalization and Terrorism. *The Journal of Social, Political, and Economic Studies*, 39(2), pp. 186–218.

Mohammad, A.Y.S. (2005). Roots of terrorism in the Middle East, in T. Bjørgo (ed.) *Root Causes of Terrorism: Myths, Reality, and Ways Forward*, Abingdon/New York: Routledge, pp. 103–118.

Piazza, J.A. (2008). Incubators of Terror: Do Failed and Failing States Promote Transnational Terrorism? *International Studies Quarterly*, 52(3), pp. 469–488.

Urdal, H. (2006). A Clash of Generations? Youth Bulges and Political Violence. *International Studies Quarterly*, 50(3), pp. 607–629.

Weimann, G. (2015). Terrorism Enters Cyberspace, in G. Weimann (ed.) *Terrorism in Cyberspace: The Next Generation*. E-book. New York: Columbia University Press.

Further reading

Abadie, A. (2006). Political Freedom, and the Roots of Terrorism. *The American Economic Review*, 96(2), pp. 50–56.

De Mesquita, B.B. (1999). An Institutional Explanation of the Democratic Peace. *American Political Science Review*, 93(4), pp. 791–807.

Doyle, M.W. (2011). *Liberal Peace: Selected Essays*. New York: Routledge.

Lee, A. (2011). Who Becomes a Terrorist? Poverty, Education, and the Origins of Political Violence. *World Politics*, 63(2), pp. 203–245.

Li, Qu. (2005). Does Democracy Promote or Reduce Transnational Terrorist Incidents? *Journal of Conflict Resolution,* 49(2), pp. 278–297.

Mueller, J. and Stewart, M.G. (2015). Terrorism, Counterterrorism, and the Internet: The American Cases. *Dynamics of Asymmetric Conflict*, 8(2), pp. 176–190.

Newman, E. (2006). Exploring the "Root Causes" of Terrorism. *Studies in Conflict & Terrorism*, 29(8), pp. 749–772.

Rosato, S. (2003). The Flawed Logic of Democratic Peace Theory. *American Political Science Review*, 97(4), pp. 585–602.

8   Choosing *organizational* terrorism

Intentional approaches to terrorist behavior assume that actors consciously decide for the use of terrorism as opposed to other tactics, and that they are not pushed or forced in any way in this direction. Furthermore, this approach assumes that actors make this choice on the background of expectations of gain. For organizations, this gain usually materializes in strategic advantages vis-à-vis the government or enemy organizations. This chapter starts off with the work of the most prominent representative of this approach as it relates to organizations, Martha Crenshaw, tracing back the origins of her approach, and then engaging with the work of other scholars along the different dimensions of this approach: purposeful behavior, gain, and strategic decision-making. Following this, we discuss strategic vs. organizational models of organizational behavior. Similar to the intentional approach to individual involvement in terrorism, there is a strong focus here on actors and their decision-making process. Consequently and different to deterministic approaches in the previous chapter, scholars here examine the behavior of organizations rather than terrorism as a phenomenon; thus, analyses are carried out at the meso rather than the macro level. External factors are considered to the extent to which they influence this particular behavior.

Martha Crenshaw (1998), in her chapter, 'The Logic of Terrorism: Terrorist Behavior as a Product of Strategic Choice', elaborates on some of the advantages of seeing the behavior of terrorist organizations through a strategic lens. Among others, she notes that the calculation of costs and benefits behind terrorist acts has remained similar over time; although evolving in its manifestations, on the background of technological innovation or changing political circumstances, the strategy of terrorism has remained the same in terms of purpose and conception. In her approach, Martha Crenshaw draws in her account of terrorism as strategic choice on the work of Harvey Waterman (1981) in 'Reasons and Reason: Collective Political Activity in Comparative and Historical Perspective'. As the title suggests, this article did not deal at the time with terrorism in particular, but with collective political violence more broadly. Waterman situates his theory in the broader context of a debate between a preexisting paradigm which emphasized external factors and psychological frustration on the one hand, and rational, 'political' explanations on the other:

> The view that crowd behavior should be seen mainly in emotional terms has crumbled in the face of study after study of crowds that have acted in quite instrumental ways. Explanations of collective action in terms of social-psychological or socioeconomic variables have repeatedly been shown to be less apt than explanations employing the components of political decisions: calculations of cost, benefit, and risk, inspired by the provocations, inducements, and newly perceived weaknesses of political elites or by the

Choosing organizational *terrorism* 109

challenges of newly mobilized competitors for status and power. The common thread running through these shifts in intellectual fashion has been a reaction against the dominant perspective of the 1960s, which turned to psychological, sociocultural, and socioeconomic explanations for political phenomena, especially in the literatures of "development," "revolution," "violence," and "political behavior." The corrective has been, in various ways, an assertion of the primacy of politics in explaining political phenomena, even those involving political action by large numbers of people not usually involved in political affairs.

(Waterman 1981: 554–555)

Waterman makes a point out of the *political* nature of the phenomena that he studied, and that those political events were the outcome of *conscious* decisions. The reason why this, in a sense, sticks out, is the fact that at the center of political events are collectivities, which are organized in some way and have a leadership which will make "instrumentally rational decisions for action in the service of objectives collectively defined" (ibid: 557–558). In more basic terms, what Waterman makes us aware of is the centrality of human agency in political violence, which thus cannot be explained by natural causes. As suggested at the beginning, this is not to say that external phenomena (or root causes in our case) do not matter, simply that their effect is filtered through the machinery and logic of collective actors, in particular, the constellation of what he calls "resources and opportunities." The *balancing of gains and costs based on resources and opportunities* is the core of the strategic model:

people will be very attentive to the extent of their own resources, the cost of what they propose to do, and the probability of the success of their action (i.e., large, powerful collectivities will be more likely to take inexpensive actions against weak governments). This latter calculation, therefore, must be the principal focus of an effective theory of collective political behavior. In sum, it is not primarily society-wide changes in well-being, levels of frustration, or ideological conflict that explain the occurrence of collective political activity; rather, the explanation lies in significant changes in the resources and opportunities of the principal contestants.

(Waterman 1981: 558)

Transposing this pre-terrorism thinking onto terrorism, intentional approaches assume that: first, terror organizations are not pushed by some unconscious or environmental factors towards terrorism, but rather that they choose it *consciously and intentionally*. Second, they do so in expectation of a *gain* (which can be material or immaterial). This gain can be similar to the 'political objective,' but can also mean shorter-term political objectives. Third, the logic of their action is strategic, that is, they are looking to obtain a *strategic advantage* over their enemies, based on a calculation of costs and benefits and on the background of resources and opportunities. As we shall see below, this strategic logic is not always 100 percent tenable, as other kinds of dynamics intervene as well, namely the ones which are internal to organizations. That is, groups will not always choose the best possible option for the achievement of their objectives, but often one that accommodates some internal need. We then talk about an 'organizational logic' of terrorist organizations. For now, it is important to remember that this theory does not assume absolute and objective rationality. Thus criticism pointing out the skewed nature of information on which decisions might be made largely misses the point, since central to the theory is not the accuracy of decision-making or the

110   *Choosing* organizational *terrorism*

accuracy of the perception of resources and opportunities, but *that* decision-making takes place, and that it is based on the perception of resources and opportunities.

'Rational' choice, gain, and strategic decision-making

As Martha Crenshaw has noted, there is little evidence in support of terrorist *irrationality*. That, however, does not mean that their rationality is perfect, which has to do with the specific human perception and processing of external information. Not all alternatives are known, the perception of reality might be skewed, or there might exist various types of contextual constraints on the rationality of calculus. Here, a useful input is the concept of 'soft rationality' introduced earlier on in this book. That is, the kind of rational calculus we are talking about here is not the abstract, game theoretical type in ideal conditions, but rather the everyday rationality, with limited knowledge and subjective interpretation, but still guided by personal gain.

Individuals hardly ever evaluate gains and costs in a perfect manner, and organizations are in the end also just a conglomerate of individuals. The model of strategic decision-making has both "strong" and "weak" variants. The strong or "substantive" variant works on the assumption that strategic decisions are based on an informed and accurate world view (McCormick 2003: 482). In this context, one could predict terrorist activity quite easily by identifying a terrorist group's goals alongside the course of action that would trigger the highest return politically. However, the weak or 'procedural' variant assumes that strategic decisions are made rationally but on the basis of "incomplete reflections of reality"; in this case, the decisions taken tend to be suboptimal and predicting terrorist behavior is more difficult (ibid: 482). Neither groups nor individuals are in fact 'perfectly' rational mainly because human knowledge is limited.

Crenshaw (1998: 10) engages in more detail with the question of what terrorists want to achieve and argues that terrorism is a means adopted by extremist organizations who "seek a radical change in the status quo, which would confer a new advantage, or the defense of privileges they perceive to be threatened." Because they are extremely dissatisfied with the policies of the government, their demands are equally extreme and involve nothing else but the "displacement of political elites" (ibid: 10). This conceptualization relates directly to the starting point in resource mobilization theory in social movements, which identifies a structure of domination that is challenged by collective actors.

In the chapter on individual motivation we mentioned the *free rider dilemma* and its solution for this particular unit of analysis, namely the expectation of immaterial or material gain and the belief that one's own action will genuinely make a difference. In the case of organizations which are relatively small groups, there would be a group interest which makes coercion or selective incentives unnecessary to achieve the collective good. This is so because some group members might have in fact a high interest in achieving the goal, members of small groups would benefit more from the return, and furthermore, the organizational costs are lower in small groups; and finally, because it is easier to influence group members in smaller units.

In order to attain their objectives, terror organizations would weigh *gains and costs*, and decide to act depending on *resources and opportunities*. Martha Crenshaw has distinguished *three rationales for the strategic use of terrorism*, where the first two are more readily subsumable under 'resources.' The first parallels the usual statements of terrorists themselves, namely that *they have no other choice*. This is perhaps the more shocking argument, since it states that terrorism is in fact the logical choice to make given the various constraints

Choosing organizational *terrorism*   111

non-state groups are confronted with, such as lack of comparable military power or mass support. Terrorism, so goes the argument, is usually adopted following the failure of other means. The reason why terrorism is sometimes adopted only after having tried other strategies would be that organizations are either slow in realizing their limitations, or that they would need to first learn from the experiences of others before trying it out themselves.

The second reason for choosing terrorism is in fact related to the first and has to do with the inferior resources of the terrorist organizations compared to the state. In other words, terrorism is the *weapon of the weak*. In general, "small organizations resort to violence to compensate for what they lack in numbers. The imbalance between the resources terrorists are able to mobilize and the power of the incumbent regime is a decisive consideration in their decision making" (Crenshaw 1998: 11). The reasons why terrorist organizations are weak in terms of resources (including supporters) are multiple, such as, for example, that their ideology is not shared by the majority population. A second reason is the inability or unwillingness to mobilize mass support due to limited resources since, as we shall see below, the existence of grievance does not automatically lead to protest. In order for protest to occur, the masses must be mobilized, which involves organizational effort. In repressive regimes, the costs of both organizing an opposition and of individual participation are significantly high. Terrorist organizations active in autocratic regimes would assume that they in fact have a broad range of supporters who, however, cannot reveal themselves out of fear. While this might be true in some cases, in the majority of instances and especially in democratic countries, these beliefs are rather the manifestation of skewed perceptions of reality, or as Crenshaw calls them 'fantasies'; thus terrorist groups are often surprised to see that, in the end, the masses in fact do not rise to join them.

The kinds of resources that might be useful to terrorist endeavors are, according to Waterman (1981), for example: numbers, wealth, skills, cohesion, and allies (ibid: 578). He refers to an older sociological study 'Insurgency of the Powerless: Farm Worker Movements (1946–1972)', where J. Craig Jenkins and Charles Perrow (1977) account, for example, for how support from the political elite counted as 'resource' for the farmers' movement at the time and was eventually decisive for mobilization. This study also offers the possibility of contextualizing the rational model in the sociological debate of the time. Similar to how current intentional approaches contest 'root causes,' an approach that was forming in the 1970s and vaguely alluded to politics and political process contested the, at the time, 'classical model.' The targets of criticism were the same as now: relative deprivation and frustration, or the more elaborated 'strain theory.' To repeat a well-known mantra of the determinism critique in social movement theory—'grievance is ubiquitous, while protest is not.' Jenkins and Perrow note that:

> Indeed, it seems more plausible to assume that farm worker discontent is relatively constant, a product of established economic relations rather than some social dislocation or dysfunction. We do not deny the existence of discontent but we question the usefulness of discontent formulations in accounting for either the emergence of insurgent organization or the level of participation by the social base. What increases, giving rise to insurgency, is the amount of social resources available to unorganized but aggrieved groups, making it possible to launch an organized demand for change.
>
> (Jenkins and Perrow 1977: 250)

A third reason is related to the recognition and exploitations of *opportunities*. This implies instances where, for various reasons and usually for a short period, the terrorist organization

112   *Choosing* organizational *terrorism*

reaches an advantageous position in relation to the state. From a military point of view, a regime or a state force can be temporarily vulnerable to attacks. This scenario goes back farther than Waterman, who cites an even older work of William A. Gamson, *The Strategy of Social Protest* (1975). He found that "violence is instrumentally used and is related to the weakness of the target" (cited in Waterman 1981: 572). Waterman gives examples such as: economic or military disasters, divisions within the government coalition, lack of control over military or police forces, or loss of support (ibid: 576). Crenshaw gives the examples of the British forces after World War I, or the American forces in Beirut in the 1980s (see Box 8.1). Vulnerability can also occur in political or moral terms, or what is usually called 'legitimacy,' at the domestic or international level. Domestically, internal repression might have reached the fine line where suffering might supersede fear. The strategic balance of power can also alter when the organization acquires new resources such as finance, recruits, or new technologies. An important element that often gives terrorist organizations an 'edge' is technological innovation, such as was the case of dynamite for the Anarchists, or the one-shot sniper for the IRA. Here, of course, one might still inquire why necessarily terrorism might be used rather than something else. The implicit rationale of the use of terrorism here would be that, for the exploitation of this window of opportunity (or 'political opening' in Waterman's terms) as it were, terrorism is simply the most effective or the only means available at that time.

Box 8.1 The Beirut barracks bombings

Unlike the 9/11 attacks of al-Qaeda on the World Trade Center in New York in 2001 which provoked the US invasion in Iraq in 2003, the Beirut barracks bombings in 1983 by Hezbollah triggered the withdrawal of US troops from Lebanon and were hence a full success for the terrorist group. In the Lebanese civil war which lasted from 1975 to 1990 and in which Palestinian and leftist Muslim guerrillas battled militias of the Christian Phalange Party, the Maronite Christian community and other groups, a multinational peace force, including 800 US marines, was ordered to Beirut in summer 1982 to support the coordination of the Palestinian withdrawal. After several attacks on US personnel over the course of the year, two suicide bombers each drove a truck loaded with explosive power equivalent to in sum 21,000 pounds of dynamite into buildings of peacekeepers of the multinational force in Lebanon, killing 241 US and 58 French personnel as well as six civilians. The incident was the deadliest single terrorist attack on Americans prior to the 9/11 attacks. Four months later, President Ronald Reagan announced the end of the American peacekeeping force in Lebanon. The success of the Beirut bombings can be seen as having inspired the terrorist attacks of al-Qaeda on 11 September 2001 on the World Trade Center in New York in the pursuit of its goal to expel the 'Zionist-Crusaders alliance' from Muslim territory as elaborated in Box 8.2.

This resources and opportunities approach builds on the work of various social movement contributors to *resource mobilization theory*, among others, John McCarthy, Mayer N. Zald, Charles Tilly, and Anthony Oberschall, who in his turn used the work of economist Mancur Olson (see Introduction). In 1977, John McCarthy and Zald N. Mayer conducted, in 'Resource Mobilization and Social Movements: A Partial Theory', a case study on social movements focusing on American left-wing organizations. The authors assume that there is

Choosing organizational *terrorism* 113

always enough discontent in a society to support a certain movement, it only depends on the effective organization of a movement and the disposal of power and resources. They furthermore argue that grievances are not directly decisive for an organization to develop but only indirectly through their definition, manipulation, and creation by movement entrepreneurs. Social movement organizations, they argue, "must possess resources, however few and of whatever type, in order to work toward goal achievement" (ibid: 1220). Such resources can be legitimacy, money, facilities, or labor. They go further to say that "the amount of activity directed toward goal accomplishment is crudely a function of the resources controlled by an organization" (ibid: 1221). Mobilization is therefore:

> the processes through which individual group members' resources are surrendered, assembled, and committed for obtaining common goals and for defending group interests. Because mobilization is facilitated or impeded by the internal organization and structure of the collectivity, group structure is a major variable in the analysis. The extent and forms of collective action taken in pursuit of collective goals depend on levels of mobilization and on repertoires of collective action.
>
> (Oberschall 1978: 306)

Closing the circle, Anthony Oberschall (2004) refers explicitly to terrorism and argues in his work, 'Explaining Terrorism: The Contribution of Collective Action Theory', that terrorism is a form of collective action and that it can be explained in the same way as other forms of collective action, like social movements, guerrillas, dissidents, or insurgencies. He applies the four dimensions of collective action to terrorism and argues that each of the following dimensions is a necessary factor for a group to get active as a terrorist collective. These are: 1) discontent; 2) ideology-feeding grievances; 3) the capacity to organize; and 4) political opportunity. First, there has to be a widespread discontent and a lack of relief. Discontent furthermore demarcates a terrorist group from a criminal gang which only acts in the pursuit of personal goals. Second, there has to be an ideology that frames discontent into grievances and that must be spread widely throughout the population. It holds political elites responsible and justifies violence as a means to change the status quo. The legitimization of the terrorist cause is important as it secures the cover for the group among the population. Third, there must be the capacity to mobilize and organize to recruit new members, acquire funds and weapons, hide safely, coordinate, and communicate with each other. This, the author argues, is only possible though if the group is perceived as legitimate and not deviant by the population. Finally, there must be a favorable political climate, a political opportunity, and public support by allies or (foreign) states that facilitate the collective action of a terrorist group.

Strategic models

Considering the interplay of resources and opportunities on the one hand, and the achievement of the desired objectives on the other, scholars have also looked more closely at the strategic logic of terrorist organizations. McCormick (2003: 481) argues that in this logic terrorists would seek to use tactics that ensure maximum gain concerning their political interests and minimal material loss (ibid: 481). Terrorism is generally an inexpensive means towards generating great impact and attention from the media and target audience, whilst also engendering more active support from some aspects of society already sympathetic to the cause. McCormick (2003) outlines four steps of strategic terrorist actions and their

114 *Choosing* organizational *terrorism*

consequences: 1) an act is carried out against a particular target; 2) the media interprets and reports on the act; 3) the media's message is received and interpreted by the target audience; and 4) the terrorist group hopes that the target will respond in a manner that will further the group's interest. Whilst the terrorist group can choose how and when to attack, they have no control over how the act is interpreted by the media and how the target interprets it and responds to it (ibid: 483). Thus McCormick argues, strategic terrorism has a 'paradoxical quality.' Terrorist attacks may have a greater political impact than the cost incurred by the group, however, the implications and consequences of the attacks are beyond the control of the terrorists. Box 8.2 illustrates these points.

Box 8.2 Al-Qaeda's strategy

Two *fatwas* were issued by Osama bin Laden in August 1996 and February 1998, which are believed to outline the motivation for 9/11. Al-Qaeda's proclaimed 'struggle' is against the so-called 'Zionist-Crusaders alliance'—namely the US, Israel, and their allies. Within the two *fatwas*, Osama bin Laden calls on all Muslims to mobilize against this alliance and defend Islamic territory and holy sites, especially Saudi Arabia, the "Land of the Two Holy Places" meaning Mekka and Medina (Bin Laden 1996) as well as to fight against the American military presence on the Arabian Pensinsula as a whole and support for Israel (Bin Laden 1998). Thus, the stated rationale behind al-Qaeda's attack was to liberate Muslims from perceived Western occupation and retaliate for blood that has been spilled at the hands of the 'Zionist-Crusader' alliance. Rohan Gunaratna (2006) argues that al-Qaeda did not foresee the possibility that the US would invade Afghanistan in response to the attacks on 9/11. This is according to the logic that the US had withdrawn troops from three key areas after jihadi-inspired terrorist attacks—namely, Beirut following an attack by Hezbollah in October 1983; Aden following an attack by al-Qaeda in December 1992; and Somalia following an attack by Al-Ittihad in October 1993 (ibid: 306). As a result, after 9/11 Aiman al-Zawahiri justified an escalation of violence in his book *Knights Under the Prophet's Banner – Meditations of the Jihadist Movement.* Such escalations included: inflicting the maximum amount of casualties against the target; the need to carefully assess the method of martyrdom operations in order to impose maximum casualties on the side of the enemy and the least amount of cost to the mujahideen; the targets, type of weapon, and method used must have a great impact on the structure of the enemy, so much so that the enemy is deterred from imposing its brutality and arrogance further on Muslim people; and finally, focusing on the domestic enemy alone is not sufficient (translated from Arabic in Gunaratna 2006: 301–302). As Gunaratna points out, "Al Qaeda was founded on the premise that it will not compromise, however long it takes, however hard the fight and whatever the losses it suffers" (ibid: 307).

Andrew H. Kydd and Barbara F. Walter (2006) suggest in their study, 'The Strategies of Terrorism', that terrorists are too weak to directly impose their will by force, therefore they use costly signals intended to persuade their audience of the credibility of their commitment. In order to accomplish their goals they need to credibly show their commitment to two main audiences, also called 'the target of persuasion.' This is first, the enemy, the governments whose policies they wish to alter, and second, their own population which consists of their own supporters as well as out-group individuals whose obedience they wish to gain. These individuals are important as they provide resources to the group (like shelter to hide and food) and must obey social and political edicts issued by the terrorist group once it gains control over the population. Kydd and Walter assign five different strategies according to three different subjects of uncertainty of the terrorist group. Uncertainty means an insecurity about an actor's willingness to fight. It can, for example, be that it is unclear whether a group has enough power, or is trustworthy. Normally, adversaries could also talk about these uncertainties in order to avoid a violent conflict, yet sometimes actors have a strategic incentive to bluff. In order to influence the behavior of an adversary, actors send costly signals. These signals are so costly that bluffers and liars would be unwilling to take them. These signals are the five strategies: attrition, spoiling, intimidation, outbidding, and provocation. Each strategy aims to achieve one of these objectives of uncertainty. It can be visualized as illustrated in Table 8.1.

According to the authors, the most important tactic of terrorist groups is attrition, which can span several years. The rationale behind this tactic is to inflict serious costs to the enemy in order to convince him to make policy concessions. The higher the costs inflicted, the more credible the threat and the more likely the target will grant policy concessions. An example here are the attacks of Hamas against the Jews in Palestine. Exerting pressure increases the cost of occupation in human lives and makes it much more unbearable. The second tactic focusing on an enemy is spoiling, the sabotage of, for example, peace talks or treaties between moderate leaders on the terrorist side and the governments targeted. The goal is to foment mistrust between the two adversaries and to secure the failing of the settlement. Kydd and Walter argue that this tactic is often chosen by terrorist groups when their objective is territorial change. An example is the kidnapping of 52 Americans in Tehran in 1979 by Iranian radicals after a handshake of Iran's prime minister with the US national security adviser. The radicals saw the danger of reconciliation of the two countries and tried to prevent it by using violence. Regarding their own population as the target of persuasion, terrorist groups often resort to intimidation. This is akin to deterrence and aims to daunt the population not to behave in an undesired way, for example, supporting the adverse government. It is mostly used when the government in power should be overthrown or when social control over the population should be obtained. An example is the assassination and massacre of thousands of people by Islamist guerillas in the Algerian civil war in 1990s because the guerillas suspected the people of switching their allegiance to the government. Outbidding is a strategy applied when two or more domestic groups compete for leadership and the population is uncertain which group best serves their interest. An example is the competition between Hamas (a Sunni-Islamist terror organization) and Fatah (a political party) in Palestine for the support of the Palestinian citizens. Finally, provocation is used when their own population should be persuaded that the incumbent government is evil and untrustworthy. Through provocation they seek to provoke the government into a military

Table 8.1 The strategies of terrorism as reviewed by Kydd and Walter

	Enemy	*Own population*
Power	Attrition	Intimidation
Resolve	Attrition	Outbidding
Trustworthiness	Spoiling	Provocation

116 *Choosing* organizational *terrorism*

dispute that harms civilians within the territory of the terrorist organization. This should generate overall support for the terrorist cause, the overthrow of the regime, and territorial change, for example, to overthrow an existing regime and to establish a new one, or the secession from a state and the establishment of a new state, or the annexation of the disputed territory by another sovereign state. An example is the attacks of ETA in Spain. With their attacks they provoked repressive measures from the Spanish government against the Basque community, which in turn helped to radicalize and mobilize its members against the Spanish government.

Pape (2003) also elaborates on the strategies of terrorism. In his article, 'The Strategic Logic of Suicide Terrorism', he focuses on suicide terrorism as strategy and shows that it follows a logic, namely to coerce liberal democracies to make territorial concessions. He shows that this strategy in the past often paid off for terrorist groups. The author analyzed worldwide suicide attacks from 1980 to 2001 and examined how terrorist organizations assessed them in terms of effectiveness. He found that first, the majority of suicide terrorism is not the random acts of insane individuals, but rather they are aimed to achieve certain political goals and occur in clusters and campaigns. Once the goals are met—at least partially—the attacks are abandoned. Second, suicide attacks mainly aim to coerce modern democracies to make policy concessions. Third, in the past 20 years, suicide terrorism has been steadily rising because it has paid off. Fourth, more ambitious suicide campaigns do not achieve greater gains. And finally, to contain suicide terrorism one must reduce terrorists' confidence in their ability to conduct terrorist attacks. Pape explains that the coercive mechanism of suicide attacks works by inflicting so much pain on the target society that they demand their government to concede or provoke them to revolt against it. This works best in democratic societies as—through the democratic form of governance—they have a leverage to influence policy-makers. In the international political arena, states are able to use sanctions or military means to coerce other states to make policy concessions. Yet terrorists are much weaker and are not able to operate in this way. Therefore, they use terrorist attacks to achieve their political goals. In this case, the coercer is the weaker part and the target is the stronger one. Lacking other resources and opportunities, terrorist organizations use punishment to inflict so much harm on the society of the adversary that they concede and make policy concessions. The willingness of terrorists to die increases the coercive effect in that suicide attacks are generally more destructive than other attacks, they are especially convincing because they signal more pain to come, and they increase their credibility because the element of suicide implies that the attackers cannot be deterred. Pape found that nearly all suicide attacks in the period under investigation 1) occurred in an organized manner in campaigns, 2) had the nationalist goal to retain control over their territory through the coercion of foreign governments to withdraw their military forces, and 3) were targeted against modern democracies. The author notes that terrorists learned that suicide attacks as a coercive strategy pay off. In fact, in the sample under scrutiny, 6 of the 11 suicide campaigns led to significant policy changes by the target state. Because coercive success for weak actors is normally relatively unlikely, a 50 percent success rate is significant. This is why suicide terrorism has been on the rise. However, he also notes that if the political costs for foreign states are too high, they rather accept high costs than abandon important political goals. Goals central to the wealth or security of states are rarely abandoned as, for example, a loss of territory would very much weaken the economic prospects of a country.

Organizational models

While strategic models look at organizations very much like a 'black box,' others consider what happens within the organization as well. In other words, here, we not only assume decision-making, but also go beyond that to understand how decisions are being made. Crenshaw (2011: 74) finds that "it is through the decision making of organizations that social conditions are perceived, interpreted, and acted upon." One of the obvious assumptions of this approach, which also parallels the intentional individual approach, is that terrorist organizations are similar to other organizations. One of the indications for this is the fact that in most cases terrorism is only one of the tactics that they employ. More broadly, however, it is apparent that they display essential qualities which are similar to other voluntary organizations: defined structure and decision-making processes; members' roles are functionally differentiated; there are leaders with formal authority; and there are collective goals with respective collective responsibility (Crenshaw 2011). In building her argument of terrorist organizations as variations of 'regular' organizations, Crenshaw draws on James Wilson's work on political organizations.

James Wilson's book was originally published in 1974 as a pioneering work in the field. Before that time, organizations as an object of study were relatively non-existent, since their role in domestic politics was not considered important. On the contrary, scholars were preoccupied with the psychology of masses, individual leaders, and lobby groups. The focus on organizations came about with the background of mere facts—such as the (long) existence of social movement organizations, but also as a matter of logic; beyond the individual characteristics of any given individual in any kind of social structure, it was thought that mechanisms pertaining to the organization they belonged to should also be taken into consideration in order to understand their behavior:

> If one were interested only in learning all about priests, then individual personality, attitudes, and class background would no doubt be of primary importance in explaining differences in priestly behavior. But if one is interested in understanding the differences between the behavior of priests and sergeants, then personality or class would probably have almost no significance or at best a marginal one. What would be of overriding importance is how the Church and the army expect men called priests and sergeants to behave.
>
> (Wilson 1995: 8)

The content we have just read is very much in tune with the overall assumption that guides intentional approaches, namely that the object of their study is not something *sui generis*, but a type of more general phenomena. Wilson goes on to specify what it is about organizations that should be studied in order to understand their behavior, namely: internal processes, how they are formed, why people join them, how leaders and policies are selected, and the strategies they employ towards other organizations and the government (ibid: 9) The terrorism literature has preoccupied itself, more or less explicitly, with all of these facets, but in particular with organizational strategies and behavior more generally. Here we can outline *organizational survival* and *competition* as aspects that have particularly captured the attention of terrorism scholars.

Wilson (1995: 10) states prominently in his book that "Whatever else organizations seek, they seek to survive. To survive, they must somehow convince their members that membership is worthwhile." In other words, in order to survive, organizations must provide their

118 *Choosing* organizational *terrorism*

members with incentives. Crenshaw has also noted this, yet it is Max Abrahms (2008) who carried on the argument along the lines Wilson originally set out. He differentiated namely between 'goal' or 'rational' models and 'natural-system' models:

> In the goal, or rational, model, the organization is defined as a collectivity oriented to the attainment of a specific purpose; its ends are given or knowable, and its central internal processes involve 'decision-making'; its success or failure is judged by standards of effectiveness and efficiency. Its ideal form is the business firm as classically conceived, an enterprise seeking to maximize profits or to achieve a target rate of return on invested capital. In the natural-system model, the organization is seen as a miniature social system in which goal attainment may be but one of several functions, the maintenance of the system is the preoccupation of its executive, and conflict among members or coalitions of members determines whether and in what way external objectives will be sought.
>
> (Wilson 1995: 11)

Max Abrahms (2008), in 'What Terrorists Really Want: Terrorist Motives and Counterterrorism Strategy', makes a point of challenging the strategic model by advocating the natural-systems model. Abrahms argues that "terrorist organizations will routinely engage in actions to perpetuate and justify their existence, even when these undermine their official political agendas" (ibid: 101–102). Abrahms essentially contests the fact that terrorist organizations act 'rational'; what he actually means is 'strategic' with respect to the attainment of goals, and explains that in line with this model, terrorist organizations primarily work to prolong their existence: 1) by making demands and carrying out actions which target governments will likely not concede to; 2) by resisting non-violent means and participation in the democratic process; 3) by rejecting settlements that may actually further their stated political cause; 4) by stating a myriad of political goals and aims that can never be fully satisfied; 5) by carrying out anonymous attacks, which prevent the possibility of coercing policy concessions from the target government; 6) by targeting ideologically similar groups that fight for the same recruitment pool; and 7) by refusing to disband even after the group has proved to have been unsuccessful for decades or its political grievances have become moot (ibid: 102). Thus, according to Abrahms, political agendas and strategy become secondary to ensuring the survival of the social unit. The author bases his argument on empirical evidence that suggests that at the individual level, terrorists are attracted to terrorist organizations because they present an opportunity to "develop strong affective ties with other terrorist members" (ibid: 96). Thus, according to this logic, the organization continuously works to preserve this social unit and attract more members (ibid).

Although Wilson presents the two as alternatives, it soon becomes clear that the two are not mutually exclusive; indeed, members can also be driven by ideological objectives. Wilson differentiates between material, specific, and collective solidarity incentives, as well as purposive incentives. The purposive incentives are: "intangible rewards that derive from the sense of satisfaction of having contributed to the attainment of a worthwhile cause" (Wilson 1995: 34). And organizational behavior also pursues the attainment of those objectives, for themselves or as a function of survival and expansion. More importantly, Wilson's functional model does not exclude rationality and does not exclude strategic thinking—albeit of a less economically strict nature than Olson originally proposed. In consequence, Wilson dedicates significant effort to the account of how organizations strategically engage government, as well as in alliances and competition with others. The difference is that the rationale behind these moves are, in this case, not systemic, but a matter of 'domestic politics.'

Competition among organizations for limited resources is also something that Wilson specifically talked about. Wilson conceded that there is competition for resources—such as in the case of political parties for example, but argues that by and large it is rather low autonomy—creating a place for oneself, which leads to competition. Terrorist groups with similar stated political goals have oftentimes targeted each other rather than their shared enemy. McCormick (2003: 488) argues that in this context, terrorist groups "act as political interest groups" that "frequently compete with each other in radical rivalries for political market share." This leads to an increase in violence as each group fights for media attention and more recruits. Thus, decisions to act can be highly influenced by the need to eliminate other rivals as well as the state (ibid). One such example of intergroup violence can be seen in the case of Northern Ireland (see Box 8.3).

Box 8.3 Inter-organizational rivalry in Northern Ireland

In Northern Ireland, the divisions have predominantly been along ethnonationalist lines, namely, between the republican groups who claimed to represent the Catholic community and the unionist/loyalist groups who claimed to represent the Protestant community. For example, the Provisional Irish Republican Army (also referred to as the IRA), was engaged in a violent rivalry with loyalist groups, such as the Ulster Defense Association (UDA) and the Ulster Volunteer Force (UVF), where each group would attack civilians in stronghold republican or loyalist areas as well as key leaders of the groups. These attacks often mobilized previously unaffiliated citizens to join one of the groups. Thus such attacks caused a swell in membership of terrorist groups in Northern Ireland, prolonging the conflict and strengthening the organizations respectively (Phillips 2015: 65–67). Whilst inter-organizational violence between two different groups with differing political goals is to be expected, rivalries between organizations that shared the same goals were also commonplace in Northern Ireland. For example, the IRA had longstanding rivalries with the Irish National Liberation Army (INLA) and the Irish People's Liberation Organization (IPLO). The latter groups fought for more extreme demands than the IRA and actively sought to disrupt the peace process with the British (ibid: 67). Brian Phillips argues that new enemies provide new missions and goals for groups, which renews their "sense of purpose" and as a consequence contributes to the increased longevity of the terrorist groups (ibid: 66).

Mia Bloom (2004) has found ample evidence for the existence and consequences of inter-organizational competition; more than that, she has shown how this competition for market share and 'outbidding' even intervenes among existing and established terrorist organizations, out to win the support of the public. She investigates in her case study, 'Palestinian Suicide Bombing: Public Support, Market Share, and Outbidding', the shift in Palestinian public support for suicide bombings by radical Islamic organizations in the Middle East since the beginning of the 21st century. She argues that the attacks against the Israeli enemy serve as a method of recruitment for these organizations within the Palestinian community and give legitimacy to militant groups who compete with the Palestinian authority as well as with other militant organizations. Bloom found that while there was an absence of attacks between November 1998 and November 2000, all major attacks since then increased public

120 *Choosing* organizational *terrorism*

support for suicide bomb attacks and decreased support for the Palestinian Authority. She criticizes the spoiler and retaliatory approach of previous studies for ignoring the internal state-building process and the competition for leadership within Palestine. This, she argues, is in fact crucial for the explanation of the absence of suicide bombings in the mentioned period and their occurrence from November 2000 onwards.

Public support in Palestine for suicide attacks increased from a third in the first period from 1994 to 1996, to two-thirds in the second period after November 2000. The author ascribes this to different political factors in these periods. According to Bloom, the empowerment of the Palestinian Authority through the election of a council and the election of Yasser Arafat as president, the smooth transition to Shimon Peres as president of Israel as well as the Oslo process made the Palestinian population hopeful and confident of a peaceful future with their own statehood and triggered a reluctance to support suicide bomb attacks. In fact, when over 70 percent of the Palestinians had faith in the peace process, the support for suicide attacks fell to 20 percent. However, at the end of the 20th century, during his second term in office, public support for Arafat decreased steadily. The peace deadlock, corruption allegations against the Palestinian Authority, the Authority's poor record on improving the daily lives of the citizens, and economic hardship triggered a wave of support for militant Islamist groups. As Arafat and his monopoly of legitimate force weakened, several militant groups started to compete and outbid each other with spectacular suicide bombings in order to gain legitimacy and leadership. The support for these groups intensified further during Sharon's time as prime minister as he stepped up nationalist policies, counter-terror tactics, and operations against Palestine, removing any faith in a peaceful settlement of the conflict. During this time (after 2000), violence was stylized as the source of honor among the Palestinian population and sacrifice on behalf of the group was rewarded with social status. Moreover, bigger groups like Hamas acted as a sort of charitable organization with a network of social services. They provided schools, mosques, and clinics and supported families of martyrs financially. This further increased their popularity. Bloom also shows that the weakening of the Palestinian state authority by Israel to weed out terrorists was counterproductive and led to the emergence of even more terrorist groups.

While these and other parallels can be drawn between regular and terrorist organizations, the latter obviously also possess specific characteristics which involve specific dynamics and outcomes. According to Crenshaw (2011), these characteristics are: the *goals*, the *means*, and, related, the *situation of illegality* (or clandestinity) *which implies a constant imperative of secrecy*. The goals are "ambitious, calling for radical change in the distribution of power in society or challenging the legitimacy of existing political and social elites" (Crenshaw 2011: 69). The means are violence, and primarily violence that is different to "regular" collective violence such as strikes, demonstrations, or riots, but "specialized, selectively directed against the institutions, officials, and symbols of the state, as well as against social classes or ethnic communities defined as the enemy," such as "propaganda of the deed" or "coercive intimidation" (ibid: 69). Crenshaw further differentiates between two different types of terrorist organizations: groups which do not rely on a broad support base and have a simpler structure, and the ones that are offshoots of social movements or political parties, or part of a legal organization and can reach out to a broader basis of support. In both cases, the locus of operational decision-making is in small operational groups, and the overall organization needs to function in a decentralized manner, due to reasons of both security and efficiency. There are furthermore different degrees of underground: full-time and part-time terrorists, which reflects the kinds of operations they pursue. The ones requiring extensive advanced planning are usually carried out by full-time cadres.

McCormick (2003) argues that clandestinity has an effect on the rationality of decision-making processes. In isolation, the members might lose their sense of reality and the way they interpret their environment and their adaptation to it. This, in turn, negatively affects their strategic decision-making process. They might, for example, be unable to calculate the costs and benefits of an alternative course of action and their view of themselves, the enemy, as well as of the society might be flawed. They might furthermore see themselves as 'soldiers' fighting a 'fantasy war' against the enemy. This self-perception is then cultivated by further group actions, a process that is conceptualized as 'auto-propaganda.' Another negative impact on the strategic decision-making process might be that they have the illusion of being a defensive actor whose actions are being justified as reacting on—real or imagined—governmental excesses like the use of state violence. The rational decision-making process might also be flawed by the perception of a need to act instead of formulating their demands. More precisely, choosing to go underground often implies leaving the non-violent path behind, which in turn continuously forces them to act (ibid: 487).

Summary

In this chapter we introduced the intentional approach to organizational terrorism and have dealt with:

- the assumption that actors rationally and voluntarily decide to resort to terrorism based on expectations of gains like strategic advantages vis-à-vis the state;
- the core elements of the intentional approach which are: rationality, gain, and strategic decision-making or weighing gains and costs depending on their resources and opportunities;
- the differentiation between strategic models and organizational models. Strategic models focus on the strategy terrorists use to ensure maximum gain and minimal material loss. Organizational models focus on the nature and workings of the organization itself.

Exercises

8.1 What might have been the strategic logic behind the terrorist attack of the 1996 Manchester bombing conducted by the IRA?
8.2 Evaluate the rationale behind the terrorist attacks in Paris in November 2015 along the lines of the strategic vs. the organizational model.
8.3 Take the specific features of terrorist organizations according to Crenshaw and see to what extent they also apply to a right-wing terrorist group.

References

Abrahms, M. (2008). What Terrorists Really Want: Terrorist Motives and Counterterrorism Strategy. *International Security*, 32(4), 78–105.

Bin Laden, O. (1996). Declaration of War Against the Americans Occupying the Land of the Two Holy Places". In Rapoport, D.C. (ed.) (2003). *Terrorism: Critical Concepts in Political Science. Volume IV The Fourth or Religious Wave*. New York: Routledge, pp. 271–294.

Bin Laden, O. (1998). Jihad Against Jews and Crusaders. In Rapoport, D.C. (ed.) (2003). *Terrorism: Critical Concepts in Political Science. Volume IV The Fourth or Religious Wave*. New York: Routledge, pp. 295–297.

122 *Choosing* organizational *terrorism*

Bloom, M. (2004). Palestinian Suicide Bombing: Public Support, Market Share, and Outbidding. *Politicla Science Quarterly*, 119(1), pp. 61–88.

Crenshaw, M. (1998). The Logic of Terrorism: Terrorist Behavior as a Product of Strategic Choice. In Reich, W. (ed.) *Origins of Terrorism: Psychologies, Ideologies, Theologies, States of Mind.* Washington: The Woodrow Wilson Center Press, pp. 7–24.

Crenshaw, M. (2011). *Explaining Terrorism: Causes, Processes and Consequences.* Oxon: Routledge

Gamson, W.A. (1975). *The Strategy of Social Protest.* Homewood: The Dorsey Press.

Gunaratna, R. (2006). The Al Qaeda Threat and the International Response. In Rapoport, D.C. (ed.) *Terrorism: Critical Concepts in Political Science. Volume IV The Fourth or Religious Wave.* New York: Routledge, pp. 298–320.

Jenkins, J.C. and Perrow, C. (1977). Insurgency of the Powerless: Farm Worker Movements (1946–1972). *American Sociological Review*, i, XLII, pp. 249–268.

Kydd, A.H. and Walter B.F. (2006). The Strategies of Terrorism. *International Security*, 31(1), pp. 49–80.

McCarthy, J.D. and Mayer, N.Z. (1977). Resource Mobilization and Social Movements: A Partial Theory. *American Journal of Sociology*, 82(6), pp. 1212–1241.

McCormick, G.H. (2003). Terrorist Decision Making. *Annual Review of Political Science*, 6(1), pp. 473–507.

Oberschall, A. (1978). Theories of Social Conflict. *Annual Review of Sociology*, 4, pp. 291–315.

Oberschall, A. (2004). Explaining Terrorism: The Contribution of Collective Action Theory. *Sociological Theory*, 22(1), pp. 26–37.

Pape, R.A (2003). The Strategic Logic of Suicide Terrorism. *American Political Science Review*, 97(3), pp. 343–361.

Phillips, B.J. (2015). Enemies with Benefits? Violent rivalry and terrorist group longevity. *Journal of Peace Research*, 52(1), pp. 62–75.

Waterman, H. (1981). Reasons and Reason: Collective Political Activity in Comparative and Historical Perspective. *World Politics*, 33(4), pp. 554–589.

Wilson, J.Q. (1995). *Political Organizations.* Updated Edition. Princeton: Princeton University Press.

Further reading

Asal, V. and Rethemeyer, R.K. (2008). The Nature of the Beast: Organizational Structures and the Lethality of Terrorist Attacks. *Journal of Politics,* 70(2), pp. 437–449.

Eilstrup-Sangiovanni, M. and Jones, C. (2008). Assessing the Dangers of Illicit Networks: Why al-Qaida May be Less Threatening Than We Think. *International Security*, 33(2), pp. 7–44.

Hoffman, B. (2006). *Inside Terrorism.* New York: Columbia University Press.

Neumann, P. and Smith, M.L.R. (2005). Strategic Terrorism: The Framework and Its Fallacies. *Journal of Strategic Studies*, 28(4), pp. 571–595.

Opp, K.D. (2009). *Theories of Political Protest and Social Movements: A Multidisciplinary Introduction, Critique, and Synthesis.* New York: Routledge.

9 Relational *organizational* terrorism

We have examined in the previous chapters a series of explanations and models which looked at organizational behavior as a result either of some external factors or as a matter of strategy. We now consider approaches which conceptualize terrorism as perpetrated by organizations in the context of broader and dynamic processes of *interaction* between various actors. Similar to Chapter 6, we refer here to studies from the social movement research tradition, as well as socio-psychological scholarship which has produced similar or complementary concepts. Different to relational approaches to individual involvement in terrorism, we see here less determinism and more strategic elements and consequently more parallels with intentional approaches to organizational behavior.

Before engaging with the bulk of the literature in this chapter, it is important to make some notes about the critical position on this question. While critical terrorism scholars have to a lesser extent carried out case studies on the behavior of organizations and their resort to terrorism, they have fully acknowledged the work of traditional scholars who have engaged in research following some fundamental critical principles, such as the multi-level analysis and the attention to context. For example, they have argued that "From a critical perspective, a focus on local context is crucial, since events and behaviour only make sense within their local meaning and context, even if this is influenced by global and transnational dynamics" (Jackson et al. 2011: 210). They have generally been very supportive of the social movement research in this area, such as, for example, the work of Mohammed M. Hafez (see Further reading). More broadly, CTS scholars have also distanced themselves from deterministic approaches, while at the same time welcoming the inclusion of structural conditions in the analysis. They argue that "the 'root causes' approach can also be deeply problematic to the extent that it decontextualizes macrolevel factors and treats them as mechanistic manifestations of 'universal categories' obeying 'universal laws'. In such a framework, local meanings and dynamics can be lost, leading to a truncated and often flawed analysis" (Jackson et al. 2010: 210). More specifically, they add to the multi-level analysis the subjective dimension or 'subjective meaning,' which differentiates them from the 'typical' social movement scholar.

Relational approaches in social movements

Relational approaches to terrorism build in part on relational approaches to social movements, which, in their turn, are part of the 'contentious' research program. The latter was initiated by McAdam, Tarrow, and Tilly (2001) as a reaction to the lack of nuance within the classic social movement research program. Tilly (2003) took this further with particular application to

124 *Relational* organizational *terrorism*

violence. Contentious politics refers to "episodic, public, collective interaction among makers of claims and their objects when (a) at least one government is a claimant, an object of claims, or a party to the claims and (b) the claims would, if realized, affect the interests of at least one of the claimants" (McAdam et al. 2001: 5). The idea of the book was to show that various forms of contention such as social movements, revolutions, strike waves, nationalism, and democratization, involve similar mechanisms and processes (ibid: 4).

The authors involved in this research program had previously contributed to the 'political process' program. Originating from a structuralist tradition and having focused on a range of 'contentious politics' in Europe and North America, the authors describe their subsequent evolution as one where they "discovered the necessity of taking strategic interaction, consciousness, and historically accumulated culture into account" (ibid: 22). They go on to explain that social communication, social ties, and dialogue should be perceived "as active sites of creation and change" rather than simply through structural, rational, and cultural explanations (ibid: 22). As such, they shifted their focus of research from the more typical social movement variables (opportunities, threats, framing, and structures), towards *explanatory* mechanisms and processes—mobilization, actors, and trajectories (ibid: 32–34). Namely, the authors examine how individual identities transform, as well as the type of actors that engage in contention (ibid: 34). In methodological terms, given that historians were involved in the classic social movement research program, the case studies tended to involve dense descriptions with historical detail. A second wave of analysts then started to distance themselves from this approach and emphasized "dynamism, strategic interaction, and response to the political environment" (ibid: 15–16). The political process program traditionally focused on "claim making" used by individuals, which became known as "the repertoire of contention" (ibid: 16). These repertoires embody the various "culturally encoded ways in which people interact in contentious politics" (ibid: 16).

Drawing on the previous work on contentious politics, Tilly (2003) specifies this approach through the lens of political violence. Contentious politics:

> consists of discontinuous, public, collective claim making in which one of the parties is a government ... Collective violence does sometimes occur quite outside the range of governments; however, above a very small scale, collective violence almost always involves governments as monitors, claimants, objects of claims, or third parties to claims.
>
> (Tilly 2003: 9)

In the preface to the volume, Tilly outlines the background of his approach and its main tenets, including some concessions to determinism and rational choice. Specifically, Tilly seeks to "correct mistakes" and assumptions he made during the 1970s regarding collective violence. Tilly argues that whilst he still rejects the notion that collective violence can be explained through "general laws," he later acknowledged that a few causal mechanisms and processes may factor into collective violence as a whole. Prior to this, Tilly was rather of the opinion that, in the majority of cases, collective violence transpired as a "by-product" of negotiations that were not fundamentally violent in themselves. Tilly additionally states that his previous work tended to exaggerate forms of collective violence, which he would rather later refer to as "scattered attacks" or "broken negotiations" (ibid: xi). The causal mechanisms and processes that Tilly refers to are at a lower level and with variable geography, as incidences of collective violence that can have similar causes but function within various combinations and settings. As Tilly states:

"Collective violence resembles weather: complicated, changing, and unpredictable in some regards, yet resulting from similar causes variously combined in different times and places" (ibid: 4). Thus, pinpointing the causes, along with the various combinations and settings, would aid in explaining a variety of incidences of collective violence (ibid: 4). In this way, Tilly's renewed approach particularly looks at how patterns of social interaction contribute to different forms of collective violence and how similar causal patterns emerge in diverse ways often "producing parallel short-term effects but yielding distinct overall outcomes as a function of their settings, sequences, and combinations" (ibid: 7). Tilly's approach is dominated by relational mechanisms, but rather than totally discarding deterministic elements, Tilly argues that the effects of social interactions on collective violence work in conjunction with cognitive, behavioral, and environmental factors (ibid: 7). Moreover, such an approach seeks to examine what causes variation in political violence over time (ibid: 19).

Tilly differentiates between several types of collective violence, whereby terrorism is a type of coordinated destruction or scattered attack. He generally avoids using the term 'terrorism' due to its connotation as the behavior of someone else. Whilst he clearly sees terrorism as a type of violence as others in the critical studies tradition do, Tilly explicitly does not include structural violence, injustice, exploitation, and oppression, as this would prevent one from asking about the causal relationships between that and physical violence, as well as hinder the possibility to investigate the role of agents (ibid: 4).

Relational scholars working on terrorism have drawn on these insights and in particular the concepts of *process*, *mechanism*, and *context*. As an introduction to the presentation of some of these studies, the brief discussion of a series of 'dimensions' of inquiry, as identified by Bosi, Demetriou and Malthaner (2014) appears useful. We shall see that the mechanisms and processes detailed later on in the chapter can be meaningfully integrated under these dynamics. These are: dynamics of movement–state interaction; dynamics of intra-movement competition; dynamics of meaning formation; and transformation and dynamics of diffusion. The dynamics between the movement and the state is important because the state is the major target, and influences movement behaviors through its actions, which can be resistance, concession, or the institutionalization of demands; scholars assume that the state is the target of most protest actions. The classic kinds of development here are spirals of violence, but can also be of other forms—one can also differentiate among various components of the state, such as prisons or the police (see Chapter 13 on the effects of repression on social movements).

Intra-movement competition can lead to 'outbidding' and thus an increase in violence as Bosi et al. (2014: 8) argue:

> when competition triggers a process in which groups try to outbid one another in winning attention and support by taking on more radical positions or by using more militant forms of action, intra-movement interactions can entail mechanisms of radicalization that contribute to the emergence and increase of political violence.
>
> (Bosi et al. 2014: 8)

This dynamic can be traced back to the assumptions of the resource mobilization approach in social movements, which argues that movements depend on the resources of participation and approval by constituencies, which are limited. In a situation of competition, movements will try to outbid each other, through differentiation in goals and means. This can include an increase in violence or the adoption of more violent means. Competition does not always

126 *Relational* organizational *terrorism*

have to entail outbidding, yet it does depend on the overall development of the movement and the interactions with opposing ones and with constituencies, state repression, or the phase in the cycle of protest. Violent outbidding is not without risk, whereby increased violence could lead to approval from the core, but disapproval from the broader constituency and audience (see Box 9.1).

Box 9.1 Revolutionary violence in Italy and the loss of support from the radical milieu

In the late 1960s a cycle of contention emerged in Italy that declined after 1982. The main actors and drivers of the dissemination of violence were the two leftist clandestine organizations, the Red Brigades and Front Line. They sought a radical political change through proletarian armed struggle and drew heavily on support from their radical milieu. The radical milieu in Italy that supported these groups consisted of the leftist students' movement, workers (especially in large factories), and intellectuals. In the 1970s, Italy's social movements were revitalized through an economic crisis and the Communist Party's strategy of compromise and the Red Brigades and Front Line enjoyed some degree of consensus and support. Thousands of demonstrators invaded city centers, sabotage occurred, proletarian appropriations proliferated, firearms circulated, and violence against property and people peaked. Yet, as the violent fringes of these groups progressed in their escalation and targeted people and resorted to assassinations, they lost the support of their radical milieu. The watershed was mainly four traumatic events: the killing of a young proletarian student, the killing of an intellectual former partisan and father of a leftist militant, the killing of a communist worker, and the killing of Italy's prime minister Aldo Moro. The leftist radical milieu started to reconsider violent repertoires and even leftist magazines and newspapers that were previously sympathetic to contentious struggles started to self-critically analyze or gave room to critical comments. Four main arguments were rationally considered by the radical milieu with respect to the legitimation of violence. First, it was argued that violence would endanger emancipatory ends. Second, the values of democracy and anti-fascist resistance were irreconcilable with violence. Third, armed struggle was perceived as political weakness. Finally, military confrontation was perceived to be counter-productive as it silenced the grievances of the masses, shrunk mobilization, and discredited communist ideals. Criticism and de-solidarization followed and the entire left reacted against the extremist violence more strongly than ever before. For example, thousands of people attended the funerals of the victims, where workers chanted slogans against the Red Brigades, mass inquiries in terrorism were organized, and surveys with the opportunity to anonymously report terrorist events and identify people involved in political violence were disseminated.

(Falciola 2015)

The dynamics of meaning formation and transformation refers to framing, which we have talked about also in the context of individual involvement in terrorism. Frames identify causes, provide solutions, and, in the process, introduce aims and objectives that are usually new to the dominant political culture. In that context, we especially focused on how frames can persuade individuals to mobilize. In this case, the focus is on how the organization frames issues in order to persuade. Finally, the dynamics of diffusion refers to "a complex multidimensional dynamic," whereby strategies, beliefs, notions, and social and cultural practices are dispersed across time, space, borders, and societies, reaching out to a variety of individuals and networks (Bosi et al. 2014: 15). This dynamic is marked by innovation, learning, transmission, and adaptation (ibid: 15). Diffusion further depends on direct interaction, geographical proximity, historical interaction, and structural similarities (ibid: 15–16) (see Box 9.2 for an example of how this could work).

Box 9.2 Indirect frame diffusion in Turkey—from the Arab–Israeli War to the Anti-Sixth Fleet demonstrations

Alper (2014) illustrates in his work, 'Protest Diffusion and Rising Political Violence in the Turkish '68 Movement: The Arab–Israeli War, "Paris May" and The Hot Summer of 1968', indirect frame diffusion of anti-imperialist frames from the US to Turkey. At this time in the West, an anti-imperialist stance developed mainly because of the Vietnam War which, however, did not spill over directly to Turkey at the time. In fact, the anti-imperialist frame was channeled through other conflicts. In 1967, the first demonstrations by Turkish students arose in the context of the conflict over Cyprus and the rising tensions between the Arab world and Israel (which was supported by the US). This coincided with a routine visit of the Sixth Fleet of the US to Istanbul which provoked further anger against the US military presence in the Middle East as it cut off the Turkish navy on its way to Cyprus. What happened then was a merging by the students of the nationalist Cyprus cause with a universal anti-imperialist stance in solidarity with the Arab people. They protested against US support for Israel and against American imperialism in Vietnam. They successfully integrated populist national feelings into a broader criticism of imperialism. The ideational diffusion of the anti-imperialist frame was furthermore followed by a behavioral one, namely demonstrations in 1967 after the first anti-Vietnam demonstrations started in the US.

Mechanisms

Building on her previous work on left-wing terrorism during the 1970s, della Porta (2013) expanded her basis of comparison to include non-European Islamist movements and ethnic-nationalist groups, in what would become a comprehensive model of involvement in terrorism or 'clandestine political violence.' Della Porta works here with the concept of 'causal mechanisms' rather than causes, which are 'action-based explanations' showing how events usually generate an outcome. She defines mechanism as "chains of interaction that filter structural conditions and produce effects" and further "a concatenation of generative events linking macro causes (such as contextual transformation) to aggregated effects (e.g., cycles of protest) through individual or organizational agents" (ibid: 24). In constructing her theory, della Porta draws heavily on Tilly and the contentious politics scholarship, yet sets a series of markers of her own, which in turn, makes her work unique. First, della Porta considers all three levels of analysis—micro, meso, and macro—and how they interact along the process. Second, along the emergent and relational features of her model, della Porta also emphasizes its 'constructed' nature, and thus the importance of subjective perceptions in understanding the emergence of political violence.

128 *Relational* organizational *terrorism*

Tilly (2003: 19–20) defined causal mechanisms originally as:

> Mechanisms are causes on the small scale: similar events that produce essentially the same immediate effects across a wide range of circumstances. Analysts often refer to large-scale causes (poverty, widespread frustration, extremism, resource competition, and so on), proposing them as necessary or sufficient conditions for whole episodes of collective violence. Here, in contrast, we search for recurrent small-scale mechanisms that produce identical immediate effects in many different circumstances yet combine variously to generate very different outcomes on the large scale.
>
> (Tilly 2003: 19–20)

Mechanisms are less than laws aiming at "selective explanation of salient features by means of partial causal analogies" (Tilly and Goodin 2008: 13). Moreover, they are neither exclusive nor sufficient, but can be central and "robust" if, despite different situations and settings, they materialize in similar forms with the same effects (ibid: 14), or in other words, those events that: "1. Involve indistinguishably similar transfers of energy among stipulated social elements. 2. Produce indistinguishably similar rearrangements of those social elements. 3. Do so across a wide range of circumstances" (ibid.). Some of the repeatedly encountered mechanisms are coalition formation and brokerage (relating groups and individuals to one another).

Mechanisms have also been classified in three categories: environmental, cognitive, and relational—whereby this scholarship clearly predominantly talks about relational mechanisms. Environmental mechanisms "alter relations between the social circumstances in question and their external environment, as, for example, when drought depletes the agriculture on which guerillas depend for their day-to-day survival" (Tilley 2003: 20). Cognitive mechanisms "operate through alterations of individual and collective perceptions, as when members of a fighting group decide collectively that they have mistaken an enemy for a friend" (ibid: 20). Finally, relational mechanisms "change connections among social units, as when a gang leader makes a deal with a cocaine wholesaler and thus converts petty protection rackets into high-risk drug merchandizing" (ibid: 20). Tilly and Goodin (2008) elaborate again on these three types of mechanisms. In terms of environmental mechanisms, they point to external conditions and settings that may have an impact on social life. Namely, words such as "disappear," "enrich," "expand," and "disintegrate" that relate to individuals' environments can manipulate social interactions. Cognitive mechanisms are depicted through words such as "recognize," "understand," "reinterpret," and "classify," as they indicate how individuals and groups perceive changes. Finally, relational mechanisms are described through words such as "ally," "attack," "subordinate," and "appease" (ibid: 16).

An example of a relational mechanism would be boundary activation, which refers to a shift in social interaction so that they organize increasingly around an "us vs. them" boundary and differentiate between within-boundary and cross-boundary interactions (Tilly 2003: 20). In the earlier book on dynamics of contention, McAdam, Tarrow, and Tilly (2001) mention a series of mechanisms, such as competition for power, diffusion, and repression. Diffusion is the shift of similar forms and 'claims of contention' across different boundaries and ideologies. Repression refers to attempts to quell contentious acts by individuals or groups (McAdam et al. 2001: 68–69). The authors argue that repression has predictable consequences on threatened groups such as: strengthening their resistance; fostering a shift in tactics to avoid detection and deterring other groups from mobilizing and acting. Moreover, repression could be "selective" and isolate the more militant groups, or repression

Relational organizational *terrorism*   129

could be "generalized" whereby more moderates start to turn towards the extremists (ibid: 69). These mechanisms especially reflect very much in della Porta's work, as we shall see below. Another relevant mechanism for our discussion is radicalization, or as McAdam et al. put it, "the expansion of collective action frames to more extreme agendas and the adoption of more transgressive forms of contention" (ibid: 69, emphasis removed). The authors explain transgressive contention as interactions between makers of claims and their objects. Namely, when:

> (a) at least one government is a claimant, an object of claims, or a party to the claims, (b) the claims would, if realized, affect the interests of at least one of the claimants, (c) at least some parties to the conflict are newly self-identified political actors, and/or (d) at least some parties employ innovative collective action.
>
> (McAdam et al. 2001: 7–8)

Della Porta (2013) differentiates between mechanisms explaining the onset vs. the persistence of what she calls 'clandestine' political violence: escalating policing, competitive escalation, and the activation of militant networks; and then organizational compartmentation, action militarization, ideological encapsulation, and militant enclosure. In terms of the kinds of dynamics mentioned earlier, the mechanisms approached here especially deal with dynamics of movement–state interaction, dynamic of intra-movement competition, and dynamics of meaning formation and transformation.

Escalating policing essentially summarizes the interaction between social movements and the state and is in effect the central explanatory mechanism for the emergence of clandestine political violence. In more positivistic terms, this would translate to the assumption that state repression causes terrorism. Bearing in mind all the caveats that we have discussed so far, such a simplistic cause–effect relationship is unlikely. However, it still remains a fact that state repression provides the initial push and further sustains the spiral of violence eventually driving groups underground. Thus:

> political violence throughout the world is intertwined with state responses to social movements in a sort of macabre dance. A mechanism of escalating policing can be identified at the onset of clandestine political violence in both democratic and authoritarian regimes. In the cases analyzed in this text, a reciprocal adaptation brought about an escalation of protest forms and approaches to policing. Policing was in fact perceived as tough and, especially, indiscriminate and unjust; transformative repressive events contributed to justifying violence and pushing militant groups toward clandestinity.
>
> (della Porta 2013: 33)

Della Porta goes on to argue that the protest becomes further radicalized mainly due to policing (ibid: 36). This mechanism was indeed first developed drawing on the developments associated with left-wing terrorism in the 1970s and it could also credibly be applied to ETA and Islamist movements in Egypt. When discussing the case of al-Jamaa, della Porta demonstrates an apt example for this mechanism within the Salafist spectrum. Namely that repression of the Muslim Brotherhood and its subsequent transformation towards using peaceful means of protest strengthened al-Jamaa as the more radical activists started to turn to militancy and action as a way to reach their political goals (ibid: 58). The complex account of how this mechanism impacts radicalization is very convincing and the examples brought

130 *Relational* organizational *terrorism*

forward are equally so. Repression acts in various ways to foster radicalization by discouraging moderates, radicalizing the moderates, cause spirals of violence or "reciprocal adaptation of tactics" (ibid: 68), the incidence of transformative and emotionally charged events, cognitive effects confirming the propaganda, or the perception that there is no other way out.

The second mechanism at the onset phase of clandestine political violence is *competitive escalation*; this mechanism is in effect similar in nature to the first one, as it refers to the increase and intensification of violence, yet it differs in terms of actors. It is not a confrontation between the movement and the state, but between the movement and opposing movements, and between parts of the same movement. As regards to the latter, della Porta concludes in relation to her cases that "the radicalization of repertoires of action was, in some movements, a competitive asset in intermovement relations" (ibid: 112). As organizations competed for support of the same constituencies, imitation, and outbidding took place.

With the *activation of militant networks*, della Porta addresses a central mechanism in radicalization; namely the continuity of social networks from earlier, less radical stages, through militancy and ultimately terrorism. In the conclusion of her case studies on this mechanism, della Porta notes first of all that networks of friends, relatives, and political peer groups are likely to highly influence political choices—radical or moderate. Thus, participation in groups with links to radical networks increases the chances of an individual being recruited into a radical movement. Specifically, in all four types of clandestine violence della Porta found that "peer groups to which individuals belonged played a very important role in determining their successive political choices (for instance, joining a more structured movement's organization), particularly in passages from low-risk to high-risk activism" (ibid: 143). Moreover, friendship often fortified the level of commitment and vice-versa. These relational processes strengthened underground groups and also created new ones (ibid: 143–4).

A further mechanism is *organizational compartmentalization*, which refers to parts of the movement splitting, going underground, and becoming more violent. Della Porta argues that splinter groups exploit environments favorable to militancy and "undergo further radicalization and eventually create new resources and occasions for violence. These radical groups, in other words, themselves become agents, or entrepreneurs, for the propagation of violence" (ibid: 147). In della Porta's analysis, organizational compartmentalization occurs as an adaptation to increasing repression and decreasing support. Aside from accounting for this dynamic, della Porta also takes the opportunity to position herself with regard to the logic of action of such organizations, namely between ideological determinism and instrumentalism, or the strategic approach. While rejecting the fact that organizational behavior might be determined by ideological content, she acknowledges the effect of internal norms on this behavior, as interests are cognitively constructed and strategic choices are both normatively constrained and dependent on the ways opportunities and resources are perceived (ibid: 148). In recognizing restricted strategic choices, della Porta draws on the broader neo-institutionalist scholarship and considers organizations as "socializing agents and as producers of norms" (ibid: 149). Moreover, the author offers here a preview of the following mechanisms: *action militarization* and *ideological encapsulation*. Violence increases and evolves from discriminate to indiscriminate violence, again under the effects of repression, but also as a consequence of internal competition for leadership, while ideology becomes increasingly obscure and an instrument for internal consumption. In describing action militarization, della Porta formulates this evolution as a transition from propaganda-oriented actions to actions which were inner-oriented and simply aimed at organizational survival (against the state)—in other words, the logic of propaganda vs. the logic of survival. Specifically, della Porta argues that "in all of the four types of clandestine violence ... the more isolated the groups and the stronger the repression, the more they gave up propaganda aims and focused on organizational survival" (ibid: 178). This mechanism manifests itself through increasing lethality and brutality with attacks becoming (more) indiscriminate; this is again traced back to decreasing support and increasing repression: "although action tended initially to propagate the aims of the clandestine organizations in the broader population, with the passing of time – and rising and more focused repression – all the groups concentrated their attention on the internal war with the state" (ibid: 202). Ideological encapsulation designates a thinking characterized by Manichean world views, overly simplified generalizations, fear of contamination, essentialization of violence as valuable per se, and so on.

Process

Unlike the work on mechanisms, process in relational approaches has been developed to a lesser extent. The difference between mechanisms and processes is highlighted by Tilly and Goodin (2008); namely mechanisms are "a delimited class of events that change relations among specified sets of elements in identical or closely similar ways over a variety of situations," whereas processes are "frequently occurring combinations of sequences of mechanisms" (ibid: 15) Bosi et al. (2014) carried out some initial work on this in relation to 'radicalization'; drawing on more general sociological understandings of process, the authors argue that radicalization processes distinguish themselves through the presence of the element of violence, which is both the outcome and the constitutive part of the process (ibid: 4); there are various types of violence and they relate and are part of "broader political struggles" (ibid: 5). The authors find that by studying radicalization through the lens of contentious politics, there is a much-needed emphasis on processes, which often entails "causal efficacy" and the ability to interpret similar causal patterns (ibid: 4). Unlike other accounts on process, we also have here a concrete and clear account of the authors' under-standing of process and the subsequent explanation, which is describing: "the unfolding of an actual process is to explain it" (ibid: 4). A social process is a sequence of events that happen over time, are in one way or another linked together, and lead to a transformation. Processes "emerge" and this emergence develops as "fluid causality," rather than "billiard ball causality" (ibid). As such, the focus is on the process of how outcomes materialize. The authors add that there is a general acceptance that outcomes may be influenced by a variety of causes. At the same time, room needs to be left for contingency, which implies the fact that the order of happenings and the timing are both very important (ibid). In thinking about process, the sequence and ordering of events is important, timing is important, and turning points occur.

Alimi, Bosi and Demetriou (2012) develop in their work, 'Relational Dynamics and Processes of Radicalization: A Comparative Framework', an explanatory framework for the comparative study of radicalization. They define radicalization as "the development of extreme ideology and/or the adoption of violent forms of contention, including categorical indiscriminate violence (or terrorism) by a challenging group" (ibid: 7). They draw on social movement theories and contentious politics and focus on a relational approach as it "depicts social reality in dynamic, continuous and processual terms, and sees relations between social terms and units as preeminently dynamic in nature, as unfolding, ongoing processes rather than as static ties among inert substances" (ibid: 7 following Emirbayer 1997). It is assumed

132 *Relational* organizational *terrorism*

that strategy, rationality, and values as well as norms are embedded in space and time and are important in the context of social relations. Structures are assumed to be "arenas of interactions" for groups with their counterparts. They emphasize that the advantage of their framework is the robust explanation that stems from the interplay of relational mechanisms. Following Tilly and Tarrow (2007) mechanisms are considered to be the key units of analysis and comparison and are defined as sorts of events that alter the relations among elements in a variety of situations. They are concatenated and form a process. Their relational mechanisms are a process constituted by relational, cognitive, and environmental mechanisms and can be broken down into sub-mechanisms. The authors propose that episodes of radicalization unfold in four arenas of interaction that are interrelated. These arenas of interaction correspond to four general relational mechanisms which do not though include all drivers of radicalization.

The first arena lies between the movement and the political environment. The political environment has an influence on the actions of social movements and is considered by movements when they develop their strategy. This arena is comprised by relations with the state and interstate institutions like international organizations, non-state elite centers of power (i.e. parties, the media), and with symbolic configurations (i.e. public opinion). The crucial general mechanism active in this arena is that of *opportunity and threat spirals.* These are actions, decisions, events, and developments that positively or negatively change the political conditions for a movement and influence its strategy of contention. What matters here is the change of the strategic positions of the movement vis-à-vis its political environment and the influence on its political leverage. As an example the authors mention court legislation that might change the space of action of the group by repositioning it in the political environment.

The second arena is the intra-movement interactive arena with opposition movements as the field of actors. Such opposition movements have common beliefs and interests, interact informally with each other, and affect each other's strategy. Movements can vary on goals, modes of action, and ideology. Internal dynamics, power relations, or the division of labor may induce tensions among movement actors. Here the central mechanism is *competition for power* among the actors that may undercut or complement each other's strategies in the battle for power and support of adherents. This mechanism is not limited to external actors but also comprises internal political competitors.

The third arena is the interaction between movement activists and security forces. This is different from the arena between movements and the political environment insofar as the security forces actually engage with movement activists on the ground. The central mechanism here is *outbidding*. This refers to action–counteraction dynamics that reciprocally raise the stakes of the actors in response to each other. This may be limited to negotiated management but might also shift to violence. Its mechanism affects the prevailing tactics (disruptive, conventional, or violent).

The last arena is the interaction of a movement with a rival movement or a counter-movement. This often occurs in times of ethnic contentions where social boundaries are subject to activation and mobilization. The central mechanism for radicalization here is *object shift* and occurs when new claims of a movement pertain to a counter-movement complementing existing claims aimed at authorities. A counter-movement that has a clear agenda of inflicting damage on the other movement opens up a new front of contention which heavily influences the process of radicalization.

The authors emphasize that it is the joint influence of each of the mechanisms that reciprocally influences each other and drives the radicalization process.

Context

Given the strong focus on interaction, for relational approaches context is paramount, however, not as an independent variable like in determinist approaches, and also not simply as a matter of detailed description of the surrounding environment. Tilly and Goodin (2008) situate themselves between positivism and constructivism, or between parsimony and post-modernism, laws and hermeneutics, reductionism and holism; in particular:

> Against the most reductive versions of parsimony, it argues that attention to context does not clutter the description and explanation of political processes, but, on the contrary, promotes systematic knowledge. Against the most exaggerated versions of postmodernism, it argues that context and contextual effects lend themselves to systematic description and explanation, hence their proper understanding facilitates discovery of true regularities in political processes. Between those extreme positions, it examines the multiple ways in which context affects *analysts' understanding of political processes*, the *extent and sort of evidence* available concerning political processes, and the very *operation of political processes*.
>
> (Tilly and Goodin 2008: 6, emphasis added)

For Tilly and Goodin, context is pieces of the puzzle, aspects which can be historical or political, for example, and which explain differences between cases, cognitive frames, or practices. They, however, do not elaborate further and understand context as something that has an influence on the mechanisms. In the attempt to develop middle-range theories and explain nuances of the mechanisms in a systematic way, they take contextual effects as not purely incidental. There are different historical, cultural, and technological settings, wherein a number of patterns and outcomes can be comprehended—these are, as the authors explain, the "rules of the game" (ibid: 25).

Bosi et al. (2014) emphasize what they call the "contextualization of violence," but not in the sense of determining factors. Rather, the argument is that political violence emerges within and out of broader political, social, and cultural conflicts. They argue that violent actions can be contextualized in three respects. First, it is acknowledged that violence as a form of confrontation is only one form within a wider repertoire of actions and strategies. When groups choose to act, they decide not only the action that matches their goals and identity orientation, but also one that corresponds to changing environments as well as the actions of their enemies. This indicates the agency of the actors involved in radicalization. Second, it is acknowledged that militant groups are embedded in a field of various actors involved in the conflict and this shapes their evolution. This relational field includes state agents, audiences, counter-movements, and other groups that belong to the movement. Finally, it is acknowledged that violent interactions occur within a wider process of political contention. This means that interactions are influenced by events and causal dynamics that are bounded together through their connection to the state that counter-positions itself. To recap, contextualization means that political violence is considered to be located "within broader political processes, relational fields, and repertoires of actions" (ibid: 2).

Social movement relational approaches to the explanation of organizational involvement in terrorism bear a series of advantages and disadvantages. Tracing back and connecting terrorism to other types of political violence, as well as setting terrorism in the context of broader protest movements and events, is useful regarding the understanding of its emergence and dynamics. At the same time, and precisely given this genealogy, there is the difficulty of distinguishing specificities of terrorism, finding mechanisms and processes which are specific to terrorism, which would be necessary in order to explain why this type of violence, as opposed to others, was chosen. This approach has clearly carried out the most elaborated account of organizational processes seen as interactions. However, given the dense description specific to this approach, it is also difficult to transpose the results of research into practical solutions. More broadly, we can observe that the *concepts* of mechanisms and processes are not yet ripe. Indeed, they proliferate with each new author; one and the same content is at times used as mechanisms, and at times as process. Another issue is the contribution of history to the social movements scholarship: on the one hand this is extremely beneficial for depth and detail; on the other hand this prevents generalizations, as often scholars tend to be case study specialists. Another problem here is the difficulty of entirely linking and integrating historical description and detail with analytical concepts.

Organizations in social psychology

Apart and beyond the social movement scholarship, social psychology has also done work in explaining group behavior in ways that fit the relational approach very well. In Chapter 6 we included some radicalization mechanisms operating at the individual level and conceptualizing the effect of the group on individual behavior. In terms of broader dynamics, we can note, for example, the parallel to intra-movement competition. McCauley and Moskalenko (2008), in 'Mechanisms of Political Radicalization: Pathways Toward Terrorism', argue that groups radicalize through several different mechanisms. Some of the 'mechanisms' they find are very similar in nature to the ones proposed by social movement scholars. At the group level, the relevant mechanisms are: "competition for the same base of support"; "competition with state power—condensation"; and "within-group competition—fissioning" (ibid).

The authors state that group radicalization *in competition for the same base of support* occurs when groups conduct more radical actions in order to increase the support of a base of sympathizers for which they compete with other groups. Such competition can, for example, be observed when more than one group claims responsibility for a terrorist attack. Groups believe that in becoming more radical, they have a higher status which in turn might attract new followers. However, if a group becomes too radical it might also lose its base of support. An example is the killing of Catholics by Catholics or Protestants by Protestants during the civil war in Northern Ireland. About a quarter of the killings during that war were the result of a competition for sympathizers among like-minded groups. The dynamics work as such because the threat from in-group competitors is similarly perceived as the threat from an out-group enemy. This creates cohesion, results in high pressures for conformity and sanctions against deviants.

Group radicalization *in competition with state power* as another form of radicalization has been in the focus of research here. It occurs when a group that displays itself publicly, for example, through protest marches, sit-ins, or other forms of disobedience, provokes state sanctions such as, for example, police responses against the activists. If the sanctions are indiscriminate or include some sort of abrogation of civil or human rights, the sympathy for the victims of state repression might increase, which in turn potentially leads to mobilization. In this respect another dynamic might be at work as well, namely *condensation.* Some of the individuals directly involved in the disobedience might give up, as for them the costs may be too high. However, activists that are not deterred, often those that bring a moral frame or personal grievance, might increase their commitment and escalate their action against the state. The interaction between the state and the non-state group results in an increased radicalization and escalation of violence. At the same time, individuals whose radicalization is not so advanced, bail out. The self-selected core of the non-state group condensates to a highly radicalized group that goes underground as a terrorist cell. A premise of radicalization by condensation is intense affective ties between group members. If one of them suffers because of state reaction (e.g. imprisonment or even death), others feel anger, become more committed, and seek to revenge the loss of the comrade. Finally, group radicalization through *within-group competition*, also called *fissioning*, is a competition for status as represented in social comparison theory and might lead to intense conflict. The personal and the political conflate and differences in political opinions lead to personal animosities or the other way around. Intra-group conflicts because of competition often lead to splits and fissions of a terrorist group into several groups. It may even trigger the desire to torture or obliterate a group member. The dynamic behind fissioning is increased cohesion which creates high pressure to agree within a group. Single individuals might not be strong enough to resist the pressure of unanimous peers, yet a group of like-minded people might, and in turn potentially face obliteration or expulsion (ibid: 424–426).

Summary

This chapter has discussed relational approaches to organizational engagement in terrorism and we have dealt with:

* the main features of these approaches, such as, for example, the emphasis on process as a matter of interaction and the genealogy of terrorism in broader phenomena of contention;
* the features of social movement relational approaches to terrorism and their origins in social movement contentious politics literature;
* dynamics of movement–state interaction, dynamics of intra-movement competition, dynamics of meaning formation and transformation, and dynamics of diffusion;
* conceptualizations of process, mechanism, and context;
* socio-psychological contributions which largely parallel social movement relational concepts.

Exercises

9.1 Do you think relational approaches are suitable to explain the emergence of terrorism?
9.2 Do you see any parallels between relational and intentional approaches?
9.3 What elements of context are most influential for the behavior of terrorist organizations?

References

Alimi, E.Y., Bosi, L. and Demetrious, C. (2012). Relational Dynamics and Processes of Radicalization: A Comparative Framework. *Mobilization: An International Journal*, 17(1), pp. 7–26.
Alper, E. (2014). Protest Diffusion and Rising Political Violence in the Turkish '68 Movement: The Arab-Israeli War, "Paris May" and The Hot Summer of 1968. In Bosi, L., Demetriou, C. and Malthaner, S. (eds) *Dynamics of Political Violence. A Process-Oriented Perspective on Radicalization and the Escalation of Political Conflict.* Surrey: Ashgate, pp. 255–274.

136 *Relational* organizational *terrorism*

Bosi, L., Demetriou, C. and Malthaner, S. (eds) (2014). *Dynamics of Political Violence. A Process-Oriented Perspective on Radicalization and the Escalation of Political Conflict*. Surrey: Ashgate.

della Porta, D. (2013). *Clandestine Political Violence*. Cambridge: Cambridge University Press.

Emirbayer, M. (1997). Manifesto for a Relational Sociology. *American Journal of Sociology*, 103(2), pp. 281–317.

Falciola, L. (2015). From Legitimation to Rejection of Violence: The Shifting Stance of the Radical Milieu in Italy during the 1970s. In Bosi, L., Dochartaigh, N.O. and Pisoiu, D. (eds) *Political Violence in Context. Time, Space and Milieu*. Colchester: ECPR Press, pp. 253–276.

Jackson, R., Jarvis, L., Gunning, J. and Breen Smyth, M. (2011). *Terrorism. A Critical Introduction*. New York: Palgrave Macmillan.

McAdam, D., Tarrow, S. and Tilly, C. (2001). *Dynamics of Contention*. Cambridge: Cambridge University Press.

McCauley, C. and Moskalenko, S. (2008). Mechanisms of Political Radicalization: Pathways Toward Terrorism. *Terrorism and Political Violence*, 20, pp. 415–433.

Tilly, C. (2003). *The Politics of Collective Violence*. Cambridge: Cambridge University Press.

Tilly, C. and Goodin, R.E. (2008). It Depends. Introduction. In Goodin, R.E. and Tilly, C. (eds) *The Oxford Handbook of Contextual Political Analysis*. Oxford: Oxford University Press, pp. 3–32.

Tilly, C. and Tarrow, S.G. (2007). *Contentious Politics*. Boulder/London: Paradigm Publishers.

Further reading

Brym, R. and Araj, B. (2006). Suicide Bombing as Strategy and Interaction: The Case of the Second Intifada. *Social Forces*, 84(4), pp. 1969–1986.

Hafez, M.M. (2003). *Why Muslims Rebel: Repression and Resistance in the Islamic World*. Boulder, CO: Lynne Rienner Publishers.

Pedahzur, A. (2006). *Root Causes of Suicide Terrorism: The Globalization of Martyrdom*. London: Routledge.

Richardson, L. and Weinberg, L. (2004). Conflict Theory and the Trajectory of Terrorist Campaigns in Western Europe. In Andrew Silke (ed.) *Research on Terrorism: Trends, Achievements and Failures*. London: Routledge, pp. 138–160.

Zulaika, J. (2009). *Terrorism: The Self-Fulfilling Prophecy*. Chicago, IL: University of Chicago Press.

10 Individual disengagement, de-radicalization and counter-radicalization

Much of this book has dealt with how and why individuals and organizations engage in terrorism. We have at times also mentioned instances where individuals or organizations stopped their terrorist activities. Indeed, it was a point made from the very beginning that neither individuals nor organizations are terrorist by nature and that this is an activity that can be taken up for a variety of reasons, or abandoned for others. The theories on individual disengagement can also be regarded through the three lenses we have introduced in this book: deterministic, intentional, and relational. The kinds of explanations we find in the literature are largely the reverse of the explanations for involvement, however, there are also a series of theories which are specific to disengagement. The reference works we discuss deal with both exit from terrorism, and from 'extremism' and extremist violence (such as hate crime); the latter is considered in the context of terrorism from the perspective of the more recent approach to counter-terrorism as a matter of counter-radicalization. This chapter introduces these after a discussion of concepts and ends with a discussion of counter-radicalization and de-radicalization policies.

What is disengagement and when does it occur?

The question of the unit of analysis approached in Chapter 1 in relation to involvement in terrorism needs to be posed here as well, namely: which kinds of behavior and individuals are relevant for the research topic of 'leaving terrorism behind'? This is by no means an easy task. As Horgan (2009b: 17) recalls, "One of the challenges that emerged from interviews was identifying when a terrorist can no longer be considered a terrorist?". We showed in Chapter 1 how involvement in terrorism means more than the mere terrorist acts and that this has an influence on the ways in which we delineate involvement in terms of activities and from a temporal perspective. This same complexity of involvement has an impact on disengagement as well, and the ways we might conceptualize and analyze it:

> involvement in terrorism goes beyond the activities that result in the most dramatic and public behaviors associated with terrorism ... Some of those interviewed are inactive in the sense that they are no longer involved in the commission of terrorist operations. But it is also the case that they have remained active in a different kind of role. That role may not involve committing violence but certainly involves behavior of importance to the aims of the terrorist group.
>
> (Horgan 2009b: 17)

138 *Disengagement and counter-radicalization*

In Chapter 1, we suggested settling on the moment when an individual joins a group or an organization and considering various types of engagement that reflect particular roles and the overall concept of 'terrorist career.' For the case of leaving, the reverse would be the moment where the individual stops acting in a particular role, breaks contact with the group, and takes up another occupation than that of 'terrorist,' and this as a permanent change rather than a break in activity, as it were. Clearly, fixing a particular moment in time is an analytically pragmatic device, as, also similar to engagement, disengagement is a process entailing several steps, fallbacks, and more often than not, especially in the earlier stages, sequences of 'small steps' which are not necessarily consciously perceived as distancing from terrorism. Also similar to engagement, the process entails cognitive and behavioral dimensions, whose dynamics and sequence in time remain idiosyncratic. In fact, scholarship has even developed separate concepts to differentiate between the two, namely *de-radicalization* vs. *disengagement*. Individuals, who leave terrorist organizations and/or stop acting in any role for the purposes of these organizations are labeled as 'disengaged.' De-radicalized individuals are the ones who, in addition to this behavioral change, have also sworn off the goals or the overall ideology of the group.

In spite of the popularity of these two concepts, it is worth questioning the utility of drawing a separation line between the two processes and between the cognitive and the behavioral dimensions, more broadly. First, it appears that disengagement and de-radicalization are closely interwoven in the course of individual biographies, and that their chronological sequence is variable. Rabasa et al. (2010) for instance review instances where disengagement occurs before de-radicalization, as a matter of initial rule abidance followed by cognitive change, but also others where the latter is a trigger for disengagement. From a methodological point of view, it is arguably difficult to establish whether or not de-radicalization, in the sense of complete abandonment of particular ideological stances, has effectively occurred. In fact, researchers tend to be skeptical about an idealized form of de-radicalization, as reverse brainwashing as it were, even being possible. Horgan (2009b: 153) notes that the term de-radicalization has the connotation that individuals can be fixed or "turned," and further argues that "we should not assume that de-radicalization assumes a return to some 'pre-radicalization' phase ... for someone who has engaged in the violent radicalization proves, there can be no returning to that original phase." From a broader perspective, it might be argued that behavior is always influenced, in one way or another, by cognitions, and the other way around. An artificial separation between processes that deal only with one or with the other would therefore make little sense. It follows that 'leaving terrorism behind' can be usefully labeled as 'disengagement,' whereas the concrete content of this concept is not limited to behavior, but includes a cognitive dimension as well.

Disengagement has been classified in typologies depending on the presence or absence of agency, or the presence or absence of publicity. Unlike involvement, which is ordinarily always voluntary, disengagement can also occur involuntarily, through an outside intervention. This is then a case where the differentiation between this and de-radicalization makes sense, since someone who disengages involuntarily is unlikely to also de-radicalize at the same time. Disengagement can thus be 'voluntary,' for instance "when an individual has made a decision that continued membership of the group is no longer as important as some overriding personal issue": it is 'involuntary,' when "an individual is forced to leave in the face of some external issue such as the reality of decommissioning, or some new legislative initiative, and the implications this has for organizational dissipation" (Horgan 2008: no page nos). Some other external reasons might have to do with organizational

Disengagement and counter-radicalization   139

circumstances, such as "organizational reshuffling, avoiding surveillance, arrest or imprisonment" (Horgan 2009b: 35). For the case of disengagement from right-wing extremism, Aho (1988) proposes a similar categorization, drawing on the cult literature which:

> distinguish[es] between three kinds of leave-taking: expulsion from the group at the behest of its leaders, forcible extraction from the group by outsiders (that is, what is known in America as "deprogramming", which often involves kidnapping the individual in question, and voluntary exiting by the member himself).
>
> (Aho 1988: 160)

Another classification of types of disengagement is according to the degree of publicity, as proposed by Bjørgo (2009: 42–44) for the case of violent groups of the extreme right: public disengagement, break with the group without breaking with the ideology, and quiet disengagement. The first exit mechanism, the "public break" is "to make a straight and public break with the racist movements, renouncing the attitudes and the ideologies it represents" (ibid: 42). It can involve switching sides to the political enemy, exposing secrets or plans of the group, or playing a role in prevention. This type of strategy is usually associated with high-ranking members, who are well known and therefore cannot withdraw undetected, but also rank-and-file members who switch to anti-racist movements. On the down side, a public break can involve confrontations with the group, security risks, death threats, or other types of punishment. On the positive side, "a clean and public breach with their past offers them an opportunity to – almost literally – begin a new life. This strategy also offers the bonus of gaining social and political support from new groups and individuals, such as family and old friends" (ibid: 42). The second option, "breaking with group without breaking with ideology", seems to be the most disadvantageous one, as individuals might end up in isolation from both the inner- and the outer-group and more often than not backslide. Exceptions to this are when the person joins a 'softer' variation of extremist group. Finally, the "quiet and gradual withdrawal" means that individuals "make themselves marginal to the group, taking less and less part in political or social activities, lose interest in the group and make the group lose interest in them" (ibid: 44). This strategy usually entails the least amount of sanctions, both from the inner- and the outer-group, but could become problematic for individuals who seek public careers at an earlier or later point in time:

> Paradoxically, for a person who has been involved with a stigmatized group, the better he or she is integrated into mainstream society and the greater the success he or she achieves professionally, the higher the risk – and the greater the fall – if the secret past is exposed.
>
> (Bjørgo 2009: 44)

How and why does disengagement occur?

Reverse motivations

The three approaches to individual motivation and processes of engagement can also be applied to a large extent to disengagement. In Chapter 4 on *deterministic* types of individual motivation we mentioned narcissistic injury which was analyzed from the perspective of belonging, externalization, and splitting. In the case of disengagement, this can work in the reverse, in that the referents of all of these three mechanisms can be replaced by their opposites, as a series of studies on violent extremism have shown. Gadd (2006: 179) argues

140　*Disengagement and counter-radicalization*

that "in order to desist from crimes that involve a symbolic 'othering' (e.g. hate crimes) offenders have to reclaim the psychic parts of themselves that are projected onto victims." The projection of the 'negative' part of the self onto enemies can be reversed, for example, in instances where the hated other contradicts previously normalized stereotypes. The reverse of 'belonging' can occur in situations where either the bonds with the group become lax, or bonds with groups or individuals outside the group gain in priority:

> If they are mainly motivated by companionship and the need to belong to a group, they are also highly vulnerable to disillusionment if the friends, the group or the leaders do not live up to the high expectations of friendship, loyalty and leadership ... For those primarily motivated by a need for belonging, alternative groups or new "significant others" might replace bonds to the radicalized group or cell. Devotion to a romantic partner outside the group or parental obligations for children may also lead the young person to leave the group due to conflicting loyalties and commitments and setting different priorities.
>
> (Bjørgo 2011: 282, 283)

The sense of belonging seems to decrease exponentially in cases where the core values of community and comradeship crumble:

> Numerous exiters from right-wing extremist groups tell of their disappointment when realizing the extent of internal bickering, self-seeking behavior, mutual suspicion, competition, and backstabbing in the group. Some tell of gradually losing the sense of attachment and of the fatigue resulting from constantly having one's level of commitment questioned. Others are abruptly disabused of their illusions, when presumed brothers turn them in or let them down in a moment of need, for example, in connection with a trial. Some even experience having their lives threatened by those they felt the closest to.
>
> (Dalgaard-Nielsen 2013: 104)

The reverse of various *intentional* elements was also considered, such as goals or selective incentives. For example, a decision to disengage could be influenced by two distinct circumstances: either the realization that these goals cannot be achieved by terrorist means, or their actual achievement. Bjørgo (2011: 280) found for instance that disengagement can occur when "the group or struggle does not further their cause or improve the plights of the population they claim to fight for." Based on interviews with 35 former ETA members, Reinares (2011: 781–782) concludes that political developments related to the transition from authoritarianism to democracy in Spain, as well as the approval of autonomy for Euskadi, followed by parliamentary elections, played a major role in their decision to abandon the armed struggle. In this case, "*It just didn't make sense any more*" (ibid: 783), since the goals that motivated involvement had been partially achieved. Bjørgo (2011: 277) argues that people engaging in terrorism or extremism do so, among other reasons, in order to "fulfill a dream, a need or an urge to do or achieve something." Failing to achieve it can result in disillusionment and subsequently lead to the decision to leave. A particular type of this disengagement mechanism seems to occur for the case of "ideologues" (see Chapter 3 on typologies), who are primarily moved by political objectives, and at some point along the way are confronted with the behavior of other members of the group who do not or cannot play into their world view:

> [They] are primarily interested in discussing ideology, producing and disseminating
> political propaganda, and building effective political organizations or even clandestine
> terrorist cells. They tend to become frustrated by belonging to a rowdy skinhead group
> where members get involved in drunken brawls with each other or in senseless fights
> with immigrants and anti-racists.
>
> (Bjørgo 2009: 37)

Disillusionment can also occur on the basis of less ideologically structured notions, but rather along the lines of the imagined life-world: "disillusionment arising from incongruence between the initial ideals and fantasies that shaped a person's initial involvement and their subsequent experiences with the reality of what is entailed by involvement – i.e. the mismatch between the fantasy and reality" (Horgan 2009b: 31). He gives examples from the IRA context; it is, however, imaginable that the same mechanism can occur in other cases as well.

Positive incentives, the sense of gain associated with particular acts, have also been associated with disengagement. Aho (1988: 162) uses the concept of private interests, by which he means two things: "the utility to the candidate of 'material' pleasures contingent upon membership in a hate group (sex, money, sociability, and power)" and "the utility to him of 'ideal' satisfactions (a sense of personal life direction, esteem, or what elsewhere we have called experiencing oneself as 'heroic')." It would make sense to assume that, in the reverse, once the group does not provide these kinds of reinforcements anymore, or when they can be obtained from outside the group, disengagement could become an option. Aho (1988: 161) mentions the possibility of social relationships outside the group having "more promissory value" and thus entailing "both a social shove from and a being allured to certain social bonds." Bjørgo (2009: 36–40) mentions among the motivations to disengage: negative social sanctions, loss of status and reputation within the group. The last of these can occur on the background of accusations of inacceptable behavior, betrayal, or generally not living up to the group's expectations. Negative social sanctions (parental scolding, social isolation, criminal prosecution, harassment or violence) seem to have ambivalent effects, depending on the intensity of the relationships with the group. A key factor, Garfinkel (2007: 1) notes, in the transformation from violence to peace is the role of reinforcement within personal relationships: "change often hinges on a relationship with a mentor or friend who supports and affirms peaceful behavior."

In terms of intentional approaches, criminological theories can also be drawn on to explain by analogy disengagement. According to social learning theory, desistance occurs as a matter of imitation of models, reinforcement, or as a direct consequence of the (intensity) of social control by various institutions (see Box 10.1 for more on these theories). The theory usefully combines social environment with variables pertaining to individual behavior, and could thus constitute an important stepping stone for further theoretical development of the disengagement *process*.

Box 10.1 Social learning

Criminologists working with social learning theory argue that the same types of mechanisms work to induce involvement in and desistance from crime. Also, the theory integrates the micro and meso levels of analysis, in that individual behavior is explained as a consequence of interaction with the social environment. Social learning theory draws on differential association theory, which emphasizes the role of

142 *Disengagement and counter-radicalization*

association with peers, and on behaviorism with its concept of operant conditioning or "reinforcement." Individual behavior in this context is explained through the imitation of models and vicarious and direct reinforcement. Warr (1998) posits that:

> The transition from criminal to conventional behavior (or vice versa), it seems, is not merely an individual conversion, but rather a social transformation that entails the destruction of old relations or social networks and the creation of new ones. If delinquency is largely a group phenomenon, it should come as no surprise that desistance is also a group process.
>
> (Warr 1998: 212)

By changing social environments, individuals basically are confronted with different role models, namely "models for conventional behavior" (ibid: 210), and different types of reinforcements. He further argues that the life-course events that other theories take as determinants of desistance are simply markers of these kinds of social processes:

> marriage marks a transition from heavy peer involvement to a preoccupation with one's spouse and family of procreation. For those with a history of crime and delinquency, that transition is likely to reduce the interaction with former friends and accomplices and thereby reduce the opportunities as well as the motivation to engage in crime.
>
> (Warr 1998: 209)

Still within this intentional approach, recently scholars have looked towards more general theories and argued that some could prove useful for the understanding of disengagement from terrorism. Altier et al. (2014) review in their article, 'Turning Away From Terrorism: Lessons from Psychology, Sociology, and Criminology', a psychological and a sociological model which they argue are useful starting points for a more comprehensive understanding of terrorist disengagement. They note that—especially the psychological model—is very much applicable to the terrorist domain, as it incorporates 'alternatives' and 'investments' as variables decisive for the satisfaction of individuals with their actual roles. It thereby allows for individual differences in how much satisfaction one derives from terrorist involvement. It furthermore accounts for individual aging-related changes in goals. Finally, it allows consideration of how variations at the macro level (e.g. state policies, amnesty, imprisonment, educational opportunity) interact with individuals and influence their disengagement.

The psychological model is *Rusbult's investment model* developed in the early 1980s, derived from interdependence theory and it incorporates traditional exchange theory constructs. It functions according to the formula:

Commitment = Satisfaction – Alternatives + Investments

where Satisfaction = Actual (Rewards – Costs) – Expected (Rewards – Costs)

This model suggests satisfaction and commitment as two components associated with individual involvement in an entity. Satisfaction is related to a positive evaluation of an aspired entity (e.g. a job, a group, a relationship) and increases commitment, which is decisive for an individual to remain in an entity and for being psychologically bound to it. Importantly, a low degree of satisfaction does not provoke low commitment, as commitment is a complex concept which is shaped by two more variables. This is the quality of alternatives (e.g. stable employment, marriage opportunities) as well as the size of the investment (e.g. time, money, energy) that has already been put into the entity. It is assumed that individuals weigh their degree of satisfaction with alternatives and investments and decide whether to stay in the group or leave it. According to this model, commitment increases when there are only poor alternatives to involvement and when they have invested heavily in the cause of the group. Individuals who derive high rewards (e.g. social bonds) and low costs like threats from their engagement in the group are likely to be highly satisfied and will not defect. Importantly, the investment model also considers emotions as a factor for commitment. High emotional costs related to involvement may provoke dissatisfaction and exit, whereas positive emotions create bonds which in turn increase satisfaction and commitment. Unlike stage models, this model is a flexible approach to understanding underlying human decision-making. It has furthermore a rich research tradition, is well regarded among psychologists, and is supported by several studies. However, as it focuses only on the exit decision as such, it says little about the exit process, which is a clear drawback. The exit process has been analyzed by Helen Rose Fuchs Ebaugh, the second model to which we will now turn.

Ebaugh's sociological role exit theory of 1988 analyzes voluntary role exit and was developed through 185 in-depth interviews with individuals who left certain roles (e.g. prostitutes, convicts, etc.). The model has been criticized for assuming that the exit process is linear and that it occurs in stages. However, it allows the re-enactment of dynamic psychological processes involved in exit processes and—as with Rusbult's model—it also incorporates satisfaction, investments, and alternatives as factors for commitment. Ebaugh emphasizes that the decision to leave a role is not suddenly made but originates long before one is fully aware of where decisions or events will lead. The process begins with the *first stage*—initial doubts—which makes dissatisfied individuals question their engagement and evaluate the perceived costs and benefits of the actual role. The *second stage* is marked by seeking and weighing alternatives. These are mental calculations which are influenced by factors such as the transferability of skills, status, friends and family, or retirement benefits. Here, people evaluate different roles through 'anticipatory socialization,' which means that they 'try them on' or test their potentially new roles. Subsequently, individuals arrive at the *third stage*, the turning point stage. Once arrived here, individuals already have viable alternatives to their hitherto existing roles and often indicate their exit externally (e.g. through a formal job resignation). This stage is also sometimes accompanied by feelings of being rootless. Finally, they enter the post-exit phase where they create a new identity that integrates their new and prior roles. In this phase, they are confronted with certain challenges as they must dis-identify with their previous role but must deal with individuals who still associate them with this prior role. Additionally, they must learn how to present oneself as an 'ex,' shift social networks, and establish new intimate relationships. This model has been criticized as no empirical research has—at the time of writing—validated the linearity of the stages. Additionally, the process might be more dynamic (interactive, cyclical) than assumed by Ebaugh. However, it allows us to understand the process individuals go through when leaving a social role.

Relational scholars have dealt to a lesser extent with disengagement, yet some insights from this perspective can also be discussed here; on a close analysis it appears that many of

144 *Disengagement and counter-radicalization*

these elements are of an intentional nature. In her analysis of left-wing terrorism in Italy, della Porta (2009) refers to the environmental opportunities and constraints for disengagement. Here, individual exit strategies can be influenced by the efficiency of oppression, but also by the "offer of conversion opportunities" (ibid: 69). In the course of the 1980s, the Italian government enacted a series of pieces of legislation such as: reductions in sentences for those who publicly abandoned the armed struggle and/or collaborated or confessed; waving accusations if the deed was merely membership and minor offences; homogeneous areas for prisoners; or the non-application of aggravating circumstances in return for collaboration (ibid: 70). In her assessment, these measures facilitated the exit process by "breaking the associative pact" in that the psychological costs of leaving were reduced (ibid: 69–70).

Relational approaches outline the idea of progression towards and also out of terrorism. As we have outlined in the chapter on engagement, such scholars consider involvement in terrorism as not a *sui generis* phenomenon, but rather as a continuation of struggle and protest by other means. Consequently, disengagement is yet another stage of the process. Della Porta (2009: 80) argues that "membership of underground organizations is only a stage within a process of radicalization of political commitment in legal forms and groups." Her sample of left-wing terrorists in Germany and Italy did not completely abandon political activities after having served their sentences or having otherwise left the organizations, but joined voluntary organizations working in the areas of social exclusion and marginalization, and political groups. A continuation of the political career can also occur for other reasons than a continuation of the fight with other means. In some other cases we might see migrations to the political opponent, or active involvement on the side of the state or civil society institutions who help combat that particular type of terrorism or extremism, or help others find their way out, all this as a sort of personal redemption.

Clearly, in della Porta's work and that of others tuned to the relational dimension, social networks are central for entry and exit. Social networks are one of the most important joining mechanisms, not simply from an opportunity availability perspective, but also through the intermediary of affective ties, the adoption of radical frames, and as a source of positive reinforcement. Social networks and social relationships can, in the reverse, also help change attitudes, or provide reinforcement for different types of behavior. Framing processes, as a majorly discursive process underlying involvement, can similarly work the other way around, through the, essentially, same mechanisms and resonance criteria. In her analysis of the material available on exit processes, Dalgaard-Nielsen (2013: 106) concludes that "Social influence [on attitudes] – direct or indirect – appears to be at work." Concretely, "A number of exiters explicitly state that though they behave differently they think the same. Others claim that even if their exit had nothing to do with ideological doubt, their attitudes gradually changed as they stopped spending time with their extremist peers" (ibid: 106). For the particular case of exit from right-wing extremist groups, Bjørgo (2009: 43) argues that "attitudes tend to change after a change of group affiliation rather than vice versa." That is, either a relaxation of the connections with the group, or the intensification of the connections with outside groups, have a transformative effect on the types of ideas that people have. The question is of course how this process works. Social movement theory would argue that this occurs through the development of affective ties, which in their turn influence commitment and the solidification of convictions. Since these mechanisms work during engagement, there is no reason why they should not work during distancing as well. Differential association theory, with its focus on the adoption of definitions favorable to crime (in this case terrorism), would also work in the reverse: through association with individuals who are not terrorists, individuals will adopt definitions which are unfavorable to terrorism. A third mechanism which explains the effect of the social environment on attitudes is one derived from the literature on cults, which is about the 'validation of beliefs' (which works in essentially the same manner as reinforcement, with the exception that it affects in this case beliefs and not behavior). Aho (1998: 161) draws on the finding that "The prototypical cult apostate first severs his bonds to the cult and as this happens the plausibility structure supporting and validating his belief system crumbles" and applied it to exit from extreme-right groups "having once cut their social links to hate groups the plausibility structures undergirding hate doctrines disappear, making reconversions to new, less hostile belief systems possible." This, we need to remember, occurs though after the decision to change social setting. We see here how the relationship between social environment, cognitions, and behavior is by no means unidirectional.

In their "age graded theory of crime," Sampson and Laub (2008: 171) similarly argue that "explanations of desistance from crime and persistent offending in crime are two sides of the same coin." The influence of the social environment is of the essence for both: "A central element in the desistance process is the 'kniffing off' of individual offenders from their immediate environment and offering them a new script for the future" (ibid: 171). In this case, however, turning points revolve around the idea of social control. Certain institutions, such as marriage/spouses, the military, school, work, and neighborhood change, "provide supervision, monitoring and social support, change and structure routine activities" and help with identity transformation (ibid: 171–2).

Motivations specific to disengagement

Apart from individual motivations and processes of disengagement which are the reverse of the ones facilitating engagement, there are a few others which are specific to disengagement. Life-course research in criminology has found that when:

> in a state of marriage, propensity to crime is lower for the same person than when not in marriage. Similar results were found for military service and steady employment. Quantitative methods of within-individual change thus give strong statistical evidence of the probabilistic enhancement of desistance associated with life-course events like marriage, military service, and employment.
>
> (Sampson and Laub 2008: 176)

Similar to desistance from crime, particular life-course events seem to also play a role in disengagement, in particular age, career prospects, family, and responsibilities (Bjørgo 2009; della Porta 2009; Horgan 2009b). Bjørgo (2009: 39) found for the case of right-wing extremists that, with the coming of age, the need for excitement decreases, while authority might be challenged by younger members "Unless they are able to define their roles in relation to the group, e.g. by acquiring some kind of managerial position or becoming a 'withdrawn elder,' they will sooner or later leave or become marginalized." The factor of an alternate family or girlfriend usually triggers a conflict of loyalty, since such groups demand "full loyalty" (ibid: 40), so that the individual would have to make a choice. Della Porta similarly notes for the case of left-wing terrorism that the young have a higher tendency towards enthusiasm and utopianism, and evidenced the relative youth of the members: "39 per cent of 1,086 activists in left-wing underground organizations active in the 1970s and observed during research in Italy were born after 1956 and another 36 per cent between 1950 and 1955" (ibid: 79).

146 *Disengagement and counter-radicalization*

A specific feature of 'life as a terrorist' is stress and uncertainty and this can trigger burnout (Bjørgo 2011: 281; della Porta 2009: 80). Bjørgo explicitly cites it as a motivation to disengage: "exhaustion and burn-out among individuals who have been highly committed over a long period, in particular if they live under high pressure and danger" (ibid: 281). In broader conceptualizations, the incidence of a desire for change and the will to lead a 'normal' life have also been noted in other works (Bjørgo and Horgan 2009; Horgan 2009a; 2009b).

Another specific feature of disengagement from terrorism is the idea of 'doubting the ideology.' The central mechanism here is 'cognitive dissonance,' the contradiction between ideology and reality, but also between for instance "violent means and political ends" or of "behavior that conflicts with one's beliefs" (Bjørgo 2011: 280–281). Cognitive dissonance can lead to doubt, but can also work in the opposite direction and lead to the stabilization or even intensification of beliefs. A second opposite mechanism is "cognitive reactance," as described by Dalgaard-Nielsen:

> people try to protect their freedom to think, act, and believe as they like. If they suspect that they are being targeted by a deliberate influence attempt—no matter how well-meaning or well-reasoned the message might be—they react by going against the perceived influence as a way of reasserting their freedom. In the process of resisting, by means of, for example, looking for flaws in the message and counterargue, bolstering existing attitudes, concocting additional evidence to support them, and so on, the original attitudes become stronger.
>
> (Dalgaard-Nielsen 2013: 107)

Some other authors also found this element of doubt relevant and furthermore argued that, given the absolutist nature of the ideology, an initial doubt could trigger a domino effect: "once doubts arise, they often quickly spread; most radical organizations are total institutions, meaning that every aspect of the group's worldview is interdependent. Thus, if one aspect is called into question, the entire belief structure tends to unravel" (Rabasa et al. 2010: 14). The question remains, however, how to induce this doubt in the first place. Some of the mechanisms and processes with a role in engagement might be useful to explain this. Doubt could be triggered by 'moral shocks' in the face of excessive violence, or other types of behaviors which contradict basic ideological principles. Dalgaard-Nielsen (2013: 104–105) for instance mentions a series of cases of disillusionment with the behavior of leaders: "Self-seeking, manipulative, cowardly, or outright incompetent leaders appear frequently in the narratives of ex-militants across different forms of extremism … Former Weathermen and RAF members point to how the leaders, despite an egalitarian and anti-materialistic ideology, reserved certain privileges for themselves." Social networks and framing processes might also play a role here, if affective ties or the credibility of the frame articulator suffices as a trigger for considering alternative interpretations. Empirical credibility directly relating to fundamental ideological principles can, in some accounts, also be of relevance:

> In some cases, the person belongs to the extremist's out-group, but acts kindly, selflessly, and justly. When this happens, a central notion in militant narratives across different forms of extremism comes under pressure: The division of the world into us and them where we are good and just and they are evil, devious, and murderous.
>
> (Dalgaard-Nielsen 2009: 103)

De-radicalization and counter-radicalization programs

Programs and initiatives aiming at de-radicalizing—in particular Islamist—terrorists have flourished all over the world. Efforts have even been invested in evaluating these programs in terms of, for example, whether or not their purposes have been achieved, or in relation to recidivism rates. In general, while the number of empirical studies on the topic has increased in recent years, abstract conceptualization and theory building remain problematic. After a review of the leading terrorism research journals since 1990, Dalgaard-Nielsen (2013) found a total of 16 articles and books on voluntary exit, and concluded that the material does not:

> establish a foundation for conclusions about causality or for building theories about exit. Though the total number of interviews is significant, the interviewees are not randomly selected, none of the studies operate with a control group, and the collection and processing of data varies from case study to case study.
>
> (Dalgaard-Nielsen 2013: 106)

To be fair, causality and methodological rigor are the Achilles heel of terrorism studies in general.

Dalgaard-Nielsen (2013: 100), in 'Promoting Exit from Violent Extremism: Themes and Approaches', differentiates in an overview of government and non-governmental organization (NGO) programs around the world between de-radicalization vs. disengagement approaches. South Eastern and Middle Eastern approaches are focused on ideological/theological re-education:

> An inculcation of a "correct" interpretation of Islam is regarded as the most effective and durable reformation a detainee might undergo. By means of discussion and dialogue with scholars, clerics, and ex-militants or other authority figures, the programs aim to convince the participants that militant Islam is theologically and ideologically wrong and instead imprint messages like "Islam is against terrorism," "acts of violence compromise the image of Islam," "the Quran views the killing of civilians as unacceptable," and "the authorities are not anti-Islamic."
>
> (Dalgaard-Nielsen 2013: 100)

European programs rather focus on "practical and economic assistance in connection with exit," and psychological counseling and assistance with "forming new social ties outside the extremist group" (ibid: 100). While this categorization is broadly accurate, a more differentiated perspective on the European programs needs to be taken, in particular with regard to the more complex prevention and de-radicalization programs such as the ones in the UK or Denmark (see Box 10.2).

Box 10.2 Governmental counter-terrorism programs in the UK and Denmark

The Channel program in the UK is an example of a project that focuses on counter-radicalization and is based on the UK Counter-Terrorism and Security Act. It provides support to people who are vulnerable to being drawn into terrorism at an early stage. It was piloted in 2007 and rolled out across England and Wales in 2012. Actors that are engaged with the provision of support are local authorities (county and district councils etc.) in collaboration with partners (i.e. the National Health Service, social workers, schools, the Home Office, immigration officials, etc.). The program aims to ensure that children and adults, irrespective of their faith, ethnicity, or background, receive support before their vulnerability is exploited by terrorist groups. This should prevent them from becoming engaged in criminal terrorist activity.

The Aarhus model is a Danish governmental multi-agency intervention program of the Aarhus Municipality and the East Jutland Police in collaboration with the University of Aarhus, the Ministry of Social Affairs and the Danish Intelligence and Security Service as external partners. It was pioneered in 2007 as a reaction to home-grown terrorism and it aims to prevent radicalization and discrimination in Aarhus. The target audience is first responders and practitioners, local community organizations, and NGOs as well as pupils, students, and youth in general. Intervention occurs on two levels, the general population and individuals and groups. On the level of the general population intervention is through presentations and workshops in order to raise the awareness of professionals and the public, and through collaboration with local communities through dialogue with mosques, cultural societies, and other major players. On the individual and group levels intervention is through first-line staff in the form of a task force that evaluates risks. Furthermore, professional staff are advised on how to deal with cases of radicalization, individuals at risk of radicalization, or those already engaged in violent extremism, who are mentored, and contingency for foreign fighters and their families is provided.

As mentioned previously, in spite of the broad range of theories explaining disengagement, policy tends to favor deterministic approaches. In his work, 'Introduction: Assessing the Effectiveness of Counter-radicalisation Policies in Northwestern Europe', Lindekilde (2012) evaluates academic assessments of radicalization prevention policy effectiveness in Britain, the Netherlands, and Denmark. The author notes that the underlying model of radicalization as a linear process is fundamentally the same in all programs. In order to develop counter-radicalization policies it is assumed that vulnerable individuals are adolescents from immigrant families who are isolated, identity-seeking, politically aggrieved, and experience a cognitive opening. This renders them to search for alternative lifestyles and ideologies. Radical groups in turn exploit this and radicalize them through the dynamics of socialization and cultivation in the group. Policies for the prevention of radicalization address those at risk and combine socio-economic integration, anti-discrimination, community building, and social cohesion.

Lindekilde also looks into the effectiveness of counter-radicalization policies and notes various important factors. First, for the balancing of security and liberty the timing of policy formulation is important. When—for example due to uncovered homegrown terrorism—the perceptions of threat and risk are strongly felt by the population, policy-makers are under public pressure to solve the problem, which in turn shapes the policy formation process through prioritizing short-term security gains. A second factor is policy design. It is important that the policies are based on correct assumptions about how the radicalization process works. Yet, this is often not the case because some policies only focus on Islam and radical Islamist ideology instead of addressing political grievances about foreign policy or cultural Islamophobia (see Box 10.3). A third factor is the presentation of counter-radicalization policies in policy texts and public debates and how this is perceived by target groups. The

Disengagement and counter-radicalization 149

discourse often problematizes entire communities instead of just a few exceptional individuals and does not take into account differences in cultural integration, religious practices, and political outlooks. This stigmatizes communities and might have counterproductive outcomes. Finally, policy implementation is important for its effectiveness. It must balance security and liberty concerns and engage with the right experts. It has, for example, been questioned by scholars whether the involvement of school teachers in preventive work is always expedient.

Box 10.3 State of exception

Heath-Kelly (2011) argues in her work 'State of Exception, State of Prevention: Radicalized British Counterterrorism Policy in the War on Terror', that the British approach was to adopt a discourse that frames Muslim communities and individuals as 'threats.' Counter-terrorism efforts used funds to finance intervention into the lives of subjects that were perceived to be 'risky' or 'at risk.' Beside more benign interventions like training exercises, more authoritarian ones were used. The Channel program, for example, performed secretive emergency interventions for more than 200 children. She argues that counter-terrorism policies are based on the assumption that radical jihadi ideas flourish in Muslim communities, take root through cognitive openings of vulnerable individuals, and that these ideas are treated in counter-terrorism policy documents like pathogens causing violence. Such ideas and also the assumption that terrorism is predominantly linked to ideas rather than political grievances or structural factors, the author notes, are irrational.

The author also identifies various challenges to counter-radicalization. The first challenge concerns the preventive nature of counter-radicalization efforts as they are difficult to observe. If preventive work is effective, nothing is observable as no political violence occurs. Therefore, control variables, which the author does not state, are important to introduce. The second challenge refers to data collection and the lack of directly observable measures of success. Ideological de-radicalization as indicated by a change of physical appearance (clothes, beards) and behavior seems untenable, and other indicators like a change in opinions and world views are difficult to assess. Underlying models of radicalization often lead to multilayered policy objectives which might result in sub-objectives and policy solutions that point in different directions. Finally, official evaluations of measures in northwestern Europe often suffer from a lack of clear indicators of success.

Summary

This chapter has been about individual disengagement and counter-radicalization and de-radicalization. It has dealt with:

- the classification of individual motives and processes within broader social science concepts which either correspond to those facilitating involvement or are specific to disengagement;
- motivations specific to disengagement and reverse motivations and processes;
- de-radicalization and counter-radicalization programs;

150 *Disengagement and counter-radicalization*

- evaluation studies of counter-terrorism initiatives that focus on individual de-radicalization and disengagement in Northwestern Europe.

Exercises

10.1 Test the theories on individual motivations to disengage and disengagement processes against the biography of a former terrorist or extremist to see which ones apply.

10.2 Do you know of any former terrorists who engaged in disengagement and de-radicalization work? How successful have they been?

10.3 Criminologists argue that an effective de-labeling by society is essential for processes of desistance from crime. Does this also apply to disengagement from terrorism? Consult the following article and discuss: Maruna, S., Lebel, T.P., Mitchell, N. and Naples, M. (2006). Pygmalion in the Reintegration Process: Desistance from Crime Through the Looking Glass. *Psychology, Crime and Law*, 10(3), pp. 271–281.

References

Aho, J.A. (1988). Out of Hate: A sociology of defection from neo-Nazism. *Current Research on Peace and Violence*, 11(4), pp. 159–168.

Altier, M.B., Thoroughgood, C.N. and Horgan, J.G. (2014). Turning Away from Terrorism: Lessons from psychology, sociology, and criminology. *Journal of Peace Research*, 51(5), pp. 647–661.

Bjørgo, T. (2009). Processes of Disengagement from Violent Groups of the Extreme Right. In T. Bjørgo and J. Horgan (eds) *Leaving Terrorism Behind: Individual and Collective Disengagement*. London/New York: Routledge, pp. 30–48.

Bjørgo, T. (2011). Dreams and Disillusionment: Engagement in and disengagement from militant extremist groups. *Crime, Law and Social Change*, 55(4), pp. 277–285.

Bjørgo, T. and Horgan, J. (2009). *Leaving Terrorism Behind: Individual and Collective Disengagement*. London/New York: Routledge.

Dalgaard-Nielsen, A. (2013). Promoting Exit from Violent Extremism: Themes and approaches. *Studies in Conflict and Terrorism*, 36(2), pp. 99–115.

della Porta, D. (2009). Leaving Underground Organizations. A sociological analysis of the Italian case. In T. Bjørgo and J. Horgan (eds) *Leaving Terrorism Behind: Individual and Collective Disengagement*. London/New York: Routledge, pp. 66–87.

Ebaugh, H.R.F. (1988). *Becoming an Ex: The Process of Role Exit*. Chicago, IL: University of Chicago Press.

Gadd, D. (2006). The Role of Recognition in the Desistance Process. A case analysis of a former far-right activist. *Theoretical Criminology*, 10(2), pp. 179–202.

Garfinkel, R. (2007). *Personal Transformations: Moving from Violence to Peace*. Washington, DC: United States Institute of Peace.

Heath-Kelly, C. (2011). State of Exception, State of Prevention: Radicalized British counterterrorism policy in the war on terror. IJCV conference, Bielefeld, Germany, 6–8 April. [Online]. Available from: www.dvpw.de/fileadmin/user_upload/ak_gewaltordnungen/2011%20De-Radikalisierung%20-%20Abstracts%20and%20bios.pdf [Accessed 29 April 2017].

Horgan, J. (2008). Deradicalization or Disengagement? A process in need of clarity and a counterterrorism initiative in need of evaluation. *Perspectives on Terrorism*, 2(4), online.

Horgan, J. (2009a). Individual Disengagement: A psychological analysis. In T. Bjørgo and J. Horgan (eds) *Leaving Terrorism Behind: Individual and Collective Disengagement*. London/New York: Routledge, pp. 17–29.

Horgan, J. (2009b). *Walking Away from Terrorism: Accounts of Disengagement from Radical and Extremist Movements*. London/New York: Routledge.

Lindekilde, L. (2012). Introduction: Assessing the effectiveness of counter-radicalisation policies in northwestern Europe. *Critical Studies on Terrorism*, 5(3), pp. 335–344.

Rabasa, A., Pettyjohn, S.L., Ghez, J.J. and Boucek, C. (2010). *Deradicalizing Islamist Extremists*. Santa Monica, CA: RAND Corporation.

Reinares, F. (2011). Exit From Terrorism: A qualitative empirical study on disengagement and deradicalization among members of ETA. *Terrorism and Political Violence*, 23(5), pp. 780–803.

Sampson, R.J. and Laub, J.H. (2008). A General Age-Related Theory of Crime: Lessons learned and the future of life-course criminology. In Farington, D.P. (ed.) *Integrated Developmental and Life-Course Theories of Offending*. New Brunswick, NJ, and London: Transaction Publishers, pp. 165–181.

Warr, M. (1998). Life-Course Transitions and Desistance from Crime. *Criminology*, 36, pp. 183–216.

Further reading

Bovenkerk, F. (2011). On Leaving Criminal Organizations. *Crime, Law and Social Change*, 55(4), pp. 261–276.

Bromley, D. (1991). Unraveling Religious Disaffiliation: The meaning and significance of falling from the faith in contemporary society. *Counseling and Values*, 35(3), pp. 164–185.

Decker, S.H. and Pyrooz, D.C. (2014). Disengagement from Gangs as Role Transitions. *Journal of Research on Adolescence*, 24(2), pp. 268–283.

Ebaugh, H.R.F. (1942). *Becoming an EX. The Process of Role Exit*. Chicago, IL: University of Chicago Press.

Ferguson, N., Burgess, M. and Hollywood, I. (2015). Leaving Violence Behind: Disengaging from politically motivated violence in Northern Ireland. *Political Psychology*, 36(2), pp. 199–214.

Horgan, J. and Braddock, K. (2010). Rehabilitating the Terrorists? Challenges in assessing the effectiveness of de-radicalization programs. *Terrorism and Political Violence*, 22(2), pp. 267–291.

Laub, J.H. and Sampson, R.J. (2001). Understanding Desistance from Crime. *Crime and Justice*, 28, pp. 1–69.

Schuurman, B. and Bakker, E. (2015). Reintegrating Jihadist Extremists: Evaluating a Dutch initiative, 2013–2014. *Behavioral Sciences of Terrorism and Political Aggression*, 8(1), pp. 66–85.

Stern, J. (2010). Mind Over Martyr: How to deradicalize Islamist extremists. *Foreign Affairs*, 89(1), pp. 95–108.

Williams, M., Horgan, J. and Evans, W. (2015). The Critical Role of Friends in Networks for Countering Violent Extremism: Towards a theory of vicarious help-seeking. *Behavioral Sciences of Terrorism and Political Aggression*, 8(1), pp. 1–21.

11 State terrorism

State terrorism is a central concern for critical terrorism scholars, and something that has preoccupied also the broader scholarship on terrorism since its early days. Significantly, state terror is a practice that predates modern terrorism by roughly two centuries. The topic remains, however, very much disputed theoretically and conceptually, while empirical research continues to be relatively scarce. This chapter walks you through the main theoretical contributions on state terrorism and discusses some of the controversies in the literature, definitions, types of state terrorism, and issues associated with its research.

While the terrorism literature looking at individuals and organizations has produced a fair amount of scholarship in all three categories: deterministic, intentional, and relational, the literature on state terrorism occupies a much smaller niche within terrorism studies. Within this literature, the intentional approach dominates and the pursuit of terrorism by states is usually conceptualized as a choice that states make, based on strategic considerations. Determinist accounts and attempts to look at state terrorism as a longer process of socialization into some ideologies are used in some historical case studies. The analysis of the French revolutionary terror is a good example here (see Box 11.1).

Box 11.1. Interpretations of the French revolutionary terror

Modern terrorism was born with the French Revolution and the first political employment of terror is linked to the 'Reign of Terror' (1793–1794). This two-year period is one of the most explored in the history of the Revolution. Why it happened and how the Revolutionaries, starting in 1789 with the Declaration of the Rights of Man and the calls to abolish the death penalty, ended in four years with the call to terror, have interested historians and social scientists for more than 200 years. Interpretations of terror in the Revolution follow largely the three approaches identified in this book. Already in the 18th century when the Revolution had just unfolded, for some observers, such as Edmund Burke, the terror was a logical consequence of the Revolution of 1789. According to him, even though it seemed that the Revolution was based on high morals and lofty principles, it would end in disaster as it was destroying the foundations of state and society. This approach was exchanged at the end of terror in 1794 with a more 'intentional approach,' concentrating on the figure of Robespierre and blaming him for the system introduced in France. This approach was dominant throughout a great part of the 19th century. In the beginning of the 20th century, Marxist historiography on the French Revolution started dominating the field and terror came to be understood as a product of certain circumstances (especially war), and as a natural part of revolution(s). This view remained predominant during the 20th century. Towards the end of the century it was challenged by the revisionist school. Scholars who belonged to this school saw terror not as a product of circumstances, but as an outflow of discourse and ideology of the Revolution with its roots in the philosophy of the Enlightenment. Yet, they were still quite firmly rooted in determinism, as they saw terror as an (almost) direct consequence of such philosophy. The post-revisionist school that developed towards the end of the 20th century took a more relational approach and emphasized both the relationship between the different groups in revolutionary France and the importance of the experiences of the revolutionaries that led them to adopt terror as a way of governing.

Deterministic approaches to terror also abound in the interpretations of the Russian Revolution. Even if it is often accepted that this particular revolution was more of a coup than a spontaneous uprising of the 'oppressed masses,' the interpretations of later periods of terror are deterministic in nature, attempting to justify these actions as a response to the international and internal conditions and the need to protect the Revolution in these difficult circumstances.

Some relational elements can also be observed in cases where state terrorism is used during and as part of a more protracted conflict. An example is historical accounts of postcolonial conflicts degenerating in or including terrorism. Paul Wilkinson, for example, finds that "it is easy to show how the violence perpetrated by autocratic and colonial regimes has almost invariably displayed a symbiotic relationship to the violence of resistance and insurgence movements" (1981: 467). In particular, he gives the example of the torturous practices of the French government and of the local authorities in Algeria at the time of the Front de Libération Nationale (FLN) (see Box 11.2).

Box 11.2 The Algerian War 1954–1962

The Algerian War, also called the Algerian War of Independence, took place from 1954 to 1962. It was a conflict between the FLN and France. The FLN sought to gain independence from France but the French viewed Algeria as an essential part of France and its culture. The movement for independence had already begun during World War I but only gained momentum when the French did not fulfill their promise to grant Algeria greater self-rule after World War II. Subsequently, in 1954, the FLN began a guerilla war against France and sought recognition at the UN to establish a sovereign Algerian state. The main fighting took place in Algiers when members of the FLN launched serious attacks, also known as 'The Battle of Algiers,' in 1956/57. France responded with the deployment of 50,000 troops and managed to regain control but only through brutal measures. This sapped the political will to continue the fight. In 1959 Charles de Gaulle declared the right to self-rule and in 1962 Algeria became independent from France. By the end of the conflict, over a million Algerians had died, with masses of European settlers being exiled. The war was an important decolonization war and was a complex conflict characterized by guerilla warfare. This war is particularly infamous due to the extensive use of torture and terror by both sides.

(Wilkinson 1981)

154 *State terrorism*

Jackson et al. (2010: 1) describe a further scenario, whereby counter-terrorism campaigns result in state terrorism "by failing to distinguish between the innocent and the guilty"—an apt example here being the recent US anti-terror campaign in Afghanistan and Iraq.

The first and perhaps ostensibly the most surprising feature of state terrorism is its formidable lethality. Chomsky and Herman quoted in Stohl (2006: 2) have characterized state terrorism as "wholesale terror," whilst terrorism perpetrated by non-state actors or "insurgents" is referred to as "retail terror." Namely, state terror is far more destructive and is executed on a larger scale than attacks carried out by non-state actors. However, despite this, retail terror "gains most public, governmental, scholarly, and media attention" (ibid: 2). Most authors agree that the numbers of victims and the intensity of psychological distress induced by state terrorism are far superior to what terror groups might ever 'hope to achieve.' Critical scholars argue that, nevertheless, state terrorism has been so far neglected and theoretically under-developed, and that there is a widespread assumption that states are primarily victims and not perpetrators of terrorism (Jackson et al. 2010: 2). Some scholars such as Stohl, however, have dedicated quite a large portion of their work to this topic.

This difference in attention may have various causes: first, and given that the majority of terrorism research is funded by state institutions, it is conceivable that states would not be particularly interested in understanding and combating their own strategies, but rather want to learn how they can stop threats coming from below. Most of the argumentation advanced by Ruth Blakeley (2007) can be subsumed under this heading. In her seminal article, 'Bringing the State Back into Terrorism Studies', she lists and analyzes in detail three reasons why terrorism practices by northern state democracies are absent from the debate, namely: the methods practiced by 'orthodox terrorism scholars,' their institutional affiliation, and the marginalization of normative approaches in international relations (IR). Blakeley argues that the problem lies in the way that terrorism has been theorized by mainstream academics as acts of violence that primarily target northern democracies. Thus, terrorism scholars tend to take a 'problem-solving' approach that does not challenge these assumptions, but rather works within the context of these widely held conjectures. As terrorism studies are highly influenced by such neo-realist and liberal approaches in IR, more normative approaches that would likely consider the oppressive behavior of northern powers on individuals in the global South tend to be overlooked (ibid: 228–229, 234). According to Blakeley, the use of these types of orthodox methods rests in the fact that terrorism scholars have a political agenda, as many academic institutions are dependent on state funding and therefore work to reinforce the dominant discourse on the perception that northern democracies are predominantly the victims of terrorism (ibid: 230, 233).

Jackson et al. (2010) also champion a more normative approach, arguing that we should study state terrorism in order to uncover such atrocities and consequently protect vulnerable populations against state violence. Because terrorism has such a strong connotation, the study of state terrorism could be "an important means of advancing a progressive political project aimed at protecting marginalized and vulnerable populations from indiscriminate and oppressive forms of state violence, whether they occur under the rubric of war or counter-terrorism" (ibid: 5–6). Furthermore, "In the present context where states are oppressing groups and individuals in the name of counter-terrorism, making the case that 'states can be terrorists too' could have a powerful normative effect of constraining state excesses and promoting genuine human and societal security" (ibid: 6).

Arguably, the terrorism perpetrated or sponsored by *other* 'rogue' states might be of interest; it is certainly named as such in political statements. For example, following 9/11 and the declaration of a War on Terror by US President George W. Bush, terror regimes such as the Taliban in Afghanistan and Saddam Hussein's Iraq were militarily targeted (Blakeley 2007; Jackson et al. 2010). Such interventions were viewed by the West as a means to contain the terrorist threat and liberate civilians from oppressive rulers. However, as Jackson et al. (2010) point out, in the eyes of the people of Iraq and Afghanistan, they were further victim to occupation and terror at the hands of the US and their allies, despite the removal of their former oppressors. Thus, the aim of CTS is to unveil state terror as a weapon of domination and demonstrate that such terror is characteristic of state behavior worldwide— regardless of whether the state is a democracy or dictatorship, or whether the state is rich or poor.

A second type of reason for the more limited attention dedicated to state terrorism is of a less 'intentional' nature, and has to do with the type of phenomenon we are dealing with. As we shall see below, the explanations for state terrorism are relatively straightforward and somewhat established, so that there is not much room for discovery in a theoretical sense. From a different perspective, there is often an entanglement of state terrorism with other forms of large-scale violence inflicted by the state on its own or other populations, such as repression, genocide, or various violations of human rights. As we shall see below, this often makes it difficult to analytically differentiate between these various types of violence. Finally, in many cases it is sometimes difficult to prove the existence of state terror at the time when it happens, since states often conduct covert operations.

A third reason and at the same time feature of state terrorism is its ambiguous legal status. Unlike terrorism perpetrated by non-state actors, it is not explicitly recognized as a crime in international law. Blakeley (2010) argues that despite this, state terrorism clearly incorporates acts which *are* crimes and that violate international humanitarian law and international human rights law. That is, "state terrorism can be defined with reference to the illegality of the acts it involves, even though we cannot argue that state terrorism itself is illegal" (ibid: 15). The author goes on to demonstrate that state terrorism is often applied in war, when the aim is to terrorize the civilian population, neither on purpose nor as collateral damage but as a 'welcome secondary effect,' so that the population turns against the regime. She gives the example of the bombardment of Basra and Baghdad in the first Gulf War, when it was hoped that the population would be "psychologically affected" and in turn provoke mass opposition to the Iraqi regime (ibid: 17). Stohl spoke in the 1980s of 'terrorist coercive diplomacy,' as a subset of coercive diplomacy, involving the use or threat of violence and argued that both superpowers at the time had used it. He cites Schelling to illustrate the point of this concept:

> The power to hurt is nothing new in warfare, but for the United States modern technology has dramatically enhanced the strategic importance of pure unconstructive, unacquisitive pain and damage, whether used against us or in our own defense. This in turn enhances the importance of war and threats of war as techniques of influence, not of destruction; of coercion and deterrence, not of conquest and defense, of bargaining and intimidation.
>
> (Schelling quoted in Stohl 1988: 171)

Stohl further argues that it is easier for states to render their threat of use of violence credible, that they have to do less than non-state actors to achieve this. The implication of this is that we need to look behind what states do to gain a full understanding of the threat. He furthermore refers to the trope 'gunboat diplomacy' (implying the display of military force) and argues that also in this case the concept would apply so long as there is a threat to hurt innocent civilians.

156   *State terrorism*

Closely related to the 'legality' of state terrorism is the apparent contradiction between state terrorism and the fact that the state has a legitimate monopoly of violence. This contradiction has been approached along the following lines: the fact that the state has a legitimate monopoly of violence does not mean that all types of violence it might choose to use are legitimate. As Stohl argues,

> If the state, and its agency the government, have a legitimate monopoly on physical violence, it may still use that violence (and its threat) in ways as unacceptable as terrorism, mass killings and other forms of repression and human rights violations. And not just 'illegitimate' governments may so act.

(Stohl 2006: 5)

In a similar analysis, Jackson et al. (2010: 3) point out that "although states have the legitimate right to use violence, this right is highly circumscribed and does not include the right to use extra-legal violence against randomly chosen civilian targets – or to commit genocide, ethnic cleansing, war crimes, and other such acts." For these authors, the criteria for deciding whether or not an act is legitimate are the legal definitions of criminal acts. In other opinions, it is a matter of morality. For example, Wilkinson asks rhetorically: "can the use of terrorism – by definition a means of violence involving the killing of the innocent – ever be morally justifiable?" Regardless of who initiates the spiral of violence, he declares: "Surely, the only consistent moral position for a liberal democrat must be unequivocal opposition to *both* the terror of the regimes *and* terrorism by factions" (Wilkinson 1981: 468).

State terrorism and non-state terrorism

Authors argue that there are significant similarities between state and non-state terrorism, and that by looking at the terrorism perpetrated by states, one can in fact, by comparison, learn something about insurgent terrorism and the workings of terrorism in general. Stohl, for example, finds that:

> while it is clear that state terrorism, violence, repression, and human rights violations are extraordinarily important in and of themselves for the death, injury, fear, and destruction they cause to individuals and the body politic, they are also important to explore because of the insights that study of the purposes, conditions, and decision matrices that state rulers use may provide for the study of insurgent terrorism ... thinking about the state's use of violence allows us to focus on the act of terror or violence rather than simply on the perpetrator and allows us to confront the political choices and potential instrumental uses of those choices, an approach which may provide considerable theoretical insight into the roots of terrorism.

(Stohl 2006: 4)

Jackson et al. (2010: 5) go further to argue that the reason why we can learn something about the causes and effects of terrorism in general is because state terrorism is the original and purest form of terrorism (see Box 11.2). Wilson (2013: 14) cites the definition of terrorism by the French Academy in 1798: "the deliberate creation and exploitation of fear through violence or the threat of violence in the pursuit of political change," and goes on to say that terrorism was indeed something that governments originally did: "Although popular usage has since shifted, in its early usages, terrorism thus belonged to the state before it belonged to the anti-state." The key issue for both types of terrorism is thus the strategy of using violence to achieve *political* aims. Jackson et al. (2010: 3) also find that the two types of actors have similar strategies: kidnapping, extra-judicial killing, bombing, torture, and so forth; and that it is also more likely for state terrorism to reach the point of actually terrorizing people.

Martin Miller's (2013) *The Foundations of Modern Terrorism*, is quite exceptional in that it tries to present the historical account of both types of terrorism throughout the two centuries since 1792. Miller sees terrorism as a type of political violence, which has at its core an attempt to "create an atmosphere of fear, insecurity and mistrust in civilian society" (ibid: 1), which also involves "dynamic interaction between groups or individuals in both government and society who choose it as a means of accomplishing specific political objectives" and finally, "terrorism is a response to the contestation over what constitutes legitimate authority within a territorial nation state in periods of political vulnerability" (Miller 2013: 1).

Thus, state and insurgent violence exist in a symbiotic relationship and in such a combination produce the most terrifying effects. Terrorism is here "a historical phenomenon characterized by the violent combat between elements in governments and societies over unresolved political issues" (ibid: 254). Since the times of the French Revolution, we see terrorism continuously reappearing either from above or from below with some groups contesting the authority of the state and the state using violence to enforce its legitimacy against such contenders. Furthermore:

> Both sides claim they are acting in the name of political progress, human rights and the amelioration of conditions for the less fortunate. Both are possessed by their fantasies of power, by the redemptive power of their goals, and by the unquestioned arrogance that the violent path they have chosen is justifiable.
>
> (Miller 2013: 257)

What is state terrorism?

State terrorism shares in principle the basic characteristics of non-state terrorism, with the difference of course that in its empirical manifestations it is far more destructive. State terrorism scholars insist that the definition of terrorism should not include the characteristics of the perpetrator, but focus on the nature of the act. Consequently, the element of inducing fear, whereby the target of the violence is not the same as the target that should be intimidated, is at the heart of state terror. This also differentiates state terrorism from other forms of state violence. In the case of genocide, mass deaths are the *main purpose*, while in the case of state terrorism, these deaths are *instrumental* (Stohl 2006). Similarly, different to repression, in terrorism it is not just about harming the direct victim, but "exploiting the opportunity afforded by the harm to terrorize others" (Blakeley 2010: 14). Wilson (2013: 14) also finds that genocide and state terrorism are different, since genocide does not aim to intimidate but to eliminate, yet cautions that in the "real world" these "processes will often overlap." For example, Blakeley (2010: 23–24) points to the example of Nazi Germany, and argues that whilst the state's primary goal was to eradicate Jews, gypsies, and homosexuals, individuals who did not belong to these groups and were not explicitly targeted were perhaps too fearful to intervene and protect the vulnerable as Hitler had threatened the same fate to his political opponents. Blakeley goes on to argue that it is unlikely "that a state involved in a genocidal policy would be too concerned about minimizing the ensuing terror among others outside of the targeted group, particularly

158 *State terrorism*

where the terror may be instrumental to its overall objectives" (ibid: 24). Thus, such classifications of genocide and state terrorism are not as clear-cut and it is necessary to examine the wider context concerning specific acts.

Regarding the actual definition of state terrorism, most authors refer to that proposed by E.V. Walter (1969) in *Terror and Resistance*, which contains three main elements:

- violence or the threat of violence;
- the distinction between two types of victims: the victim of direct violence vs. the terrorized victim;
- the expectation that the latter would directly or indirectly do or refrain from doing something as desired by the regime.

Jackson et al. propose a definition which effectively limits the scope of the analysis to intentional approaches:

> the rational choice use or threat of violence by state agents or their proxies against individuals or groups who are victimized for the purpose of intimidating or frightening a broader audience. The direct victims of the violence are therefore not the main targets, but are instrumental to the primary goal of frightening the watching audience who are intimidated through the communicative power of violence. The intended effects of the violence are the achievement of specific political or political-economic, as opposed to religious or criminal, goals.
>
> (Jackson et al. 2010: 3)

Manifestations of state terrorism

Forms of state terrorism have been identified by Stohl (2006: 7) and Blakeley (2010: 19–20) by the kinds of targets, means, and purposes envisaged. In all cases, state terrorism can occur either directly through state agents, or indirectly through the employment of state or private groups, such as paramilitary or vigilante groups. State terrorism can thus be:

- against the state's own population, in order to maintain order and quell political opposition, and can involve disappearances, illegal detention, torture, and assassinations, the prime example here being Operation Condor (see Further reading);
- against the population or governments of other states, in a limited form, such as limited campaigns or assassinations, or on a large scale, involving the destabilization of other societies in order to cause the collapse of government; the latter could be in the form of torture, the killing of enemy combatants, the targeting of civilians, hijackings, kidnappings, illegal detentions, or torture;
- employment of surrogates to engage in warfare with other nations to provoke international incidents, alarm, destroy morale, cause the diversion of resources into security budgets, sabotage, and provoke repression and reactive strategies or revolutionary overthrows;
- support of foreign insurgents or states which use terrorism against their own population, or against the population or governments of other states; this support can be ideological, financial, or military, or simply, in a broader framework, cooperation.

As to the strategic reasons to employ terrorism, these are in essence the same as those pursued by non-state actors (Stohl 2006: 8–12):

- publicity for the cause: "a message of strength (at least relative strength), a warning designed to intimidate and to demonstrate the willingness to use violence and thus to engender compliance without the need to physically touch each citizen" (ibid: 8);
- win concessions through coercive bargaining;
- create or enforce obedience of the broader population or the ruling party;
- provoke overreactions by the regime or the insurgent—the 'agents provocateurs';
- create and then eliminate a threat from an opposing political movement or possible political movement to demonstrate the need for greater resources and powers for 'law and order' campaigns.

Paradoxically and different to non-state terrorism, these strategic considerations also work for strong, not just weak, states: "Weak states have chosen terrorism when they thought themselves vulnerable (they had no other means to employ) but strong states have chosen terrorism because they thought it was an efficient use of their power and they felt invulnerable to any backlash against employing terrorism" (Stohl 2006: 12).

In terms of *process*, Stohl (2006: 13) draws on Gurr's (1986) *The Political Origins of State Violence and Terror: A Theoretical Analysis*, to outline three conditions affecting the decision-making process: situational, structural, and dispositional. These are detailed below, along with other individual conditions (Stohl 2006: 13–16) that can be usefully classified therein:

- Situational conditions refer to the position and strategies of challengers and the elite's own political resources for countering those challenges, such as regime strength and police apparatus. The government would have to weigh up the costs of using terrorism against alternative means. Such costs in this case would be economic and psychological—that is the cost of weapons and resources as well as the (negative) effect of the state behaving in a manner that might be deemed inappropriate by their citizens. The latter is usually neutralized through the dehumanization of the victim and the justification that the use of terror is in the best interests of the state. However, this depends on the distance between government and the victimized group. Stohl notes that in almost all cases of state terror, there has been a campaign by the government to dehumanize the targeted group prior to taking any action.
- Structural conditions allude to the state's position in the international system as well as the nature of social stratification and the elite's position within it. In the case of marginalized groups, it is possible to minimize public attention and present the terrorist strategy as politically acceptable. An advantage here is also the fact that such groups usually do not enjoy external support. A lack of transparency internationally can also increase the likelihood of terrorism occurring: "as regime vulnerability to international pressure is greater, terrorism is more likely to be secretive, and, concomitantly, is less likely to be as extensive. Thus state terrorism appears to be greatest in reclusive states" (ibid: 16).
- Dispositional conditions refer to norms supporting the use of violence, which in turn are determined by previous experience with violence. Previous experience with violence can also lead to learning effects (see also Box 11.3).

Box 11.3 Perpetuating terror

Joan Wardrop (2010) details a case of continuous state terror in the case of Zimbabwe and argues that current terror is made possible by past terrors, first the terror perpetrated by the colonial regime, followed by that carried out and still carried out by the government. Colonialism and its psychological, cultural, and physical violence "facilitated the construction of a culture of violence through which the terror of the colonial state could be perpetuated by the post-colonial state" (ibid: 111). She includes in her analysis not only actual acts of violence, but also what she labels:

> structural violence of systematic neglect of the basic needs of human survival, [given that the] consequences are similar: the construction of a shared state of fear and apprehension, the continual and constant expectation of arbitrary and illegal acts by agents of government, the deprivation of means of life, the individual body reduced to an emancipated cipher, the loneliness of unnoticed death, through disease, through the batons, firearms or instruments of torture of the security forces.
>
> (Wardrop 2010: 107)

Beyond this structural violence, though, it was the post-colonial campaign against Matabeleland that ensured the perpetuation of terror up to the present date. In Matabeleland, "state terror was deployed as a deliberate strategy of state building through the politicization of ethnicity" (ibid: 109). These massacres "made conceivable by a traumatized past, in turn made continued state terror feasible, the anonymity of its victims became a guarantee of continuance" (ibid: 110). In a telling citation from an official report:

> The very men who tortured people in the 1970s used the same methods to torture people again in the 1980s. Both times they got away with it and were never punished. Some of these men still hold senior positions in the Zimbabwean Government and armed forces.
>
> (Wardrop 2010: 116)

Beyond these, she argues, it is the stories, the narratives of the past which re-enact the horrors in the present and in their turn then melt with the ones of the present, serving to perpetuate 'cultures of terror.'

Also similar to non-state terrorism, there are two conditions for seeing other means as ineffective (Stohl 2006: 13): either the public is not receptive to the state's message, or the state does not have the capacity to mobilize. It is therefore a question of resources and resonance. States tend to have few resources when they are new, weak, or fragile states, and there is a lack of receptivity when there is a larger population group and commitment to conflicting values.

Democracy and state terrorism

While in principle any state could make use of state terrorism, there is ardent debate in the literature as to whether this is also the case for democracies. Indeed, democratic governments enjoy a high level of legitimacy—which however, as we have seen above, is not necessarily a guarantee for the fact that their individual actions will also be legitimate. Apart from this fact, the actions of democratic governments are regularly submitted to checks by the other powers in the state, namely the parliament and the judiciary. This is, however, not always the case; in particular, in times of national emergency—not least in the age of the War on Terror, executive powers are significantly increased and their actions increasingly opaque. In the opinion of some authors, state terror would thus be a matter of exception:

> The cases in the domestic realm in which stable democracies resort to repression or even clandestine acts of terror within their borders have almost all occurred during times of defined extremis or in specific regional crises, which while "explicable" go beyond what we expect the behavior of democracies to be, particularly when looking from a distance of either years or miles.
>
> (Stohl 2006: 19)

Wilson's (2013) assessment here is quite different in tone. He draws attention to the fact that state terror is not just the feature of the 'paradigmatic cases' of revolutionary France, Hitler's Germany, Stalin's USSR, and Mao's China, but that there are also the 'democracy's gulags,' such as Guantanamo and Bagram. By looking at the number of states using torture in present times, he concludes that "state terrorism is no aberrational lapse in the modern state, but rather one of its constitutive modes of operation" (ibid: 15) (see also Box 11.4).

Box 11.4 The terror foundations of the modern state

In a historical account, Wilson (2013) shows how, during the 19th century, state terrorism became integrated in military operations of pacification and the police state. The legacy of the 1792–1815 wars was "a stunning growth in governmental power and capacity for control" (ibid: 19). This power, he argues, was increased and maintained not through violence but fear, thus achieving public order inside and outside prisons. The lasting success of the counter-revolution in 1948–1949 was insured by the "state of intimidation," a "rule not by demonstrative atrocity but by system: of spies, informers, identity checks, press seizures and quiet deportations" (ibid: 20). The regimes of terror of the 20th century were characterized as totalitarian due to the total control they exercised on the individual. However, Wilson observes that "All modern states involved themselves more closely in the lives of their populations as the twentieth century progressed; welfare has advanced relentlessly behind warfare. Totalitarian states merely did it earlier than most" (ibid: 22). The anti-imperialist wars and the Cold War saw the proliferation of further terror:

> The effect of the Cold War was thus to inflame many areas of the globe left conspicuously untouched by the world wars. Thus, the Superpowers invested in elaborate state repression and torture where they chose to intervene directly (Afghanistan, South Vietnam). But they also supervised, advised and

162   *State terrorism*

> bankrolled state repression in client states. Soviet and East German security experts assisted the Ba'ath in Iraq, for example: just as their American counterparts were to do for their regimes across Latin America.
>
> (Wilson 2013: 25)

Finally, the War on Terror opened the terror box again:

> Indeed, what was striking about the period following the 9/11 attacks was the ease with which some Western governments introduced various forms of internment and, indeed, torture. In both the USA and Great Britain, the outer defenses of the *Rechtstaat* crumbled quickly under a "blitzkrieg against the concept of due process."
>
> (Wilson 2013: 26)

Studying state terrorism

Studying state terrorism can be problematic due to a number of methodological issues. For example, as terrorism perpetuated by the state is covert, it is difficult to empirically substantiate incidences of state terror. Furthermore, it is challenging to effectively ascertain whether such acts of violence by the state are predominantly driven by the need to instill terror or whether terror is a secondary effect of a different policy. Precisely the element of instilling fear in others is problematic in terms of empirical verifiability, given the lack of publicity concerning acts of state terror. As we well know, publicity is usually seen as the 'oxygen of terrorism' and conditions essential elements of its definition, in the case of both non-state and state terrorism. Blakeley (2010: 18) shows that "For torture to constitute state terrorism it must be aimed at, or have the effect of, terrorizing an audience beyond the direct victim." For example, in the Guatemalan insurgency in the 1970s to 1980s, newspapers were allowed to publish pictures of dead torture victims. She argues that if there is no audience to the torture and no evidence that the state condones it, then it is a criminal act. The problem here of course is that in most cases of state torture—and state terrorism in general—there is little to no publicity. As a case in point, the Bush administration did everything to avoid public exposure of the abuses in Guantanamo and Abu Ghraib. However, Jackson et al. argue that one should not focus on the publicity as such, since it is only a means to a purpose, which is communication:

> It is communication to an audience which is one of the key elements of terrorist violence, not necessarily publicity. For non-state actors lacking societal penetration, publicity is the easiest way to communicate, but this is not the case for states whose violence does not necessarily require publicity to reach its intended audience.
>
> (Jackson et al. 2010: 4)

Another issue related to the lack of publicity often encountered in the case of state terror is the difficulty of showing intent. In principle, in order for an act to constitute state terror, the state needs to actually aim to provoke harm and instill fear. The problem is how to identify agency—whether the state sanctioned the act or not, and motive—whether or not terror was actually intended as such. Blakeley (2010: 20–22) argues that the way to ascertain whether these two elements existed at the time of the commission of the terrorist act is to examine the circumstances around the event. Agency can be evaluated by criteria such as: the way states respond to those acts, whether or not they prosecute the responsible, and the existence of evidence for other such incidents or for instances when the state did sanction them. While terrorism as a secondary effect of other measures can be difficult to evaluate in terms of motive, a criterion here would be the "reasonably anticipated likely consequences of an act" (ibid: 22). Blakeley goes further to argue that unintended consequences of repressive policies should be considered state terrorism "if a state seeks to commit genocide, for example, against a specific group, are they not assisted because others outside of that group are sufficiently fearful of the consequences for themselves if they are to intervene in an attempt to prevent the genocide?" (ibid: 24).

Summary

In this chapter we elaborated on state terrorism and have dealt with:

- the classification of its scholarship as a primarily intentional approach;
- the definitions and forms of state terrorism;
- the debate around democracies as perpetrators of terrorism;
- the difficulties associated with the study of state terrorism.

Exercises

11.1 Why do you think there are no deterministic approaches to the explanation of state terrorism?

11.2 Think about the Abu Ghraib and Guantanamo incidents. Could they be categorized as state terrorism? If so, why?

11.3 Apply the process matrix to Saddam Hussein's campaign against the Kurds in 1987–1988.

References

Blakeley, R. (2007). Bringing the State Back into Terrorism Studies. *European Political Science*, 6, pp. 228–235.

Blakeley, R. (2010). State Terrorism in the Social Sciences. Theories, methods and concepts. In Jackson, R., Murphy, E. and Poynting S. (eds) *Contemporary State Terrorism. Theory and Practice.* London/New York: Routledge, pp. 12–27.

Gurr, T. (1986). The Political Origins of State Violence and Terror: A theoretical analysis. In Lopez, G. and Stohl, M. (eds) *Government Violence and Repression: An Agenda for Research.* London/New York: Greenwood, pp. 45–71.

Jackson, R., Murphy, E. and Poynting, S. (2010). Introduction: Terrorism, the state and the study of political terror. In R. Jackson, E. Murphy and S. Poynting (eds) *Contemporary State Terrorism. Theory and Practice.* London/New York: Routledge, pp. 1–11.

Miller, M.A. (2013). *The Foundations of Modern Terrorism. State, Society and the Dynamics of Political Violence.* Cambridge: Cambridge University Press.

Stohl, M. (1988). States, Terrorism and State Terrorism: The role of the superpowers. In Slater, R.O. and Stohl, M. (eds) *Current Perspectives on International Terrorism.* Basingstoke, Hampshire: Macmillan, pp. 155–205.

Stohl, M. (2006). The State as Terrorist: Insights and implications. *Democracy and Security*, 2(1), pp. 1–25.

164 *State terrorism*

Wardrop, J. (2010). The Politics of Convenient Silence in Southern Africa. Relocating the terrorism of the state. In Jackson, R., Murphy, E. and Poynting, S. (eds) *Contemporary State Terrorism. Theory and Practice*. London/New York: Routledge, pp. 104–123.

Walter, E.V. (1969). *Terror and Resistance.* Oxford: Oxford University Press.

Wilkinson, P. (1981). Can a State be 'Terrorist'? *International Affairs*, 57(3), pp. 467–472.

Wilson, T. (2013). State Terrorism. An historical overview. In Duncan, G., Lynch, O., Ramsay, G. and Watson, A.M.S. (eds) *State Terrorism and Human Rights: International Responses since the End of the Cold War*. London/New York: Routledge, pp. 14–31.

Further reading

Byman, D. (2005). *Deadly Connections: States that Sponsor Terrorism.* Cambridge: Cambridge University Press.

Chomsky, N. (2001). The United States is a Leading Terrorist State: An interview with Noam Chomsky by David Barsamian, *Monthly Review*, 53(6), [Online]. Available from: http://monthly review.org/2001/11/01/the-united-states-is-a-leading-terrorist-state/ [Accessed 29 April 2017].

Herman, E.S. (1999). *The Real Terror Network: Terrorism in Fact and Propaganda.* Boston: South End Press.

McSherry, J.P. (2005). *Predatory States: Operation Condor and Covert War in Latin America.* Plymouth: Rowman & Littlefield.

Schelling, T. (1966). *Arms and Influence.* New Haven, CT: Yale University Press.

12 Terrorism in time and space

We have discussed so far various approaches to the definition and understanding of terrorism, and the various ways in which it has been studied by scholars and combated by government. We have thereby taken an analytical perspective and dissected approaches to identify the main theories, concepts, and methods used, and how they could be traced back to earlier, broader theories. In this chapter, we take a historical stance to look back in time at *how terrorism has developed empirically* and *how it has been studied academically*. We relate back to the initial chapters of this book to follow the dividing line between positivists and critical scholars. Depending on which paradigm dominates any particular scholarly discourse, there will be different views on these two major questions. In short, positivists would take terrorism as a given, as a phenomenon out there, and inquire to what extent it has changed in time. Whether there is a 'new' terrorism at all constitutes a major point of debate for this approach. Historical overviews are quite present here; at the same time, social movement scholars looking at the contextualization of terrorism in time and space—namely, how these variables influence the unfolding of terrorism, would naturally use methods specific to this type of scholarship. Critical scholars, starting with the premise that terrorism is a social construction, will not look into how it has changed in time, but into how it has been 'constructed' in time, and also use historical analysis, as well as various types of discourse analysis.

Positivist time and space

One of the major positivist scholars looking at the evolution of terrorism in time and space is David C. Rapoport who elaborated in his 2004 work, 'The Four Waves of Modern Terrorism', on how modern terrorism has emerged and changed over the course of the past century. The author argues that terror is nothing new; to the contrary, it is persistent and has always been present in history in the form of rebel (non-state) terror. The 'newness' of terrorism rather lies in the characteristics of the waves in which it occurs, each being unique in some way. Rapoport uses the concept of waves to explain the change in terrorism as cycles of activities in a given period of time that are characterized by expansion and contraction phases. Importantly, each wave has international features which are given by the interactions of five principal actors, namely: terrorist organizations, diaspora populations, states, sympathetic foreign publics, and from the second wave on, supranational organizations.

Rapoport demarcates the different waves of terrorism as 'anarchist,' 'anticolonial,' 'New Left,' and 'religious,' which often overlap for a certain period of time. The first three waves lasted for about 40–45 years. Each wave has its own momentum and the first three waves, the author states, lasted about a generation each, which might be linked to the political

166   *Terrorism in time and space*

themes and dreams in the general culture of a generation and the loss of appeal for the following one. An overriding aim in every wave, Rapoport notes, is revolution. Revolutions were meant to radically reconstruct the dominant authority and to create a new political legitimacy, in the past mostly national self-determination.

The first wave: The 'anarchist wave'

In Rapoport's (2004) account, modern terrorism initially appeared in 1879 in Russia and spread within a decade to Western Europe, the Balkans, and Asia. This was the so-called 'anarchist wave,' which was the first global and international terrorist wave in history. The idea of anarchy (a Greek word stemming from *anarkos* meaning 'without a chief') emerged at the time especially in Europe, Russia, and America and the ideology aimed to abolish all governments and to organize society by voluntary cooperation rather than force. The origin of the movement was the search of the industrial working class for a political voice given the background of the failure of democratic reform (see Box 12.1). Changes in communication and transportation patterns facilitated the momentum of the first and successive waves. The telegraph, daily newspaper, and railroads made it easier for information to be spread and to inspire sympathies and groups in other countries. Additionally, new modes of travel facilitated emigration within a short period of time, and the creation of diaspora communities. Another facilitating factor was the strategy of terror created by Russian revolutionaries and novelists, for example, Sergei Nechaev, Nikolai Morozov, and Peter Kropotkin and which was used, improved, and transmitted by successors. Traditional revolutionaries used pamphlets and leaflets to generate uprisings. The creators of modern terrorism used actions, also called 'propaganda by the deed,' to communicate with the masses. In order to reach the aim of destroying and undermining unfair conventions and policies, anarchist terrorists provoked governments through their deeds to overreact in order to thus prove conventions invalid. The ultimate aim was to provoke uprisings and revolutions. Vera Zasulich, who shot and wounded a Russian police officer because he abused political prisoners, can be mentioned here as an example. With her deed she aimed to use the trial to make the wrongdoings of the officer public and to instigate the masses. The assailants usually called themselves 'terrorists' and used dynamite as the weapon of choice against political targets. Russian rebels also trained Armenian and Polish nationalist groups and anarchist terror developed in the West too when Russians joined Russian diaspora colonies there. The high point of this first international wave of terrorism was the 'Golden Age of Assassination,' when prime ministers, monarchs, and presidents where murdered by assassins who crossed international borders.

Box 12.1. Czar Alexander II and the failed transformation of the system in Russia

Predating the initiation of the anarchist wave is the failed attempt of the Czar to transform the system in Russia. In 1861 he freed the serfs and promised to provide money which would allow them to buy land. In 1864 he even declared limited local self-government, westernized the judicial system, ended capital punishment, and relaxed censorship as well as control over education. The people were hopeful but felt that their hopes were not fulfilled fast enough as the available funds for serfs were insufficient. Because of this disappointment, assassination strikes against government officials began and culminated in the death of the Czar himself. Subsequently, the rebels trained other groups (even if they had different political aims) and the insurgencies spread to Armenia and Poland, where nationalist groups resorted to assassinations, and even terrorist activities in India were influenced by the Russian anarchist terror (Rapoport 2004).

The second wave: The 'anticolonial wave'

This wave began in the 1920s with the Treaty of Versailles (signed 1919) that ended World War I and lasted for approximately 40 years. The ideology behind this wave was anti-colonialism and its aim was to achieve self-determination. The victors of the World War broke up the empires of the mostly defeated European states by applying the principle of national self-determination and created mandates for countries which were not deemed to be ready for independence. As empires dissolved, the wave abated too. Terrorist activity at this time was crucial to establishing the new states of Ireland, Israel, or Cyprus, to mention a few. It was fought in territories where non-engagement was not an option because political problems, like conflicting aspirations of different ethnic groups once the imperial power had withdrawn, were still present. The Turkish community in Cyprus, for example, did not want to be put under Greek rule. As the Cold War developed, the process sped up, as the Soviets helped would-be rebels. Organizations in this wave preferred to be called 'freedom fighters' who fought against the terror of their government, since the designation 'terrorist' was negatively connoted. 'Freedom fighter' implied a certain extent of legitimization and therefore attracted potential political supporters. Governments on the other side described all violent rebels as terrorists. With this wave, terrorist tactics changed as well. Diaspora communities contributed more money and bank robberies were less common. Martyrdom and the assassination of public figures were regarded as counterproductive while the police, which were perceived to be spies of the government, became a main target. The main strategy was a hit-and-run guerilla-like tactic and some groups gave warnings in order to limit civilian casualties. In this wave, foreign states with kindred populations acted suppor-tively, and with an international court and the League of Nations drafting conventions on the containment of terrorism, supranational organizations came into play too, though neither came into effect as two League members, Hungary and Italy, blocked the anti-terror efforts. The anticolonial cause of the freedom fighters gained more attention when increasing numbers of former colonies became new states and were admitted to the UN (see Box 12.2).

Box 12.2 The group Irgun Tz'va'i Le'umi and the struggle against the British

The anticolonial wave can be exemplified by the fight of the Jewish 'National Military Organization,' also known under their acronyms Irgun or Etzel in Israel. This armed Jewish underground organization was founded after World War I in 1931 and was primarily concerned with the struggle against the Arabs. Yet, after the British published their White Paper in 1939, which set out the establishment of an inde-pendent Palestinian state, they directed their activities against the British mandatory authorities. In 1944, after some internal splits, the group, led by Menachem Begin, finally declared war against the British administration. They blew up British military and government offices and attacked police stations. In 1947 they hanged two British sergeants after four of their group members were executed. The group finally disbanded when the independence of the Jewish state was declared and its members were integrated into the army of the new Jewish state, which was finally achieved in 1948.

Jewish Virtual Library (2017)

The third wave: The 'New Left wave'

This wave followed the 'anticolonial wave' and diminished by the end of the 20th century. Only a few groups of this wave are still active in Nepal, Spain, the UK, Peru, and Colombia. The ideology behind this wave was the 'New Left' and nationalism. The aim was to combat the oppression of the Third World by imperialistic First World countries. The triggering event of this wave was the Vietnam War where the Viet Cong, the combatants of the Vietnamese National Liberation Front, fought with primitive weapons against First World America with its modern technology. It was especially the youth—also in Western countries—who questioned the value of the existing system and many groups saw themselves as fighters of and—in the West—for, the Third World. The Soviets encouraged the uprisings against the values of the existing system and supported the groups with training, moral support, and weapons. As in the first wave, women played an active role: they became leaders and fighters. Theatrical targets, such as airplanes, replaced the military targets of the second wave; international hijackings to secure hostages and kidnappings occurred en masse during this wave. Kidnappings occurred in 73 countries and the abandoned practice of assassinating prominent individuals was revived again. What differed from the first wave though was the purpose of the assassinations. In the first wave people were assassinated because of their public office; in the third wave they were assassinated to punish them for their policies. This wave was also very international as some groups conducted more attacks abroad than in their home countries and on their own territory they often attacked individuals with international significance. Americans became the most favored target because of their new importance in world politics during the Cold War. American citizens were targeted in countries in Latin America, Europe, and the Middle East where the US supported governments that were confronted with terrorism. During this wave, involvement with foreign groups led some terrorist organizations to neglect domestic constituencies and sometimes the revolutionary ethos alienated domestic and foreign liberal elements during the Cold War. In order to maintain control, states began to sponsor certain groups and even America, itself a preferred target, supported terrorist groups in several countries such as Nicaragua and Angola. The 'New Left' wave started to diminish in the 1980s when revolutionary terrorists were defeated in several countries and because international cooperation, like the imposition of an arms embargo by the European Community in Libya or the bombings by the US with British aid in Libya became effective. The UN's stance on terrorism changed immensely in this time period as new states increasingly viewed terrorist activities as threats to their interests. New conventions against hijackings, hostage taking, and financing international activities named these as crimes. The term terrorism was preferred and the name freedom fighter was abandoned by the UN.

Box 12.3 Weathermen aka Weather Underground and their 'Declaration of War' against the US

The Weather Underground was an American militant left-wing underground organization, which was active between 1969 and 1977. They originally organised as a faction of Students for a Democratic Society, the most prominent revolutionary group of the epoch, with the goal of creating a clandestine revolutionary party in order to oust the U.S. government. Furthermore, the group supported the Black Power movement, and were staunchly critical of US military involvement overseas, in particular the Vietnam War and the invasion of Laos. Their first public demonstration on 8 October 1969, was a violent riot in Chicago to protest against the Vietnam War, and was timed to coincide with the trial of the 'Chicago Seven,' who had previously been involved in anti-Vietnam War protests. Not long thereafter, three of their members died while making bombs in a Greenwich village safe house, which led the group to go fully underground. This is where their aka-name Weather Underground was derived from. The group fully rose to prominence in 1970 after they issued a 'Declaration of a State of War' against the U.S. government. During their active time, they conducted several attacks, such as the bombing of the US Capital in 1971 which caused major damage but no deaths, and the bombing of the Pentagon on 19 May 1972, on Ho Chi Minh's birthday. A central belief shared by group members was that violent action was required to change the course of imperialistic powers and to achieve equality in the US. In 1974, the organisation's leading members collaborated with Clayton Van Lydegraf, an important left-wing social activist of the time, to publish a manifesto entitled Prairie Fire: The Politics of Revolutionary Anti-Imperialism, taking the name from a Mao Zedong quote, 'a single spark can set a prairie fire.' The manifesto's influence led to the establishment of the Prairie Fire Organizing Committee in numerous US cities. Nonetheless, frictions led to the development of a more radical wing in 1976. Five WUO members were arrested for planning to bomb the office of John Briggs, a State Senator in California. It was later revealed that the FBI had had undercover agents in the group for almost six years, after two of these agents testified against the core members, and that the infiltration had led to these arrests. The group disbanded not long thereafter and the majority of the Weather Underground emerged voluntarily from underground and rejoined mainstream society. They were not subjected to serious federal charges.

The fourth wave: The 'religious wave'

This wave emerged in 1979 and is predicted by Rapoport to disappear by 2025 when a new wave might emerge. In his view, religious elements had played a role in modern terror before, because they often overlap with ethnic identities, but religion today has a different significance as it supplies justifications and organizes principles for a state. Central to this wave, he argues, is religion, and Islam in particular. The aim of Islamist terrorism is to liberate Muslim countries from Western occupation and these groups are responsible for the most deadly and significant international attacks. The political events that provide hope for this wave also originated in Islam. The fourth wave was mainly triggered by the Iranian Revolution and the Soviet invasion of Afghanistan. This wave involved huge Sunni

170 *Terrorism in time and space*

resistance and the successful eviction of the Soviets from Afghanistan with the help of the US, as well as the subsequent disintegration of the Soviet Union in 1989—seen as a victory of religion over a secular superpower. Formerly Russian lands with a large Muslim population became important territories for Islamic rebels. Suicide bombing was a tactical innovation because it was most deadly. During this wave the number of terrorist groups declined from about 200 in the 1980s to 40 in the 1990s. The American role changed too during this wave. The US became the 'Great Satan' for Iran and the main enemy for al-Qaeda. The latter collapsed in Afghanistan after the US invasion, which was supported by more than 100 states (including Iran).

Debating 'newness'

At the core of Rapoport's classification is novelty in terms of ideology, aims, strategies, and tactics. Isabelle Duyvesteyn has famously questioned this in relation to religious terrorism. In her view, the aims, instruments, and effects of religious terrorism are not fundamentally different to previous waves. In her 2004 work, 'How New Is the New Terrorism?', she focuses concretely on features like the transnational nature of the perpetrators and their organizations, their religious inspiration and fanaticism, their use of weapons of mass destruction, and their indiscriminate targeting. The first 'new' feature of religious terrorism she questions is the transnationality and network-like organization of these groups, as opposed to previous organizations which were supposedly national and territorial in focus, as well as hierarchically organized. Other scholars have also delved into this debate with particular reference to al-Qaeda (see Further reading for the dispute between Hoffman and Sageman).

As for Duyvesteyn (2004), she argues that the actors of the 9/11 attacks also focused on national and territorial aspects, as traditional terrorists did; and traditional terrorists also acted transnationally, and finally, their organizations were also structured in networks. Thus, 'new' terrorist groups like al-Qaeda aim to establish a caliphate, which is clearly a territorial aim. They intend to govern a territory that stretches from North Africa to Southeast Asia and is presently inhabited by a community of believers, the Umma. Furthermore, they are against the occupation of their holy land by the US and the US support of Israel and its policies toward the Palestinians. These are concerns that are highly national and territorial. Duyvesteyn also contests the novelty of aims as religious fanaticism. She argues that traditional terrorists were not areligious either and religiously inspired terrorism with the aim of killing others has existed for millennia. In fact, there have been cases in history where the main audience for terror attacks was a deity (see below for the case of the Thugs). Furthermore, she emphasizes that the motivation of new terrorist organizations is political and religious at the same time. They, *inter alia*, intend to provoke, gain publicity, and hurt the enemy. On close inspection of bin Laden's teachings, Duyvesteyn states that not Islam as religion but Islam as political interpretation is dominant. Finally, with regard to instruments and effects, it is stated in the 'new terrorism' discourse that the means of attacks and that their targets have changed; they no longer kidnap individuals, hijack airplanes, or use car bombs. Instead, scholars of this school argue that new terrorists use, among other things, weapons of mass destruction, intend to inflict as much damage as possible and kill many innocent civilians. As a result, the number of victims has risen. Yet, the author counters that terrorists still rely on conventional arms and explosives, the targets are still largely selected for their symbolic value (like buildings), and the number of victims is already on the rise since the beginning of the 1980s. These aspects can therefore not be classified as features of the new terrorism.

Duyvesteyn's points (2004) become more clear when we look at ancient terrorist groups and their mode of action. Rapoport (1984) provides in his work, 'Fear and Trembling: Terrorism in Three Religious Traditions', a good overview over three different ancient groups who, in the pursuit of their goals, resorted to acts of terrorism, much like the 'new' terrorists. The Thugs existed from the 7th until at least the 13th century in India and are said to have killed about a half million to a million people; more than any known terrorist group before or after. Their primary audience was Kali, the Hindu goddess of terror and destruction. The Thugs believed that Kali required blood to keep the world in equilibrium, so they killed in order to meet her demand. They terrorized cities for months, though they avoided publicity and did not claim responsibility for their acts as their killings were meant solely for her. Their primary targets were travelers in India. As traveling in India was very dangerous at this time, people used to travel in large groups in order to feel safer. The *modus operandi* of the Thugs was to disguise themselves as travelers and to travel with these large groups, often for months, before they attacked them. For these expeditions, they often received outside support from princes in the form of international sanctuaries. This constantly exacerbated international relations between states, which the British authorities tried to improve by seizing and punishing the Thugs in accordance with international law on piracy. Out of obscure religious reasons they never threatened institutions and only killed travelers; women, vagabonds, the blind, the mutilated, and lepers, as well as members of certain artisan crafts, were immune from attacks as they believed them to be descendants of Kali; it was also taboo to kill European travelers, which was why they could escape attention. The Thugs only retired when they were physically no longer able to participate in expeditions and new recruits were exclusively their offspring. It is not clear if they had political objectives and they were finally exterminated by the British authorities.

The second group of ancient terrorists were the Assassins. This group, also known as the Ismailis-Nizari, existed from the 11th to the 13th century in Persia and had its roots in Shi'ism. Contrary to the Thugs, they clearly had political objectives, namely to deliver a moral message, to fulfill or purify Islam, whose political and religious institutions they saw as inseparable. Moreover, they not only attacked individuals but also seriously threatened governments of several states, above all the Turkish Seljuk Empire in Persia and Syria. The international feature of this terrorist group even went so far as to aim to reconstitute Islam into a single supranational community again, spanning the whole region and one that could not be implanted into an existing Islamic state. This again strengthens the argument of Duyvesteyn (2004) who asserts that not only new but also traditional terrorists transcended international boundaries. Contrary to the Thugs, the Assassins were very much interested in gaining publicity and attention from the community to gain its sympathy. This was easy to accomplish as they attacked prominent victims such as orthodox religious or political leaders in venerated sites and courts, mostly on holy days when a lot of people could witness their deeds. Yet they hardly ever attacked Christians. During their education and training they became prepared to die in the course of an attack; they were even instructed that it would be shameful to survive it. Those who died were promised freedom from the guilt of all sins and to be allowed to go to paradise. In this sense, suicide terrorism existed before, which further indicates that the concept of modern terrorism is not characterized by entirely new features. Again strengthening Duyvesteyn's (2004) claim, the Assassins operated already in an organized network of cells in sympathetic urban centers, they implicated enemies as accomplices, and gained support from key people in the establishment by bribery and intimi-dation (Rapoport 1984). The Assassins become very well known in the Western world, legends were built, and it is said that even the English King Richard Lionheart allegedly

172 *Terrorism in time and space*

employed Assassins to kill Conrad of Montferrat, a north Italian nobleman and de facto king of Jerusalem in the 12th century. They are also known in the contemporary world as the main characters in the video game *Assassin's Creed* (Taylor and Gautron 2015). However, their damage never reached the extent of the Thugs and they inflicted only marginal economic damage (Rapoport 1984). Their method was ineffective against the conquering powers in the Middle East at this time and they were finally eliminated by the Mongols in Persia in 1256 (Taylor and Gautron 2015).

The third group of actors were the Zealots-Sicarii, a religious, Jewish terrorist group active for about 25 years in mid-1st century Judea (Rapoport 1984). They had an extreme doctrine, 'No Lord but God,' and killed members of the Jewish community that acted against this credo (Taylor and Gautron 2015). Their main objective was to fight Roman oppression and subsequently to hinder attempts at reconciliation between the Jews and the Romans (Rapoport 1984). Their targets were Jews, mostly prominent leaders like priests, who cooperated with Roman authorities or other foreigners. In fact, they degraded their Jewish opponents to the status of foreigners or enemies not worth more than Romans. They carefully chose their victims, people from the social and religious elite, known for their high symbolic political value, in order to disrupt the flow of important information from Jewish leaders to the Romans. They aimed to isolate the Romans and to drive a wedge between the Jewish population and their traditional leadership who were thought of as corrupt (Tayler and Gautron 2015). Their goal was to provoke a massive uprising in the population. They resemble the Assassins as they also sought maximum publicity, were promised to get to paradise after their death, had an international character as they transcended state boundaries, used daggers for their terrorist acts, and attacked in daylight on the most holy days. They did not have a particular group leader, but rather there existed several organizations, and various other groups participated in the struggle (Rapoport 1984). Some of the Zealots-Sicarii fled from Judea to Alexandria in Egypt and sought to provoke an uprising against the Roman authority there but failed to do so (Taylor and Gautron 2015). In fact, this even led to the extermination of Jewish centers there (Rapoport 1984). The Zealots-Sicarii had a huge impact on events at the time and sparked the First Roman–Jewish War. However, their ideology and their extreme violence alienated the wider population and facilitated their extinction (Taylor and Gautron 2015). This terrorist group is another example that strengthens the claim of Duyvesteyn (2004) that traditional terrorism has some resemblances to modern terrorism. Taylor and Gautron (2015: 33) even suggest that the Sicarii resemble al-Qaeda and ISIS insofar as they "sought both political and religious outcomes through their actions."

The arguments so far with respect to religion and terrorism and the very separation between the concepts of terrorism and religion seem to rely on the assumption that terrorism is political whereas religion is not. Relatedly, it is assumed that terrorism is driven by an *ideology*, which is again, separable from the concept of religion. On closer inspection, it appears, however, that the two might be in some ways similar, in particular concerning their *function*. Ours is not a textbook on religion or ideology, for which reason we will not delve too much into this topic. It is, however, still useful for scholars of terrorism to ponder some broader considerations on these two elements.

According to Hovorun (2016) in his article *Ideology and Religion*, ideology was an invention of the 18th century formulated as an alternative to religion to have the same impact on the minds and behavior of people. The author traces the roots of ideology back to the French philosopher, Antoine Destutt de Tracy, who lived during the French Revolution (1754–1836) and who constructed ideology as a sort of cognition of the truth without religious bias, that is, as an anti-religious cognition. Karl Marx (1818–1883) criticized the concept of ideology in his work by arguing that it promotes the interests of elite social groups with political and capital power. However, Marxism that struggled with idealist ideologies in the end became an ideology itself. Carl Schmitt (1888–1985) characterized ideology as a secularized epitome of theology, that is, a secular religion with intellectuals as priests. He stated that it could offer a holistic world view, mobilize masses, have the power of a myth, and could supplement religion or replace it. After World War II, the consequences of totalitarian ideologies led to a crisis of ideologies. This was further exacerbated through the emergence of post-modernism, a discourse that was constructed to weaken the impact of totalitarian ideologies on the masses. However, it soon itself became an ideology called 'relativism' (an ideology that posits that views are relative to differences in perception without absolute truth and validity). The 'end of ideology' in the post-modern era led to an epoch of ideologies of a new type. Samuel Huntington defined ideologies in 1957 as a system of ideas regarding the political and social values that define the identity of a group; a cultural software that helps to shape social and political action. This new framework was a binary one, with two opposite parties reflecting the American political system: liberalism and conservatism. Liberalism as ideology holds that all individuals are free and equal and repressive hierarchies are refused. Conservatism assumes that people need strong leaders and strict moral codes to keep them under control. From an anthropological point of view, liberalism is said to be open and optimistic with regard to the capability of people to handle their freedom without external assistance and the paternalism of the state. In fact, freedom is seen as an ultimate value. To the contrary, conservatism is said to be closed and pessimistic with regard to this aspect, denies people the ability to handle freedom responsibly, and even sees it as a source of evil and therefore tries to limit it through state paternalism.

Historically, ideology and theology have had a dialectical relationship, meaning that ideology is emancipated from theology but also influences it. Especially after the 18th century when churches in the West and East, because of their interference in politics, were under the permanent influence of several ideologies, this led to an 'ideologized theology,' "unable to clearly see objective theological truths: it mixes them up with various political desiderata" (Hovorun 2016: 30). This often divided churches along ideological lines, yet not necessarily along the lines of conservatism and liberalism as such. Another concept of ideologization is the concept of 'political Orthodoxy,' which is often coined in conjunction with 'political Islam.' It means the "mobilization of Islamic identity in pursuit of particular objectives of public policy, both within an Islamic society and in its relations with other societies" (ibid: 31). With regard to the conjunction between ideology and politics, Hovorun argues that "The intention of the adherents of 'political Orthodoxy' precisely fits the definition of ideology as a form of the translation of beliefs into social and political action" (ibid: 31).

Critical time and space

CTS scholars have also taken a stance on the notion of 'new terrorism,' however, their critique does not relate to empirical manifestations of terrorism, but to the ways in which terrorism scholars have conceptualized and researched terrorism. A mechanism through which these constructions have been approached and criticized is the concept of 'subjugated knowledge' from Foucault (see also the related concept of 'exclusion' introduced in Chapter 1). In his article, 'Unknown Knowns: The Subjugated Knowledge of Terrorism Studies', Richard Jackson (2012) argues that there exists a range of potentially important subjugated

174 *Terrorism in time and space*

knowledge which has to be released in order to improve the quality of terrorism studies. Following Foucault, the author states that there exist two kinds of subjugated knowledge. First, endogenous knowledge which is present within terrorism studies, that is generated within the practices of the field of terrorism studies but unacknowledged, unreferenced, and not systematically engaged with, so it is buried by more dominant forms of knowledge. It has, for example, been known for several years that terrorism can be employed by both state and non-state actors, that state terrorism is far more deadly, that terrorism is driven by political grievance or opposition to oppressive policies, that non-state actors acting as terrorists are rather unlikely to use weapons of mass destruction, and that terror acts are not necessarily rooted in religious ideology, individual pathology, or hatred. However, this knowledge has been subjugated by the concept of the 'new terrorism' discourse which assumes that terrorism is primarily a violent conflict strategy of non-state actors, that Western states do not practice terror, or that new terrorism must be attributed to processes of radicalization or religious extremism of individuals which are incorrigible and are not open to political dialogue or negotiations. This, of course, has implications for solutions to the terror threat, legitimizing coercive and repressive counter-terrorism strategies. Second, subjugated knowledge can be exogenous to terrorism studies. Contrary to the first type of knowledge, this type has been disqualified and excluded by scholars as naïve, inferior, or insufficiently scientific. This might be knowledge of other scientific fields such as anthropology, criminology, sociology, or history but also non-scientific and subjective experiential knowledge from individuals, communities, terrorists themselves, peacemakers working in conflict zones, journalists, or individuals who have experienced counter-terrorism policy directly. Jackson (2012) states that the most important source of exogenous subjugated knowledge is knowledge generated within peace and conflict studies. This field has produced a huge amount of knowledge, especially on the connections between physical, structural, and cultural violence, human-needs based conflicts, escalation cycles, and so on. However, this knowledge, he argues, is largely unknown in terrorism studies.

In her book, *Disciplining Terror: How Experts Invented "Terrorism,"* Lisa Stampnitzky (2013) also takes a critical but historical approach to the question of how the terrorism discourse emerged and evolved over time. Stampnitzky thus offers historical context and empirical evidence for the circumstances which led to some of the assumptions criticized by Jackson, such as the downplaying of grievance as the cause of terrorism, or of terrorist rationality. She worked qualitatively and used multiple sources and types of data such as archives, a database of sponsors, participants and themes at 150 of the most important terrorism conferences and textual sources, as well as interviews with university-, think-tank, and government-based experts. Furthermore, she used conference reports to investigate the development of the field, and compiled a data set on biographical data on more than 2,000 participants in 150 conferences held between 1972 and 2002. She also used archival materials from government committees and papers of key experts from the US government and research centers such as RAND. She examined three core journals in the field of terrorism research to analyze the changes in the nature of substantive content of research and insiders' views of the development of the field. Finally, she conducted 32 interviews with current and former terrorism researchers on their career paths and their views of the field and attended several conferences, talks, meetings, and seminars on terrorism as an observer.

Stampnitzky found that terrorism was created as a new object in the 1970s. Hijackings, hostage takings, and political violence had already occurred from 1968 to 1972 but it was the massacre at the Olympic Games in Munich in 1972 that is said to be the event that inaugurated the era of modern terrorism. The attack was conducted during the New Left wave which began during the 1960s, as suggested by Rapoport. It was conducted by Palestinian terrorists who took 11 hostages of an Israeli sports team and demanded the release of Palestinians imprisoned in Israel as well as the release of the RAF terrorists, plus Kozo Okamoto, a Japanese left-wing terrorist. However, religious motives played a role in some way too and therefore, there might have been an overlap with the religious wave.

Following this attack, terrorism came to be regarded as a problem in the public sphere and an object of expert knowledge; the term was subsequently used frequently in the media. However, it was not yet entirely clear what the phenomenon 'terrorism' entailed exactly and officials often spoke of 'crimes' and 'assaults' or 'depredations.' Previous studies suggested that the terrorism discourse arose because terrorist attacks appeared as a new problem and because it was enhanced by interested elite parties in Western states and experts whose theories reflected the interests of these elites. Yet, Stampnitzky questions these assumptions and notes that although a dramatic shift of political violence occurred (for instance a rise of hijackings as a new tactic) to non-state actors in the 1960s and 1970s, these incidents were not purely novel and once the term 'terrorism' had been coined, experts also assigned it to past events. She argues that, in fact, the popularity of the discourse on terrorism increased because of changes in three dimensions and their interaction: new sorts of terrorist events occurred, new sorts of experts appeared, and specific forms of techniques of knowledge were applied. A new feature of terrorist events was their transnational character, violence spilling over from local conflicts into the international sphere; this was the key factor that drew attention to the problem. This led to the appearance of new experts, the formation of actor networks, and specific forms of knowledge, factors that are elaborated on in more detail below.

The discourse advanced when US President Nixon began to establish the Cabinet Committee to Combat Terrorism (CCCT) as the first governmental body concerned with terrorism, which comprised high-ranking officials and became a major sponsor of terrorism expertise in the 1970s. Subsequently, an associated working group of the Committee formed, which funded a number of research projects and sponsored conferences on terrorism. Also, research institutes like the RAND Corporation were established. The author notes that in the early 1970s there were only a few, if any, experts on terrorism. This was because the topic was perceived as being too controversial and poorly defined to become a basis for academic study. But with governmental initiatives and independent interest from academia, the production of terrorism expertise increased and within a couple of years terrorism as a hitherto scholarly neglected problem (nothing was published on the subject prior to 1960) was transformed into a topic around which journals, institutes, and conferences were established. By 1977, 161 books had been dedicated to the topic. Also, the connections among terrorism experts increased. Conducting a network analysis, Stampnitzky shows that there was not only a quantitative increase in knowledge-producing activities, but also a growth of relationships between the soon to become terrorism experts. Whereas at the first three conferences from 1972 to 1973 there were no linkages between individual presenters, at conferences in 1976 there were already multiple overlapping ties. Her analysis shows that the majority of the ties were created by a small minority of presenters. From the late 1970s onwards, terrorism studies took shape as a new networked social arena. The numbers of conferences, experts, and publications increased massively. Moreover, there was a qualitative shift in the types of experts and expertise and a shift in the meaning of terrorism. The perception of terrorism as a new problem coincided with the creation of a new type of expert, coming from fields such as collective behavior, social movements, or social psychology, but also from eclectic fields such as arts, medicine, or law. Yet, many of them

176 *Terrorism in time and space*

did not constitute the core of the terrorism studies community in later years. Later prominent experts like Martha Crenshaw, J. Bowyer Bell, and Brian M. Jenkins had often already conducted research on the topic. They came from fields such as political science, intelligence, or counter-insurgency. By the mid- to late 1970s, networks of experts, which Stampnitzky termed the 'terrorism mafia,' formed as the core of the field and established terrorism as an object of knowledge, a legitimate field of study, and organized projects, organizations, and activities. They also funded the major journals *Terrorism* (1977), *Conflict* (1978), and *Terrorism, Violence, Insurgency* (1979). This was at the time when the religious wave, which, according to Rapoport started around 1979, began. Her analysis indicates that terrorism studies as such were not an outgrowth of a pre-existing discipline or institutionalized field, but were a coalescence of individuals and knowledge from various backgrounds that joined the community accidentally. Stampnitzky's work shows that knowledge on terrorism evolved from the interplay of hybrid actors, namely academia, the state, and the media, meaning that not all experts were academics.

In tracing back the origins of terrorism as a field of study, she found that terrorism took its cues from the discourse on insurgency and emerged over the 1970s as a new framework, differentiated from previous understandings of political violence. When the terrorism discourse began, the discourse on insurgency was already in decline because, *inter alia*, of a state-sponsored dubious research project in 1965 that was cancelled before it got off the ground. Yet, the insurgency framework was coherent enough to serve as a basis for the terrorism discourse and some of the new terrorism experts had roots in the field of insurgencies. There were even some continuities that were carried over from one discourse to the other. Terrorism, at its beginning, was seen more as a tactic than a morally defining act. Also, initially, the main role of grievances as a trigger for insurgencies remained central in early analyses of terrorism, even in US governmental reports and especially the unresolved Middle East question. As a result, it was acknowledged that in order to fight terrorism one must first act upon the grievances. But this changed by the late 1970s when a reconceptualization of terrorism occurred and the role of grievances and political motivations as triggers became highly contentious. Rationality was no longer attributed to terrorists, terrorism was then rather seen as barbarism, naïve, fanatical, truly irrational, as psychopathology. Experts who focused on a certain 'understanding' of terrorism even exposed themselves to moral judgments about their 'sympathy' with terrorists and faced difficulties presenting their work as legitimate. From the late 1970s onwards, a moral evaluation was intrinsically built into terrorism and its discourse. The former notion, that a terrorist could be a freedom fighter, was no longer valid. According to the author, this shift in the perception of terrorism can be explained through government elites who wanted to advance their political agenda and therefore shifted the phenomenon as a problem into the public sphere, such as the media. Stampnitzky found evidence in transcripts from congressional hearings of 1974, where members of Congress were likely to label terrorism as evil and irrational, whilst expert witnesses varied in their approach and stressed the role of political grievances. Additionally, terrorism was perceived as more of an imminent threat to the domestic US population because it targeted US Americans and sites of international connection. Furthermore, there was a shift in criminological policy from a framework of rehabilitation to a punitive framework. There was then also the question whether terrorism, being irrational, was susceptible to rational analysis. This impacted on the possibility of terrorism expertise itself. The author concludes that the new discourse on terrorism became problematic as an object of expert knowledge along three axes in terms of the possibility of creating expert knowledge and in terms of conceptualizations of terrorism and terrorists.

Terrorism in time and space 177

These dimensions are rationality, morality, and politics. Contrary to insurgencies, terrorism was necessarily seen as immoral, irrational, and political motives and goals were strongly questioned. With regard to terrorism experts, there was a requirement to condemn terrorism, value-neutral research as well as a rational analysis was questioned, and the possibility of an apolitical expertise was also continually in question. To the contrary, the neutrality of studies towards insurgencies and guerilla warfare was common in the 1960s and 1970s. Prior to 1972 every definition of terrorism referred to state violence; subsequently, the definitions referred to insurgent violence or included both insurgent and state violence.

Summary

This chapter has traced the emergence of terrorism in time and space along the lines of two different approaches: the positivist or traditional school and the critical terrorism studies school. It has dealt with:

- the overview of the four waves of terrorism;
- the debate over the newness of modern religious terrorism;
- subjugated knowledge in terrorism studies;
- the creation of the terrorism discourse in time and space.

Exercises

12.1 Analyze four terrorist organizations and examine them by looking at the features specific to the four waves.
12.2 Identify the features of ancient terrorist groups that contradict the novelty in the various waves.
12.3 What are the differences between religion and ideology?

References

Duyvesteyn, I. (2004). How New Is the New Terrorism? *Studies in Conflict & Terrorism*, 27(5), pp. 439–454.
Eckstein, A.M. (2016). How the Weather Underground Failed at Revolution and Still Changed the World. [Online]. Available from: http://time.com/4549409/the-weather-underground-bad-moon-rising/ [Accessed 29 April 2017].
Hovorun, C. (2016). Ideology and Religion. *Kyiv-Mohyla Humanities Journal*, 3(2016), pp. 23–35.
Huntington, S.P. (1957). Conservatism as an Ideology. *The American Political Science Review*, 51(2), pp. 454–473.
Jackson, R. (2012). Unknown Knowns: The subjugated knowledge of terrorism studies. *Critical Studies on Terrorism*, 5(1), pp. 11–29.
Jewish Virtual Library (2017). *Irgun Tz'Va'I Le'umi (Etzel): Background and Overview.* [Online]. Available from: www.jewishvirtuallibrary.org/background-and-overview-of-the-irgun-etzel [Accessed 6 April 2017].
Rapoport, D.C. (1984). Fear and Trembling: Terrorism in three religious traditions. *The American Political Science Review*, 78(3), pp. 658–677.
Rapoport, D.C. (2004). The Four Waves of Modern Terrorism. In Cronin, A. and J. Ludes (ed) *Attacking Terrorism: Elements of a Grand Strategy*. Washington, DC: Georgetown University Press.
Stampnitzky, L. (2013). *Disciplining Terror. How Experts Invented "Terrorism."* Cambridge: Cambridge University Press.

178   *Terrorism in time and space*

Taylor, D. and Gautron, Y. (2015). Pre-Modern Terrorism. The cases of the Sicarii and the Assassins. In Law, D.R. (ed.) *The Routledge History of Terrorism*. Abingdon/New York: Routledge, pp. 28–44.

Further reading

Austenfeld, T., Daphinoff, D. and Herlth, J. (2011). *Terrorism and Narrative Practice.* Vienna/Zürich/Berlin: LIT Verlag GmbH & Co KG.

Bolt, N., Betz, D. and Azari, J. (2008). *Propaganda of the Deed: Understanding the Phenomenon.* London: Royal United Services Institute.

Burleigh, M. (2009). *Blood and Rage: A Cultural History of Terrorism*. New York: HarperCollins.

Jensen, R.B. (2004). Daggers, Rifles and Dynamite: Anarchist terrorism in nineteenth century Europe. *Terrorism and Political Violence*, 16(1), pp. 116–153.

Hoffman, B. (2006). *Inside Terrorism*, 2nd ed. New York: Columbia University Press.

Hoffman, B. (2008). The Myth of Grass-Roots Terrorism: Why Osama Bin Laden still matters. *Foreign Affairs*, 87(3), pp. 133–138.

Hoffman, B. and Sageman, M. (2008). The Reality of Grass-Roots Terrorism [with Reply]. *Foreign Affairs*, 87(4), pp. 163–166.

Ranstorp, M. and Normark, M. (2015). *Understanding Terrorism: Innovation and Learning. Al-Qaeda and beyond*. Abingdon: Routledge.

Sageman, M. (2008). *Leaderless Jihad: Terror Networks in the Twenty-first Century.* Philadelphia, PA: University of Pennsylvania Press.

13 Counter-terrorism

Asta Maskaliūnaitė

The topic of terrorism has generated an extensive library of books and articles, the amount of which has been increasing exponentially since the 9/11 attacks. A smaller fraction of these studies has been dedicated to the analysis of terrorism's alter ego—counter-terrorism. Until the beginning of this century there were very few works that aimed to systematically address the successes and failures of counter-terrorism policies, and more generally, the ways in which terrorist campaigns end. The reasons for this imbalance in attention are manifold. First, as we have already noted in the initial chapters of this book, most literature on terrorism is sensationalist in character, the topic is flashy, and counter-terrorism successes may often seem anticlimactic. Second, data collection can prove to be similarly challenging to studies dealing with terrorism; while terrorist groups are known to be difficult to access, counter-terrorism officials can be just as secretive, if not even more so, than their adversaries, making it difficult to produce scientific studies with verifiable data and results. Third, also related to the nature of counter-terrorism, counter-terrorism officials who could have most to say about the topic tend to concentrate on the prevention of the next attack rather than reflect on the nature of their own work and the policies that they implement. Finally, because of this focus on prevention, the work on counter-terrorism policies and strategies is mostly concentrated on case studies evaluating what works and what does not work in counter-terrorism and on quantitative analyses that try to assess the effects of different measures. Holistic views of the terrorist challenge and the responses to it are less commonly found.

The studies that do exist and approaches that are taken can be organized in the same categories as discussed in the previous chapters: deterministic, intentional, and relational. This chapter will follow this same categorization, recognizing the difficulty of sorting these often pragmatic approaches into neat, well-defined boxes. For example, as we will see below, scholars and practitioners looking at the short-term preventive measures often also indicate that some long-term political solutions are needed to eradicate terrorist groups. Inversely, scholars who are interested in tackling root causes concede that incentives to participate in terrorism should also be curbed by policing and other methods, which increase the costs of participation in terrorist organizations, thus assuming that terrorist (organizations) are rational, calculating actors whose decision-making can be influenced.

Building on the discussion in Chapter 12 on terrorism in time and space, we first consider from a *historical* perspective the question of how terrorism campaigns end. Here, the focus will be laid on how and why these campaigns end, the role of the individual/group agency therein, and the environmental factors that lead to their demise. Second, we elaborate on the *deterministic* approaches to counter-terrorism. These approaches often involve looking for and addressing the 'roots of terrorism' and trying to devise grand strategies to deal with this challenge. The third part discusses approaches to counter-terrorism through the *intentional*

180 *Asta Maskaliūnaitė*

perspective and therefore examines measures that aim to change opportunity structures or otherwise either encourage disengagement from terrorism or discourage engagement in it. The fourth section addresses the *relational* approaches to counter-terrorism and the last part of the chapter especially considers CTS approaches to counter-terrorism. The CTS was born partially as a response to abuses of power in the name of counter-terrorism and the critique of its policies is one of the cornerstones of this school of thought. In this last section these critiques are discussed.

How terrorism ends

Terrorism often generates so-called 'black swan' events: rare occurrences which have a disproportionate influence on policies, of which the 9/11 attacks are probably the best example, and that give the impression that each new attack or group is uniquely dangerous and requires an entirely new set of measures to tackle it. Remember the new terrorism–old terrorism debate in Chapter 12. To some of the proponents of the 'new terrorism' thesis, groups motivated by religious fundamentalism that have risen to prominence since the 1980s and 1990s have culminated in such seemingly omnipotent actors as al-Qaeda and ISIS, which are fundamentally different from those which preceded them: the Irish Republicans, the Basque separatists, or the Leftist radicals. This view was popular in both policy circles and the academic community at the beginning of the century, marked as it was with such spectacular events as the 9/11 attacks.

With time and with enough distance from these attacks, both policy-makers and researchers started looking more deeply into history and exploring what it could teach us about countering such violent groups. Three works in particular can be distinguished here, each using statistical analysis in combination with in-depth case studies to show how terrorist groups demise (see Table 13.1).

Table 13.1 Comparison of three studies into the end of terrorism

	Jones and Libicki (2008)	*Cronin (2009)*	*Weinberg (2013)*
Data used	648 groups in RAND-MIPT database	457 groups from MIPT database	433 groups from University of Haifa's National Security Studies Centre database, the US Department of State Patterns of Global Terrorism Project, MIPT, and information from Schmid (2011)
How groups end	• Policing • Military force • Splintering • Politics • Victory	• Capture or killing of the group's leader • Entry of the group into a legitimate political process • Achievement of group's aims • Implosion or loss of the group's public support • Defeat or elimination by brute force • Transition from terrorism to other forms of violence	• Defeat • Success • Transformation

These and other investigations reveal a number of misconceptions that are prevalent in the public discourse on terrorism. Four of these misconceptions are addressed in this section: the notion that terrorist groups are strong actors and often achieve their aims; the idea that leadership decapitation leads to a terrorist group's demise; the notion that military force defeats terrorism; and the idea that states do not negotiate with terrorism or that such negotiations lead to more terrorism.

Victory to terrorists?

Probably the largest of these misconceptions concerns the strength of terrorist groups and their abilities to achieve their aims. Public discourse is teeming with demands not to allow terrorists to win, to destroy 'our lifestyle' and similar. According to Weinberg's interpretation of statistics, though, only around 4.5 percent of the groups active in the period between 1968 and 2006 managed to attain their objectives (Weinberg 2013: 31). Jones and Libicki's (2008) study puts this number as high as 10 percent, but their 'victorious' groups contain such actors as the Action Front for the Liberation of the Baltic Countries, which only appeared on the scene with three bombings in 1977. To connect this group's actions with the eventual regaining of independence of the Baltic states in 1990 would be farfetched.

The differences in these statistics indicate how difficult it is to judge a terrorist group's achievement of its aims, especially on the strategic level. Looking deeper into other case studies it appears that the achievement of such aims often happened not because, but despite of the use of terrorism. The most notorious cases of success include Irgun Zvai Le'umi and the establishment of the state of Israel, the African National Congress and the end of Apartheid in South Africa, and the FLN in Algeria. Of the less-publicized cases, the suffragette bombers in the UK could be mentioned (see Box 13.1). In all of these cases the peaceful political movements advocating for such changes were strong and there are powerful arguments to suggest that the violence only slowed down the process already under way (Cronin 2009). The conclusion from research thus seems to suggest that even though many groups achieve some tactical successes, the strategic victories of terrorists are very rare.

Box 13.1 Suffragette bombers

At the juncture of the 19th and 20th centuries, the movement for women's right to vote, or the suffragist movement, produced some notable successes around the world. The British colonies in Australia and New Zealand introduced the right to vote for women at the end of the 19th century. In Europe, Finland was first in 1907 and Norway followed in 1913.

The movement for the introduction of the vote for women was spread throughout the world and mostly the struggle for women's rights proceeded along the lines of peaceful protest. Britain was a notable exception. Here, the suffragette movement produced an organization which was inspired by the anarchist notion of 'Propaganda by the Deed' and insisted on the need to complement political action with violence to achieve the women's vote. The Women's Social and Political Union (WSPU), led by Emmeline Pankhurst, started its campaign with peaceful demonstrations, but progressed along a more militant path with arson attacks on empty houses, window smashing, and even bombings, culminating in the June 1914 bombing of Westminster Abbey.

> This violent side is often forgotten in the histories of the movement, yet current history shows that the use of violence had a detrimental effect on the advance of the the women's vote in Britain, postponing its actual introduction rather than helping it along. The tactics used by the WSPU and by extension the women's movement were seen in parallel to those of the Irish nationalists, creating fears that giving in to women's demands in such circumstances would encourage the Irish to use violence even more extensively.

Leadership decapitation as a way to end terrorist groups

The role of leader capture or elimination became one of the most discussed issues in the field when the tactic of targeted killings started to play an ever-more important role in the playbook of US administrations. For example, the National Strategy for Combatting Terrorism of 2006 puts leadership decapitation as the first among the priorities of action (Jordan 2009). The strategy continued to play a prominent role during the Obama administration with drone strikes used extensively to target terrorist leaders. This debate bled into an eternal social sciences problem of primacy of structure or agency. For example, authors like Jenna Jordan (2009) have doubts about the utility of leadership decapitations and these doubts stem largely from their reservations about the potential impact one individual may have. They dismiss leadership decapitation as a useful tactic and their research suggests that it is not these individuals themselves, but rather the grievances, the incentives, the group dynamics, in other words, structural aspects, that drive the phenomenon of terrorism. Individuals here are trapped in a web of causes and consequences over which they have little control.

On the other side of debate there are those who, like Patrick Johnston (2012), believe in the benefits of 'leadership removal' and are implicitly arguing that the strategic, operational, or tactical skills that leaders bring matter, thus favoring agency over structure. The truth, as is so often the case, is somewhere in between. It is clear that there are some groups which are very dependent on the leaders and there are groups for which particular leadership matters less. The typical examples of heavily leader-dependent groups include the Sendero Luminoso, or Shining Path, in Peru and the Japanese cult-cum-terrorist organization Aum Shinrikiyo. Both organizations were effectively destroyed by police action targeting their leaders. Such successes, however, are few and far between, as most organizations have mechanisms to ensure the transition between leaders and, even when suffering from a loss of expertise, do not experience a collapse. While the debate on the effectiveness of targeted killings is still raging, the evidence of its usefulness for the elimination of terrorist groups is controversial.

Use of military force to deal with terrorism

During the history of terrorism, military force was regularly employed to tackle this challenge and is often one of the first reflexive responses to terrorist attacks. As Cronin writes, "Answering the threat of terrorism with repression, a state's strongest means of defending itself, is natural – even instinctive" (Cronin 2009: 115). She adds that "Sanctimonious statements about the foolishness of force reveal an ignorance of history, or at least selective memory" (ibid: 115). Examples here include the airstrikes on ISIS targets in retaliation for the Paris attacks in November 2015. Arguably, the strikes had a rather symbolic function, as the actual perpetrators of the attacks were later apprehended in France and Belgium. Thus, while it is true that the use of military force has often been a reflexive answer to the terrorist challenge, it is also true that the use of military force has ended only a small fraction of terrorist campaigns. According to Jones and Libicki (2008: 19), this fraction is as low as 7 percent. Again, as with decapitation, the usefulness of military force against a terrorist campaign depends on circumstances.

Authors (for example, Jones and Libicki 2008) suggest that the use of such force is both necessary and efficient when the terrorist threat starts evolving into an insurgency. Where the terrorist group becomes powerful enough as to challenge the state not only by symbolic acts of violence but with the actual take-over of territory, the military becomes a primary responder. The cases where this has happened include the fight against the Liberation Tigers of Tamil Eelam (LTTE) in Sri Lanka, the Russian fight against the Chechens, Peru's against Sendero Luminoso and Uruguay's against the Tupamaros. Yet, even in cases where terrorism evolved into insurgency with its larger-scale capabilities for violence and territory control, only 25 percent of groups ended because of military defeat (ibid). The use of military force has often had little more utility than psychological reassurance (Silke 2005).

In most cases where the military was employed to tackle the terrorism challenge, victory came at a cost of enormous destruction and human suffering. As Cronin (2009: 136–137) writes, "There is a point at which military force, particularly when used internally against a threat within one's territory, succeeds in destroying terrorism because it destroys *everything*." Jones and Libicki (2008) add that military force is too blunt an instrument to be employed against groups which typically contain not more than 100 members. In democratic countries, the use of such force inside one's own state has an additional effect of degrading institutions, often serving as a stepping stone for the establishment of undemocratic regimes, as the examples of Peru, Uruguay, and Russia can testify.

Negotiating with terrorists?

States often insist on a 'no negotiation' policy regarding terrorism, yet of the 43 percent of groups that end their campaigns 'through politics,' the majority do so through some kind of negotiating process. Indeed, rhetoric notwithstanding, the majority of the governments engaged in dealing with long-term terrorist campaigns engage in negotiations at some point during the period of struggle.

Negotiation periods are used by both sides to get respite and regroup and thus do not automatically lead to the end of terrorism. In the cases where they do lead to the end of terrorism, certain factors have to be present. First, the situation needs to reach what William Zartman (2005) calls a "mutually hurting stalemate." Both sides have reached a point where they can hurt one another, but without much chance of tipping the scales in one or other direction. Second, both sides should possess strong leaders capable of imposing their vision on the followers and tackling 'spoilers.' There should be an understanding that even where there is a general will to achieve a negotiated end, there will be 'spoilers' who do not want the end of struggle. Third, having some sponsors of the process helps as the outside backers of peace may work to create trust between the parties, impose some discipline on them, and even provide sticks and carrots for continuing the peace process. Fourth, the changes in the international environment and the perception of the utility of violence can have an influence. As terrorist campaigns are often concerned with nudging history along the path that it already takes, changes in the environment which make history seem to go the other way can be very influential (see Cronin 2009: 62–71).

184 *Asta Maskaliūnaitė*

To conclude, the analysis of the demise of terrorist groups helps us deal with some of the misconceptions around terrorism and the way it may end. The analyses discussed here show that some groups self-destroy few achieve victory; few are ended by the use of military force; negotiations, despite rhetoric to the contrary, end a significant number of campaigns; and the verdict on the impact of leadership decapitation on the group's demise is not yet in. In the rest of this chapter, theories of counter-terrorism and the best approaches to counter-terrorism policy are assessed, following the same typologies as used earlier in this book: that of deterministic, intentional, and relational approaches, finishing with the CTS contribution in this area.

Deterministic approaches to counter-terrorism: Tackling the root causes

As was discussed earlier, deterministic approaches to terrorism see it as a derivative of certain structural conditions, often described as 'root causes.' Counter-terrorism, using such an approach, focuses thus on the long-term perspective, emphasizing the change in these structural conditions and creating an environment that is less conducive or less supportive to terrorism. In military strategy, these are identified as 'hearts and minds' campaigns designed to 'drain the swamp' from which terrorists get their recruits and financial and moral support.

After the 9/11 attacks, most states (all, according to Karin von Hippel 2005: 268) declared in public the need to tackle the root causes of terrorism. The EU, UN, and the Organisation for Economic Co-operation and Development's counter-terrorism strategies put significant emphasis on the 'root causes,' primarily in the form of socio-economic reforms in the countries producing terrorism (von Hippel 2005). The US also introduced the element of tackling root causes in its 2003 counter-terrorism strategy.

The one-year anniversary of the 2004 Madrid bombings was commemorated with the meeting of Club de Madrid, a gathering of former heads of state and prominent policy-makers as well as researchers on terrorism. The gathering sought to explore the question of the root causes of terrorism and, after having identified such causes, propose methods to tackle them. A part of their conclusions focused on long-term developmental measures to decrease the level of terrorism, with the notion that economically advanced societies with a well-developed middle class, run democratically, and based on the principles of equality among groups, are the best recipe for tackling terrorism (see Box 13.2).

Box 13.2 Club de Madrid: Tackling the socio-economic and political causes of terrorism

- Creating development strategies that "mitigate the impact of rapid socioeconomic change on vulnerable segments of the population in poorer countries."
- As education without job opportunities is seen as dangerous, redistribution of new wealth among the population in the form of education and corresponding job opportunities was proposed.
- Promoting women's literacy, education, and economic and political participation.
- Encouraging governments of heterogeneous societies to reduce group discrimination and barriers to domestic socio-economic mobility.
- Designing strategies to reintegrate "weak globalizers" into the world economy.

- Enlisting the cooperation of non-governmental bodies including the corporate sector, financial institutions, and donor NGOs in long-term socio-economic reform efforts.

- Promoting the growth of the middle and professional classes and their organizations. Middle-class civil society groups usually have strong incentives to support non-violent politics and to discourage militants from terrorist actions.

- Facilitating democratic reform, because long-run socio-economic and political policies that reduce the risks of terrorism are easier to implement in democracies than autocracies.

(Club de Madrid 2005)

In general, deterministic approaches to counter-terrorism can be divided into two categories: some that assume a correlation between broader socio-political development and terrorism; and some that are narrower in focus and concern the root causes of terrorism per se, as they look at terrorism as part of conflict and counter-terrorism as part of conflict resolution. The broad approaches in their turn could be divided into two groups: those that focus on socio-economic conditions and their improvement; and those that look to democratization as a means to prevent and limit terrorism.

The first type of investigation often starts from the poverty–terrorism nexus, which was popular immediately after the 9/11 attacks. In spite of this idea being soon dismissed due to lack of evidence, a similar idea, namely, that an increase in development could limit the incidents and support for terrorism, persisted. Thus, as Patrick Cronin (2004) discusses in an article about foreign aid, foreign aid for the US had a long tradition of being used as an instrument of preventing radicalization. This idea was born out of the Marshall Plan to reconstruct Europe and later employed for the same purpose primarily in Latin America. Cronin suggests that foreign aid should be linked to commitment to good governance, therefore allowing the influx of money to be used as a stick (withholding it) and carrot (providing it as a reward for performance) for governments, while at the same time ensuring that these funds are used for the strengthening of institutions and communities, which may work as a first line of defense against terrorism.

The second type of broader approach, the focus on democratization as a means of inhibiting terrorism in the long run, is also persistent. Lack of democracy, transparency, and social justice are identified as grievances which tend to fuel violent resistance and terrorism. Therefore, dealing with these aspects is seen as a way of responding to its 'root causes.' Consequently, for example, Alex Schmid (2005: 226) argues that prevention of terrorism, at least in the political sphere, should be based on four principles: good governance, democracy, rule of law, and social justice.

The proponents of narrower approaches look at terrorism as a part of a larger socio-political conflict and argue that terrorism can be eradicated by addressing the underlying causes of conflict. Addressing root causes through conflict-resolution type engagement, i.e. addressing concrete grievances, has potential in localized conflict situations and, especially when combined with the negotiations, has been proven successful in lessening the impact of terrorist campaigns. The oldest European terrorist groups, the IRA and ETA, have been significantly weakened by political reforms acknowledging the legitimate grievances of the groups they claimed to represent. In the Northern Irish case, the gradual empowerment of the Catholic minority, and in the Basque case, the process of devolution of power to enhance

186 *Asta Maskaliūnaitė*

Basque autonomy after the Spanish transition to democracy took wind out of the sails of the supporters of violence and demonstrated that political aims could be achieved by using non-violent means. In both cases, it could be argued that the policies had a long-term beneficial effect on reducing the challenge of terrorism, but a significant amount of time lapsed until the campaigns actually ended. Yet, though it is difficult to argue against such overarching approaches to counter-terrorism, as, indeed, people everywhere in the world would benefit from improved standards of governance, democracy, and socio-economic conditions, some criticism has also been voiced. First, as von Hippel (2005: 269) writes, the rhetoric notwith-standing, few practical steps were taken to implement them in practice. Western countries did not manage to influence the realities on the ground in their counter-terrorism target area of the Greater Middle East and failed to support changes in, for example, education policy and access to high-quality public education in these countries (ibid).

Second, while the long-term perspective of improving governance is a laudable aim, it is questionable whether it should be subsumed under counter-terrorism. As has been discussed previously, the causal relations between these structural conditions and terrorism are hardly proven, and indeed, studies show that transitional periods, for example, to democracy, make countries most vulnerable to terrorism.

Finally, as terrorism itself tends to generate high emotions, these sometimes spill over to the debate on the root causes. As Alan Dershowitz (2002) contends, for example, attempting to understand and deal with the causes of terrorism gives terrorist tactics their legitimacy and thus increases incidents. His proposal thus is that "We must take precisely the opposite approach to terrorism. We must commit ourselves never to try to understand or eliminate its alleged root causes, but rather place it beyond the pale of dialogue and negotiation" (ibid: 24–25). Lisa Stampnitzky (2013: 187) shows how this position of what she calls anti-knowledge became dominant in the first years after the 9/11 attacks. Terrorism here is understood as the ultimate, biblical evil and "[e]xplanation itself came to be seen by some as profane." Consequently, analytic "attempts to explain [terrorism] would be taken as justifi-cation, and attempts to understand would be elided with sympathy" (ibid: 191). Even though currently the pressure has eased on the scientists to conform to this rigid interpretation of terrorism as evil which has no causes other than itself, and the political nature of terrorism is now largely accepted, the root causes debate still sometimes invites accusations of sympathy for terrorism and disrespect to its victims.

Intentional approaches to counter-terrorism

While tackling the root causes may be a fruitful long-term strategy, with the caveats discussed in the previous section, the short- and medium-term approaches to dealing with it tend to rely on some type of intentional thinking. Two major lines here would be the different rational choice approaches to counter-terrorism and the organizational dynamics of the counter-terrorist.

Rational choice approaches to counter-terrorism: Increasing costs, decreasing benefits

A large part of practical activity and by extension research into counter-terrorism focuses on stopping the next attack, decreasing both vulnerabilities and potential rewards for the attacks. Protection of infrastructure, detection devices in airports, and similar measures are thus supposed to have an effect not only in directly dealing with potential attacks, but also are expected to serve as a deterrent to such attacks in the future. In this respect, both theory

Counter-terrorism   187

and practice follow rational choice models and, contrary to the rhetoric, assume that (potential) terrorists and their organizations are rational actors, which are engaged in cost–benefit calculations, leading them to adopt one or another course of action.

Generally, models based on rational choice in counter-terrorism are built to show how the calculations of costs and benefits by a terrorist organization can be affected and use this background material to evaluate which of the measures has more likelihood to affect the calculation in the direction desired by the counter-terrorist and which may have the opposite effect. The thinking about costs and benefits leads also to two types of strategies proposed: deterrence and defense against terrorist attacks, thus focusing on the increasing costs; and inducement of disengagement for the members of the terrorist organizations, thus adding some benefits for leaving.

First, the increasing costs side of counter-terrorism focuses on the deterrence of terrorism or defense against potential attacks. Deterrence measures include increased sentences for terrorism and other increased legal measures against the potential recruits of terrorist organizations. Use of retaliation, including by military strikes after attacks, is also supposed to serve as an example to deter future terrorist acts. In terms of defense, active and passive measures are distinguished. The active measures include pre-emption and prevention by use of force, while the passive measures include hardening the targets and thus diminishing the chances of a terrorist attack. Measures included here are the use of metal detectors at airports to reduce the incidents of skyjacking, or the fortification of embassies to increase security for diplomats, or even building walls to separate physically warring communities, like in Belfast or between Israel and the Palestinian territories.

The second type of strategy here is measures that create benefits for alternative action, i.e. leaving the terrorist organization and choosing another means of political participation. Examples inlcude legal measures to induce defection from terrorist groups (such as the famous Italian *Pentiti* and *Dissociati* laws; see Box 13.3).

Box 13.3 Italian legal inducements to quit terrorist organizations

During the 1970s Italy suffered from one of the most intense terrorist campaigns in the Western world: 4,362 events of political violence resulted in 351 deaths, among them the prime minister, Aldo Moro, assassinated by the Red Brigades after being held captive for 55 days. Success for the government came with the introduction of new legislation that offered inducements to quit terrorist organizations. The so-called *Pentiti* (repented) law introduced in 1979 allowed a reduction in prison sentences and the possibility of early release for all those who confessed to the crimes committed while in the organization and offered evidence against their comrades. The second system known as the *Dissociati* (disassociated) system allowed for the reduction in sentences and ease in prison conditions in exchange for the severing of links with the terrorist organization, but did not demand either confessions or any new information from the person choosing this path. The system proved very successful in prompting the defection of numerous members of the organizations, effectively destroying the groups within a couple of years of their introduction. Yet, attempts to repeat the same success did not always bring positive results. The Spanish program of social reinsertion, modeled on the same principle, is often seen as unsuccessful, even though it helped dismantle at least one terrorist organization, ETA(pm) (where 'pm' stands for politico-military, a smaller splinter group of ETA, which decided to turn to politics

188 *Asta Maskaliūnaitė*

> after the Spanish transition to democracy). To mitigate the effects of this legislation, the remaining ETA organization issued death threats against all who would take advantage of the scheme and managed to effectively stop the program with some high-profile killings, including that of their former leader, Maria Dolores Gonzalez Katairan.

Criticism of these measures are similar to those regarding terrorist rationality in general. Just like terrorists, governments also tend to make mistakes in assessing the outcomes and effects of their actions. Neither of them functions with complete knowledge of the situation and can only assume what the reaction of the target audiences will be. Actions may be based on wishful thinking rather than strategic calculation. Psychological mechanisms come into play here as well. As Andrew Silke (2003: 228) convincingly demonstrates, the logic of retaliation, for example, has been consistently employed, overlooking the evidence that it does not deter terrorism. Terrorism tends to produce strong emotional responses and lead to pressure on the state to act forcefully and immediately, even when it is not compatible with its long-term rational objectives.

In addition, the measures themselves can have unintended consequences. Enders and Sandler (2011: 133) explore the effects of various measures against terrorist attacks and show the effects of 'transference' when "government policies designed to thwart one type of terrorist behaviour can induce increases in other types of terrorism." As rational actors, terrorists evaluate the price of their attacks and move to 'cheaper' (not only in material terms, but also in terms of effort) types of attack. A paradoxical result of this interaction is often that the civilians of the countries affected become more vulnerable as the terrorists look for 'softer' targets. Similarly, Enders and Sandler suggest that the governments of various states should coordinate their responses to international terrorism, because when one state makes its targets less accessible, the terrorists may move on to those in neighboring states.

Organizing counter-terrorism

The rational choice approach outlined above has the terrorist and terrorist organization at its center and looks for ways to influence them without delving deeper into the internal dynamics of counter-terrorist institutions and indeed often assuming that the state engaged in counter-terrorism is a kind of unitary actor. A small fraction of the literature, however, tries to unpack this black box of counter-terrorism and looks into the dynamics of interagency cooperation and rivalry, examining how these shape the outlook and outcomes of the fight against terrorism. This is in a sense the flipside of the organizational approach to terrorism (see Chapter 8). The works that focus on these aspects show that, first, counter-terrorism policy is never a unitary stable plan, but is an outcome of the process of negotiation and rivalry between different agencies and other governmental and even non-governmental actors; and second, that because of this continuous negotiation and re-negotiation, the outcome of counter-terrorism policy is never based only on the objective assessment of the threat.

In her analysis of counter-terrorism policy and its relation to political process, Crenshaw (2013: 183) argues that "American counter-terrorism policy is not just a response to the threat of terrorism, whether at home or abroad, but a reflection of the domestic political process." She shows how counter-terrorism policy is born out of interactions between the executive branch, its various agencies and Congress, each of which has a preference for one or another type of policy solution. As in democratic politics, none of these institutions has a complete domination of the process, the resulting policies are an outcome of difficult compromises, and consequently, no administration develops "a consistent policy based on an objective appraisal of the threat of terrorism to American national interests" (ibid: 190).

This lack of objective appraisal of threat is most apparent in the discussion of the 9/11 attacks and the missed possibilities to stop them. According to Parker and Stern (2002: 607), the agencies responsible for the fight against terrorism in the US at the time, according to the authors, suffered from the psychological effects of their previous successes, resulting in the overvaluation of those successes, overconfidence, and insensitivity to warnings about their current policies. In addition, past terrorism incidents lured them into wishful thinking that terrorism was something that happened abroad (ibid: 607). Politicians, on their part, also failed to take terrorism seriously enough and did not create robust frameworks for its prevention.

In terms of bureaucratic dynamics, the organizations responsible for terrorism were too numerous, they lacked a well-developed cooperation and coordination structure, failed to share information between themselves, and were engaged in strong interagency rivalries (ibid: 610–614). In addition to these factors, the agencies were limited by standard operating procedures and simply had difficulty in distinguishing real signals from noise, also continuously trying to balance between underreaction and overreaction. Such findings were largely echoed in the 9/11 Commission report, which found miscommunication between different agencies at the heart of the failure to prevent the attacks.

In the US, the establishment of the Department of Homeland Security was supposed to address such issues. Yet, as shown above with regard to the aims of terrorist organizations, one of those aims is survival. The same aim applies also to the organizations dealing with counter-terrorism. As the literature on bureaucratic politics shows, governmental agencies are also wired for survival and expansion. The exaggeration of the threat of terrorism by counter-terrorism organizations in order to justify their existence and expansion is one of the dangers of which this theoretical approach warns.

Relational approach

In the chapters dealing with the relational approach to terrorism, it was shown that this approach entails looking at terrorist emergence and evolution through the prism of interaction between different actors. Relational approaches are largely found in the realm of social movement studies and more specifically their application to terrorism arises in the frame of contentious politics within the relational approach. Contentious politics is furthermore defined as consisting of "discontinuous, public, collective claim making in which one of the parties is a government" (Tilly 2003: 9). The centrality of the government in the discussions of contentious politics defines the importance of this approach to counter-terrorism. Yet, the studies using this approach tend to focus on the side of the contenders and use government action as an external trigger for the activities of a group. Governmental agencies and the development of their involvement with terrorism are largely left aside. The government and its agencies' actions, such as the use of police violence, are treated here as if they were independent variables which explain some of the variation in the dependent variable, which is the presence of terrorism.

The terrorist groups themselves place a strong emphasis on the potential overreaction of the state in their strategies, using some variant of the action–reaction–action model in their thinking. The role of the state is discussed in this way particularly in the approaches of those following the social movements perspective. On the individual level, encounters with state violence are seen as a rite of passage, propelling an individual on the path towards greater radicalization. The interaction, however, is not unidirectional, the counter-terrorism forces are also learning organizations and, as is noted in, for example, Cronin's research (2004, 2009), though they often start by overreacting and making mistakes, in most cases they end up adapting to the new challenge and adopting a more measured approach to the issue. Here, the counter-terrorist organizations are learning organizations which follow the impacts of the measures they take as much as terrorists themselves try to avoid being impacted by those measures. Similarly, in Art and Richardson's (2007) *Democracy and Counter-terrorism: Learning from the Past*, the wax and wane of the popularity of terrorist groups is seen as a product of the interaction between the audiences they try to influence, their own acts or mistakes, and actions or mistakes of the governments (see Box 13.4).

Box 13.4 Playing to the audience

As mentioned previously, the terrorists need support in terms of money, recruits, and even simple encouragement. Similarly, the counter-terrorists needs to prove that what they are doing is advancing a public good, that their actions are actually beneficial for society. In democratic societies, especially, their funding depends on the satisfaction or dissatisfaction of parliaments with their work. In this respect, both terrorists and governments play to the audience and hope for their support.

For example, in Northern Ireland, support for the IRA and the government fluctuated in this pattern. The IRA's popularity rose with events such as the introduction of internment and hunger strikes. Evidence of the practice of 'shoot to kill' or the collusion of police with the loyalist paramilitaries also increased its popularity. The IRA was looked at less favorably and the government's position improved with the IRA attacks that indiscriminately killed civilians. The most powerful example of the latter being the Omagh bombing in 1998, which killed 29 people and injured 220 others, which proved decisive in turning public opinion against the violent republicans.

In India, the two attempts to dislodge the Sikh militants from the Golden Temple complex show such a learning process and the recognition of the importance of the reactions of the audience. The first such attempt, in 1984, used regular armed forces and killed more than a thousand people, including many civilians. As a result, even moderate Sikhs were outraged, divisions between the Hindu and Sikh communities deepened, and violence escalated. Four years later in similar circumstances, only special forces were used and the attack ended with 30 terrorist deaths and no civilian deaths. This time, the actions of the terrorists, widely covered by the media, created outrage and undermined support for them.

One of the best examples of relational approaches to counter-terrorism can be found in Beatrice de Graaf's study (2011) on the performative power of counter-terrorism. De Graaf proposes looking at both counter-terrorism and terrorism as communication strategies. This approach has significant similarities with social movement theory's take on framing, as discussed in Chapter 6. Counter-terrorism is seen here "not as a coherent strategy to start with, but a process in which objectives can fluctuate between different institutions, political parties and change along the tide of public interest or discontent" (ibid: 13–14). Looking at these political processes and at counter-terrorism officials as at any other officials in the state, she identifies three areas in which they want to have an impact: setting the agenda, organizing support, and framing discourse (ibid: 14). To analyze how effective counter-terrorism is in these aspects, different measures to the absence or presence of terrorist attacks are needed. Here, de Graaf introduces the notion of performativity, "the extent to which a national government by means of its official counterterrorism policy and corresponding discourse, is successful in selling its representation of events, its set of solutions to the terrorist problem, as well as being able to set the tone for the overall discourse on terrorism and counterterrorism" (de Graaf and de Graaff 2010: 261).

It is thus the 'process and performance of counter-terrorism' that needs to be evaluated and that can be done by taking five aspects into account:

1   Whether the question was politicized;
2   Whether it was defined as directly threatening public safety and security;
3   How broad or narrowly the government defines the threat? For example, are only the perpetrators of the acts considered guilty of terrorism, or also supporters and sympathizers?;
4   The extent to which the counter-terrorism measures have a mobilizing impact on society;
5   How the fight against terrorism is presented. Is it relentless strife against a "broad circle of terrorists and their sympathizers, or [is] violence ... seen as a part of larger social movement with some legitimate grievances?" (ibid: 268).

Perhaps, counter-intuitively, the lower the performative power of counter-terrorism, the more successful the counter-terrorism action. The decline in such power corresponds to the decline in the number of terrorist incidents and vice versa. Yet, high-profile incidents with many victims necessarily increase the visibility of terrorism and at the same time the perfor-mativity of counter-terrorism. The two thus have a symbiotic relationship and influence one another in the process. The end of terrorist violence in this explanation is linked to the "decrease of political and public relevance attached to terrorism and counter-terrorism" (ibid: 270).

To prove that counter-terrorism performativity has an influence on the levels of terrorism and not only the other way around, the author analyses the cases of the Netherlands, Italy, Germany, and the US in the 1970s. In these accounts, she convincingly shows that the reduction in the performative power of counter-terrorism actually preceded the decrease in terrorist violence, not vice versa. The Dutch situation appeared a little different, but here the level of violence and performativity were both quite low compared to the other countries and the role of terrorism in public debate was very limited throughout the period under analysis (de Graaf 2011: 138–139).

Critical approaches to counter-terrorism

Relational approaches suggest that terrorism should always be viewed in context and that its significance cannot be disentangled from broader political issues and cleavages. Counter-terrorism actions and tools are also constrained by this context and, the more salient the issues at stake, the less room for maneuver the counter-terrorist has. In this respect, CTS follows this tradition of research with the significant addition of 'bringing the state back in' to such analyses.

192　*Asta Maskaliūnaitė*

CTS scholars start their analysis of counter-terrorism with two major premises: that terrorism and counter-terrorism are "symbiotic cultural constructs" and that counter-terrorism should be seen as a "discursive and cultural construct" (Holland 2016: 203). Starting from such premises, they thus aim to deconstruct discourses and to locate the practices of counter-terrorism in their particular relational contexts. Three major lines of investigation can be distinguished here: first, emphasis on the terrorism threat as exaggerated and the threat and practice of state terrorism as underestimated; second, critical evaluation of foreign policy discourses and practices of Western countries since 9/11; and finally, the dynamics within the 'counter-terrorist complex' and the critique of 'experts' as a significant part of this complex. These are now examined in turn.

Threat of terrorism

CTS studies aim to show that the non-state terrorism threat is exaggerated, that it is not 'existential' in nature, and thus does not require 'state of exception' type responses; second, on the flip side, that state terrorism is a much more significant problem. They argue that the enormous amount of resources spent on the counter-terrorism effort is wasteful, as the security risk posed by terrorism to an ordinary citizen of contemporary states (outside the zones of conflict) is minute. Statistics shows, for example, that the probability of an average American citizen dying in a terrorist attack is approximately the same as that of being hit by an asteroid (Jackson et al. 2011: 133).

Given such levels of actual threat, CTS scholars argue that the 'state of exception' which is used to rationalize the deterioration of the human rights regime is unwarranted. In this respect, they particularly criticize the use of force in counter-terrorism and show how this use has increased significantly since the attacks of 9/11 and consequently reduced the human security of those at the receiving end of counter-terrorism practices, primarily people in the so-called global South (see Chapter 11).

Analysis of counter-terrorism as discursive practice: Foreign and security policy discourses

As the theories looking at the organization of counter-terrorism explore the ways in which interaction between different actors produce contingent systems, the discourse analysis proposed by some critical studies scholars suggests looking at the *genealogy of counter-terrorism* and exploring the roots of its practices in order to better understand its shape and form in the present. In so doing it also explores the *meanings* of both terrorism and counter-terrorism that are abandoned in the process and looks at these potential alternative histories to show the contingent nature of current counter-terrorism. Looking at counter-terrorism in a broader context, continuities can also be explained and in this case, counter-terrorism is analyzed as part of the cultural environment. The analysis of popular culture artifacts, such as films, TV shows, books, graphic novels, etc. is proposed here to show how the image of a terrorist is constructed and how such images travel from one context to another (Stump and Dixit 2013: 119–140).

In particular, a large part of CTS is focused on the foreign and security discourses of Western states since 9/11. As Jackson et al. contend:

> rather than asking how terrorists who are opposed to Western foreign policy can be defeated, it might instead be asked how and why Western foreign policy provokes

Counter-terrorism 193

violent responses. In taking this approach, critical scholars challenge the view that Western societies are simply innocent victims of terrorism, suggesting instead that the best way to respond to terrorism might be to review and revise oppressive policies which provoke violent resistance in the first place.

(Jackson et al. 2011: 243)

Looking at them through the lens of discourse, CTS proposes to examine how the practice of counter-terrorism and the language used to justify this practice create new social realities, for example, how terrorism was transformed from a minor law-and-order issue into a major existential threat following the attacks of 9/11. These studies are also interested in showing how differences in seeing terrorism and counter-terrorism efforts emerge due to varied cultural settings in which these discourses are produced. Finally, they aim to demonstrate the hegemonizing effort of these discourses and the consequent silencing of the opposing discourses, especially in the immediate aftermath of the 9/11 attacks (see Box 13.5).

Box 13.5 Three foreign policy discourses after 9/11

In his study of foreign policy discourses of the UK, Australia, and the US, Holland (2013) uses a three-step framework to show how these discourses came into being and to discuss their practical implications. The first premise in this framework is that politicians use language to paint a certain picture of the world, they identify friends and enemies and give them 'geographical addresses.' Second, they cannot do that the way they please, but have to plug into the pre-existing cultural knowledge of the target audience. Third, the language of national interest and national identity makes resistance difficult and alternative discourses are silenced.

All three states he analyzes used similar rhetoric in their initial response to these attacks. They claimed that the attack on the US was an attack on all of them, that the attack presented a moment of rupture, and that the response should be focused on al-Qaeda and its host, the Taliban regime in Afghanistan. Despite starting from the same premise, the discourses they produced were different due to different historical and cultural settings. In the US, the binary of good vs. evil prevailed; in the UK, the rationality of British leadership and its continuous importance on the global stage was emphasized; and the Australian response involved a mixture of 'emotional and practical solidarity.' In all three cases, the strength of official discourses made it difficult for opponents to have their voices heard as any criticism of concrete policies was deemed unpatriotic and, in a Manichean version, outright evil.

The problem-solving focus of counter-terrorism and the role of experts

One of the major criticisms by CTS scholars of 'mainstream' terrorism studies is its instrumental nature, problem-solving focus, and state-centric approach when dealing with the subject. The narrow focus on the immediate problem does not allow the counter-terrorist to look at the broader picture, to view terrorism within a context, and to evaluate the relations between the different actors which lead to violence. Here the role of 'terrorism experts' becomes important and a part of CTS thus focuses on their failure to adopt a "critically reflexive attitude" and to take seriously "ethical challenges and consequences of conducting research on political violence" (Jackson et al. 2009: 220).

194 *Asta Maskaliūnaitė*

This is particularly demonstrated by the failure of researchers to "condemn particular counterterrorism policies such as targeted assassination, rendition, torture" etc., the "co-option of researchers into government-determined research programs," and the "tainting of researchers with the suspicion that they may be working for the security services" (ibid: 221). Looking back at the start of the CTS project, Richard Jackson (2015: 198) argued that it was conceived as an "anti-expertise movement" and as such "sought to challenge and contest the very notion and basis of 'terrorism expertise' and the 'terror expert' itself," thus subjecting "orthodox terrorism studies and expertise to systematic critique of its problematics, concepts, procedures, practices and, most importantly, accepted knowledge" (ibid: 193).

In his 2016 article, Jackson argues forcefully that:

> In such conditions, where counterterrorism causes widespread suffering and is an obstacle to progressive change and social justice, it can be argued that working directly with state counterterrorism is akin to medical professionals who collaborate with torturers in an effort to improve prisoner welfare; while there may be some benefit to individual prisoners who perhaps suffer less as a consequence, the broader impact of their participation is the perpetuation and legitimization of the overall system of torture, and their involvement does nothing to fundamentally change an inherently immoral set of practices.
>
> (Jackson 2016: 122)

The critical scholar should thus not seek to engage with the state, but to "embrace our 'outside theorizing,' 'anti-hegemonic' identity, recognizing that in truth we have no voice in the structures of power anyway, nor are we likely to ever have any real influence over the way state power operates" (ibid: 124).

It must be admitted that Jackson's is one of the more radical positions in CTS. Other significant members of the project, such as Jaroen Gunning and Harmonie Toros, are more inclined to find accommodation with the policy-makers and have their voices heard. For them, too, it is difficult to deal with the tension inherent in such a desire to be heard and the need, implied by critical theory, to be emancipatory and anti-hegemonic. Yet, the role of the expert and expertise in the development of counter-terrorism seems to be one of the major dividing lines between the critical studies of terrorism and their more 'traditional' variety.

Summary

This chapter explored the different avenues for analyzing counter-terrorism. It has dealt with:

- the premise that all terrorist groups eventually end and it looked at the ways in which this end can be facilitated;
- the deterministic approach to counter-terrorism, which looks at the root causes of terrorism and proposes long-term strategies to eradicate it;
- the intentional approach, which looks at the cost–benefit analysis of terrorist groups and how this can be affected, as well as looking into the dynamics of counter-terrorist organizations and showing how the interaction between different actors produces certain contingent results;

- the relational approach, for example, de Graaf's notion of 'performative power' as a measure of counter-terrorism effectiveness was introduced here and CTS approaches to counter-terrorism as discursive and cultural constructs were discussed.

Exercises

13.1 What are ways of looking at terrorism from the counter-terrorist perspective other than the dichotomy of terrorism-as-crime vs. terrorism-as-war?
13.2 What are the advantages and disadvantages of dealing with root causes as part of counter-terrorism?
13.3 If decreasing performativity leads to more successful counter-terrorism, how can this decrease be encouraged?

References

Art, R.J. and Richardson, L. (2007). *Democracy and Counterterrorism: Lessons from the Past.* Washington, DC: US Institute of Peace Press.

Club de Madrid (2005). *Addressing the Causes of Terrorism.* The Club de Madrid Series on Democracy and Terrorism, Volume I. Madrid: Club of Madrid.

Crenshaw, M. (2013). *Explaining Terrorism: Causes, Processes and Consequences.* London: Routledge.

Cronin, P. (2004). Foreign Aid. In A.K. Cronin (ed.) *Attacking Terrorism. Elements of Grand Strategy.* Washington, DC: Georgetown University Press, pp. 238–261.

Cronin, A.K. (2009). *How Terrorism Ends: Understanding the Decline and Demise of Terrorist Campaigns.* Princeton, NJ: Princeton University Press.

de Graaf, B. (2011). *Evaluating Counterterrorism Performance: A Comparative Study.* London: Routledge.

de Graaf, B. and de Graaff, B. (2010). Bringing Politics Back In: The introduction of the 'performative power' of counterterrorism. *Critical Studies on Terrorism*, 3(2), pp. 261–275.

Dershowitz, A.M. (2002). *Why Terrorism Works: Understanding the Threat, Responding to the Challenge.* New Haven, CT: Yale University Press.

Enders, W. and Sandler, T. (2011). *The Political Economy of Terrorism.* Cambridge: Cambridge University Press.

Holland, J. (2013). *Selling the War on Terror: Foreign Policy Discourses after 9/11.* London: Routledge.

Jackson, R. (2015). On How to Be a Collective Intellectual. Critical Terrorism Studies (CTS) and the Countering of Hegemonic Discourse. In T.V. Berling and C. Bueger (ed.) *Security Expertise: Practices, Power and Responsibility.* London: Routledge, pp. 186–203.

Jackson, R. (2016). To Be or Not to Be Policy Relevant? Power, emancipation and resistance in CTS research. *Critical Studies on Terrorism*, 9(1), pp. 120–125.

Jackson, R., Smyth, M.B. and Gunning, J. (2009). *Critical Terrorism Studies. A New Research Agenda.* London: Routledge.

Jackson, R., Jarvis, L., Gunning, J. and Breen-Smyth, M. (2011). *Terrorism: A Critical Introduction.* Basingstoke: Palgrave Macmillan.

Johnston, P. (2012). Does Decapitation Work? Assessing the effectiveness of leadership targetting in counterinsurgency campaigns. *International Security*, 36, pp. 47–77.

Jones, S.G. and Libicki, M.C. (2008). *How Terrorism Ends. Lessons for Countering al-Qaeda.* Santa Monica, CA: RAND Corporation, HV6431. j65, 17.

Jordan, J. (2009). When Heads Roll: Assessing the effectiveness of leadership decapitation. *Security Studies*, 18, pp. 719–755.

Parker, C.F. and Stern, E.K. (2002). Blindsided? September 11 and the origins of strategic surprise. *Political Psychology*, 23(3), pp. 601–630.

Schmid, A. (2005). Prevention of Terrorism: Towards a multi-pronged approach. In T. Bjorgo (ed.) *Root Causes of Terrorism: Myths, Reality and Ways Forward*. London: Routledge, pp. 223–240.

Silke, A. (2003). *Terrorists, Victims and Society: Psychological Perspectives on Terrorism and its Consequences*: Chichester: John Wiley & Sons.

Silke, A. (2005). Fire of Iolaus: The role of state countermeasures in causing terrorism and what needs to be done. In Stampnitzky, L. (2013). *Disciplining Terror. How Experts Invented "Terrorism."* Cambridge: Cambridge University Press, pp. 241–255.

Stampnitzky, L. (2013). *Disciplining Terror. How Experts Invented "Terrorism."* Cambridge: Cambridge University Press.

Stump, J.L. and Dixit, P. (2013). *Critical Terrorism Studies: An Introduction to Research Methods*. London: Routledge.

Tilly, C. (2003). *The Politics of Collective Violence*. Cambridge: Cambridge University Press.

von Hippel, K. (2005). *Europe Confronts Terrorism*. London: Springer.

Weinberg, L. (2013). *The End of Terrorism?* London: Routledge.

Zartman, W. (2005). *Need, Creed and Greed in Intrastate Conflict: Rethinking the Economics of War. The Intersection of Need, Creed, and Greed*. Washington, DC: Woodrow Wilson Center Press.

Further reading

Bigo, D. and Tsoukala, A. (2008). *Terror, Insecurity and Liberty: Illiberal Practices in Liberal Regimes after 9/11*. London: Routledge.

Bjørgo, T. (2013). *Strategies for Preventing Terrorism*. London: Springer/Palgrave.

Byman, D.L. (2006). Friends Like These. Counterinsurgency and the War on Terrorism. *International Security*, 31(2), pp. 79–115.

Crelinsten, R.D. (2002). Analysing Terrorism and Counter-Terrorism: A communication model. *Terrorism and Political Violence*, 14(2), pp. 77–122.

Crelinsten, R. (2013). *Counterterrorism*. New Jersey: John Wiley and Sons.

Crenshaw, M. and LaFree, G. (2017). *Countering Terrorism*. Washington, DC: Brookings Institution Press.

de Wijk, R. (2002). The Limits of Military Power. *The Washington Quarterly*, 25(1), pp. 75–92.

English, R. (2016). *Illusions of Terrorism and Counter-Terrorism*. Oxford: Oxford University Press.

Erlenbusch, V. (2016). Terrorism Knowledge, Power, Subjectivity. In P. Dixit and J.L. Stump (eds) *Critical Methods in Terrorism Studies*. London: Routledge, pp. 108–120.

Joseph, J. (2016). Reading Documents in their Wider Context. Foucauldian and realist approaches to terrorism discourse. In P. Dixit and J.L. Stump (eds) *Critical Methods in Terrorism Studies*. London: Routledge, pp. 19–32.

Sederberg, P. (1995). Conciliation as Counter-Terrorist Strategy. *Journal of Peace Research*, 32(3), pp. 295–312.

Silke, A. (2010). The Psychology of Counterterrorism. Critical issues and challenges. In A. Silke (ed.) *The Psychology of Counterterrorism*. London: Routledge, pp. 1–18.

Sinai, J. (2005). A Conceptual Framework for Resolving Terrorism's Causes. In T. Bjorgo (ed.) *Root Causes of Terrorism. Myths, Reality and Ways Forward*. London: Routledge, pp. 215–222.

Van Dongen, T.W. (2013). Law Enforcement as Politics by Other Means: Lessons from countering revolutionary terrorism. *Police Practice & Research*, 14(5), pp. 428–441.

Index

Abu Ghraib 16, 162–3
Action Front for the Liberation of the Baltic
  Countries 181
Afghanistan 14, 37, 96, 105, 114, 154–5, 161,
  169, 170, 193
Agency xii, 2–5, 21, 23, 39, 44–5, 47, 50, 77,
  80–1, 94, 104–5, 109, 133, 138, 148, 156,
  162–3, 179, 182
Aggression 13, 35, 44, 54, 60–2, 80, 92, 151;
  frustration-aggression 44–5, 49, 51, 61–62
Algeria ix, 115, 153, 181
Algerian War ix, 115, 153
Al-Qaeda viii, 37–8, 49, 62, 98–9, 101–2, 112,
  114, 170, 172, 178, 180, 195
Al-Jamaa 129
Anarchist terrorism 178
Anarchists 96, 112
Anticolonial 165, 167–8
Arafat, Yasser 23, 120
Assassins 166, 171–2, 178
Attribution error 58–9
Attrition xii, 115
Aum Shinrikiyo, 182

Baader-Meinhof 23, 58
Beirut, barracks bombings viii, 112, 114
Bin Laden, Osama 99, 114, 121, 170, 178
Black September Organization 30
Bush, George W. xvii, 98, 154, 162

Career 40, 42, 54, 96, 138, 144–5, 174
Causality 2, 8, 16, 57, 71, 103, 131, 147
Causal mechanisms 104, 124, 127
CCCT xi, 175
Civil liberties 16, 19, 96, 98
Civil war 28, 35–6, 112, 115, 134
Clandestine organization xii, 78, 126, 131
Club de Madrid ix, 184–5, 195
Cognitive restructuring xii, 15, 80

Cold War 37, 161, 164, 167–8
Collective political violence 108
Colonialism xii, 160, 167
Conservatism xii, 173, 177
Constructivism xii, 133
Contentious politics xiii, 78, 123–4, 127, 131,
  135–6, 189
Contest 3, 73, 111, 194
Counterculture 79, 82–4, 92
Counter-terrorism i, vi, viii, 1–4, 8, 14, 16, 18,
  21, 24, 28, 42, 48, 58, 61, 74, 91, 94, 103,
  137, 147, 149, 150, 154, 174, 179, 180–9,
  190–6
Critical discourse analysis viii, xiii, 16
Critical terrorism studies, CTS xi, 3, 6–8, 18–9,
  20, 25–6, 28, 33–5, 37, 47–8, 77, 123, 155,
  173, 180, 184, 191–5
Critical theory xiii, 3, 5, 8, 11, 16, 18, 22, 194

Democracy 5, 18, 24, 29, 36, 48, 66, 98, 99,
  100, 104–7, 126, 140, 155, 161, 163, 185–6,
  188, 195
Democratic peace theory viii, 98, 107
Deprivation 6, 50–2, 59, 61, 65, 96–7, 160
Deprivation, relative xvi, 5, 50–1, 53, 56–7, 62,
  85, 96–7, 104, 111
De-radicalization v, 137–8, 147, 149, 151
Desistance 141–2, 145, 150–1
Deterministic approach 2–5, 7, 37, 44–5, 47, 50,
  57, 60, 62, 65, 67, 70, 77, 92, 94, 104, 106,
  108, 123, 148, 153, 163, 179, 184–5, 194
Discourse analysis 8, 16, 22, 48, 165, 192
Differential association theory 141, 144
Disengagement v, 2, 14–5, 23, 137–9, 140–9,
  150–1, 180, 187
Dissociati 187

Economy, political 195
Economy, world 184

198 *Index*

Ethniki Organosis Kyprion Agoniston, EOKA xi, 90–1
Ethnographic methods 20, 48
Ethno-nationalist terrorism 105
Europe i, x, xv, 9, 12, 24, 40, 49, 53, 70, 76, 92, 124, 136, 148–9, 150–1, 166, 168, 178, 181, 185, 196
Euskadi ta Askatasuna, ETA x, xi, 27, 36, 41, 116, 129, 140, 151, 185, 187–8
Exit from terrorism 137, 151
Extremism x, 9, 11, 23, 42, 54, 56, 63, 76–7, 89, 92, 96, 104, 128, 137, 139, 140, 144, 146–8, 150–1, 174

Failed state 101, 107
Fatah 115
Fatwa xiii, 114
FBI xi, 22–3, 63, 169
French revolutionary terror viii, ix, 28, 152
Front de Libération Nationale, FLN xi, 153, 181
Frames viii, xiii, 71, 73, 79, 80–2, 85, 113, 126–7, 129, 133, 144, 149
Framing viii, 2, 14, 61, 70, 78–9, 81–2, 92, 124, 126, 144, 146, 190–1
Framing theory 2, 70, 78–9, 81
Freedom fighter xiii, 23, 25, 35, 84, 167–8, 176
Free rider dilemma xiii, 7, 46, 110
French Revolution xiv, xvi, 27–8, 30, 152, 157, 172
Frustration 44–5, 50–2, 54, 56, 61–2, 70, 86, 99, 100, 108–9, 111, 128
Fuerzas Armadas Revolucionarias, FARC xi, 11
Fundamentalism 180

GDP xi, 96
Genealogy 2, 5, 134–5, 192
Genocide xiv, 155–8, 163
Globalization 97, 99, 100–1, 103, 107, 136
Global south 154, 192
Greed 45, 196
Grievances 4, 6, 12–3, 18, 30–1, 43–5, 60–3, 99, 100–2, 105, 111, 113, 118, 126, 134, 148–9, 174, 176, 182, 185, 191
Grounded theory, GT viii, xi, 17, 70, 76
Group polarization xiv, 88
Grupos Antiterroristas de Liberación, GAL xi, 27, 36
Guantanomo Bay 14, 16
Guerilla warfare 153, 177

Hamas xi, 51–3, 102, 115, 120
Hezbollah 37, 95, 112, 114

Human rights xvi, 16, 20–1, 48, 102, 134, 155–7, 164, 192
Humiliation 50–3, 99

Identity xvi, 5, 38–9, 40, 50, 54–7, 59, 60–2, 64, 67, 78–9, 83–6, 89, 90, 92–3, 99, 133, 143, 145, 148, 161, 173, 193–4
Ideology xii, xiv, 4, 11–2, 15, 42–4, 60–2, 70, 73, 78–9, 80, 83–6, 92, 99, 100–1, 103, 111, 113, 130–2, 138–9, 141, 146, 148, 153, 166–8, 170, 172–4, 177
India 97, 167, 171, 190
Insurgency 30, 35, 111, 122, 162, 176, 183
Intelligence x, 41, 63, 148, 176
Intentional approach 2–4, 6–7, 37, 44–8, 60, 65, 70, 72, 75, 77–8, 80, 82–4, 92, 105, 108–9, 111, 117, 121, 123, 135, 141–2, 152, 158, 163, 184, 186, 194
International conventions xiv, 26
International relations, IR xi, 20, 154
International terrorism 8, 19, 22, 163, 188
Internet 42, 49, 62, 75, 85, 102, 106–7
Interviews 20, 48, 51, 54, 58, 67–8, 70, 76–7, 90, 137, 140, 143, 147, 174
Iraq xi, 16, 80, 96, 98, 104, 112, 154–5, 162
Iran 96, 170
Irish National Liberation Army, INLA xi, 119
Irish People's Liberation Organization, IPLO xi, 119
Irish Republican Army, IRA viii, xi, 38, 41, 49, 70, 106, 112, 119, 121, 141, 165, 190
ISIS xi, 96, 172, 180, 182
Islamic State xi, 11, 81
Israel viii, xi, 51, 67, 89, 99, 105–6, 114, 120, 127, 167, 170, 175, 181, 187
Israel Defense Forces, IDF xi, 51
Italy viii, 13, 54–6, 59, 68, 77–8, 90, 92, 126, 136, 144–5, 167, 191

Jihad xiv, 53, 61–3, 72, 81, 84–6, 92, 96, 98–9, 102, 106, 121, 178
Just war theory xiv, 32–3

Knowledge xii, xiii, xv, 16–9, 39, 67, 71, 75, 62, 110, 133, 173–7, 186, 188, 193–4, 196

Labeling 3, 11, 13–4, 16–7, 21–2, 25, 34, 39, 40, 47, 150
Left-wing terrorism 13, 39, 54, 78, 127, 129, 144–5
Legitimacy 14, 100, 112–3, 119, 120, 157, 161, 166, 186

Liberalism xiv, xv, 99, 173
Liberation Tigers of Tamil, LTTE xi, 183
Lone-wolf terrorists 31

Mechanism/s 4, 7, 14–5, 23, 42, 44, 47–8, 62, 72, 78–9, 80–1, 83, 87, 90, 92, 94, 104, 117, 124–5, 127–9, 130–4, 136, 139, 141, 144, 146, 182, 188
Media 11–2, 18, 28, 30, 32, 42, 53, 58, 102–3, 113–4, 119, 132, 154, 175–6, 190
Methodology 6, 70, 74, 76, 104
Michel Foucault 15
Middle East xi, 13, 62, 96, 99, 104–5, 107, 119, 127, 168, 172, 176, 186
Middle East and North Africa, MENA xi, 96
Modernization 99, 100, 103
Moral disengagement theory 14

Narcissism xv, 50, 53–4, 56, 59, 60–3
Narcissistic injury 54, 59, 139
Nationalism xiv, 100, 124, 168
Natural-system model 118
New Left xv, 100, 165, 168, 174
New terrorism 170, 173–4, 176–7, 180
New terrorism-old terrorism, debate 180
Non-governmental organization, NGO xi, 147
Northern Ireland viii, 38, 119, 134, 151, 190
Nuclei Armati Rivoluzionari, NAR viii, xi, 55

Obama, Barrack 182
Occupation 21, 40, 52–3, 59, 71–2, 95, 99, 101, 104–5, 114–5, 118, 138, 142, 155, 169, 170
Occupational change i, x, 9, 71–2, 76, 92
Occupational choice theory 73
Operation Condor 158, 164
Opportunities 4, 6, 7, 72, 96, 98, 106, 109–13, 116, 124, 130, 142–4, 184
Opportunity structure 75, 180
Organized crime 11, 31
Oslo accords 51

Palestine Liberation Organization, PLO xi, 51–2
Palestinian Authority 51–2, 119, 120
Pentiti, 187
Performance 185, 191, 195
Peterborough Adolescent and Young Adult Development Study, PADS+ xi, 74
Polarization xiv, 88
Positivism xv, 133
Poverty viii, 22, 44, 48, 52, 86, 95–6, 106–7, 128, 185

Power xiii, xiv, xv, 3, 5–6, 8, 14–9, 20–1, 26, 38, 46, 71, 87, 89, 90–1, 98, 101, 105, 109, 111–3, 115, 120, 128, 132, 134, 141, 155, 157–9, 161, 167, 173, 180, 185, 190–2, 194–6
Preventing terrorism 196
Process, 4–5, 7, 13, 20–1, 27, 39, 42, 47, 49, 65, 67, 73, 81, 83–4, 104, 125–7, 131–2, 134–5, 138, 163, 167, 181, 183, 189, 190–1; counter-terrorism, of 191; decision-making 108, 121, 159; democratic 118; desistance, of 145, 150; devolution of power, of 185; disengagement, of 141; exit 143, 150–1; group 142; identity formation, of 56; involvement of, in terrorism 50, 65–6, 68, 82, 85, 144; negotiation, of 183, 188; occupational change i, x, 9, 70–2, 76, 92; Oslo peace 51, 120; peace 119, 120, 183; political 31, 48, 111, 124, 162, 180, 188; political contention, of 133
psychotherapeutic xii; radicalization, of 43, 54, 61–2, 72, 78, 90, 132, 135–6, 144, 148; reintegration, of 150; resisting, of 146; social 19; socialization, of 61, 152; state-building 120; terrorism 47, 60, 69
Propaganda of the deed 120, 178
Provisional Irish Republican Army, PIRA xi, 38, 40–1, 43
Psychology xiii, xiv, 5, 14–5, 17, 20, 22, 44, 51, 60, 63, 65–6, 68, 70, 76–7, 87–9, 92–3, 117, 134, 142, 150–1, 175, 195–6
Psychological warfare xv, 102

Qualitative comparative analysis, QCA xi, 58, 64
Qualitative methods 48
Quantitative methods 6, 47, 145

Radicalization 2, 40, 42–3, 47–9, 50, 53–4, 56–7, 60–3, 70–4, 76, 78, 87, 90, 92–3, 102, 106, 129, 130–6, 138, 144, 148–9, 174, 185, 190
Radical milieu viii, 43, 126, 136, 146, 175
Rational choice xvi, 2, 5–7, 45–6, 66, 70, 72–5, 78–9, 80, 105, 110, 124, 158, 186–8
Rationality viii, xvi, 6, 38, 45–6, 65, 70, 73, 79, 105, 109–10, 118, 121, 131, 174, 176, 188, 193
Red Army Faction, RAF xi, 12–3, 23, 103
Red Brigades, RB xi, 68, 90–1, 96, 126, 187
Recruitment 40–2, 46, 49, 52, 67, 83–4, 118–9
Reign of Terror xvi, 28, 152
Relational approach 2–5, 7, 44, 46–8, 60, 77–8, 83, 85, 91–2, 123, 131, 133–5, 144, 153, 179, 180, 184, 189, 190–1, 195

Index

Religion 42, 44, 62, 85, 90, 92, 99, 101, 106, 169, 170, 172–3, 177
Repression 13, 48, 112, 125–6, 128–9, 130–1, 134, 136, 155–8, 161–3, 182
Resource mobilization theory 6–8, 110, 112
Resources viii, xv, 6–7, 23, 50–1, 97, 105, 109–13, 115–6, 119, 121, 125, 130, 158–9, 160, 192
Revolutionary terrorism 105, 196
Right-wing extremism 42, 56, 139
Right-wing terrorism 55
Rogue state xvi, 154
Root causes 44–5, 47–8, 50, 94–5, 97–8, 103–4, 106–7, 109, 111, 123, 136, 179, 184–6, 194–6
Russia ix, 166, 183

Salafi jihad xiv, 84, 86, 99
Sampling bias xvi, 58
Situational action theory, SAT viii, xi, 72–4, 76
School schootings 12, 24
Selective incentives xvi, 7, 65, 70–1, 110, 140
Social contract xvi, 27
Social learning theory 17, 141
Social movements xiii, xvi, 2, 6–8, 42–3, 47, 68, 72, 77–9, 81–2, 85, 92, 110, 112–3, 120, 122–6, 129, 132, 134, 190
Social movement theory 47, 60, 65, 70, 78, 83, 97, 111, 144, 190
Social cognitive psychology 14–5, 17, 22
Social psychology xiv, 51, 60, 77, 87–9, 92–3, 134, 175
State of exception viii, 149, 150, 192
State terrorism i, v, 2–3, 6, 14–5, 20–1, 42, 48, 103, 152–9, 160–4, 174, 192
Strategic decision-making 108, 110, 121
Strategic model 109, 118
Structure xii, xiv, xv, xvi, 2–4, 17, 41, 44–5, 47, 49, 50, 55, 72, 75, 77, 79, 86, 89, 97, 110, 113–4, 117, 120, 145–6, 182, 189

Subculture xvi, 43, 56, 85–6
Subjectivity xvii, 3, 8, 44, 72, 91, 105, 196
Subjugated knowledge 173–4, 177
Suffragette bombers ix, 181
Suicide bombing 119, 122, 136, 170
Suicide terrorism 76, 101, 106, 116, 122, 136, 171
Surveillance 69, 75, 139

Targeted killings 20, 182
Terrorist Organization Profile, TOP xi, 101
Thugs 170–2
Torture 16, 20, 29, 135, 153, 157–8, 160–2, 194

Ulster Defence Association, UDA xi, 119
Ulster Volunteer Force, UVF xi, 119
Uncertainty 89, 90, 92–3, 115, 146
United Arab Emirates, UAE xi, 104
United Nations, UN xi, 11, 100, 153, 167, 168, 184
United States of America, US ix, xvi, xvii, 12–4, 16, 22–3, 37, 49, 54, 56, 59, 61, 80, 88, 96, 99, 101, 112, 114–5, 127, 150, 154–5, 164, 168-9, 170, 174–6, 180, 182, 184–5, 189, 191, 193, 195, 200

Vietnamese National Liberation Front 168
War on Terror xvii, 15, 21, 37, 98, 149, 150, 154, 161–2, 195
War on Terrorism 14, 196
Wave 85–6, 100, 121–2, 124, 165–9, 170, 174–6
Weathermen, the ix, 88, 146, 169
West, the 9, 21, 56, 60–3, 80, 92, 95–7, 99, 127, 155–6, 168, 173
Women xviii, 100, 168, 171, 181
Women's Social and Political Union, WSPU xi, 181–2

Zealots-Sicarii 172